The 64-Square
Looking Glass

The 64-Square Looking Glass

THE GREAT GAME OF CHESS
IN WORLD LITERATURE

Edited by Burt Hochberg

TIMES **T** BOOKS

RANDOM HOUSE

FOR CAROL

Library of Congress Cataloging-in-Publication Data

The 64-square looking glass: the great game of chess in world literature / edited by Burt Hochberg.—1st ed.
p.   cm.
ISBN 0-8129-1929-7
1. Chess—Literary collections.   2. Chess—Fiction.   I. Hochberg, Burt.   II. Title: Sixty-four square looking glass.
PN6071.C45A614   1992
809'.93355—dc20   92-53664

DESIGN BY LAURA HOUGH
Manufactured in the United States of America
24689753
FIRST EDITION

Contents

Contents

♦

Contents

◆

Burt Hochberg

Preface

Despite prolonged investigations and profound contemplation by poets, philosophers, psychologists, psychoanalysts, and enough other -ists to staff a medium-size research institute, the lure of chess remains a mystery, even to chessplayers. Chess fascinates people of all ages, all cultures and nationalities, all levels of education. It is simple and impossible, intricate and grand. It is a pleasant pastime, a challenging game, a demanding sport, an inexhaustible passion. There is no joy like winning a chess game, no misery like losing one.

Game, sport, art, science, passion, madness, recreation, obsession—chess is no one thing but all of these things: It is a world. The writers whose work appears in this book have looked at chess from many different angles and have shown it in as many lights. Yet all have this in common: they show human beings in the act of being human. Chess, like love, like music, has the power to let us see ourselves.

This is hardly the first anthology of chess belles-lettres, and I want to express my appreciation for the best of those that have gone before. The earliest of the "modern" anthologies in English is a charming little book edited by Edwin Valentine Mitchell entitled *The Art of Chess-Playing* (1936), in which I first read Alfred Kreymborg's memoir. The anthology most eagerly sought by collectors is Jerome Salzmann's *The Chess Reader* (1949), where I, and no doubt a great many other chessplayers, discovered Stefan Zweig's *The Royal Game.* In 1975, Marcello Truzzi edited *Chess in Literature,* an excellent collection of short stories that he augmented with references to many other stories he was unable to include—a valued gift to later anthologists.

In England, there were the interesting but flawed anthologies *Chess Pieces* (1949, second edition 1968), edited by Norman Knight, and *King, Queen and Knight* (1975), edited by Norman Knight and Will Guy. I found Andrew Waterman's collection *The Poetry of Chess* (1981) of particular value. And *The Complete Chess Addict* (1987), an entertaining assortment of chess oddments edited by Mike Fox and Richard James, sent me on more than one fruitful research expedition.

The present anthology was undertaken in part to rectify an omission. Nowhere is there to be found a collection of fully realized chess scenes and complete stories and essays drawn mostly from the works of contemporary writers. *Chess in Literature* contains only short stories, and most of the other anthologies, for all their many virtues, consist mainly of brief excerpts, sometimes hardly more than a sentence or two, and interminable stretches of ancient poetry.

Assembling an anthology as ambitious as this one required the generous assistance of a number of friends and colleagues. I owe a special debt of gratitude to Judge Dan O'Hanlon, the best friend a chess anthologist could have. Despite the hundreds of miles that separate us, he invited me to rummage around in his library by mail and telephone, joined eagerly in the search for undiscovered nuggets, and was as delighted as I with every new find.

Berta Klaif Tabbat, poet, journalist, chess fan, and friend of long standing, attacked my request for possible leads with enthusiasm and came up with a number of titles I had forgotten or never knew.

In various ways, important help was provided by International Grandmaster Andy Soltis; International Master Anthony Saidy; Hanon W. Russell, owner and curator of the Russell Collection, a massive archive of original chess-related documents; the renowned chess teacher and writer Bruce Pandolfini; Dale Brandreth, a leading specialist in out-of-print chess literature; Emanuel Sztein, a scholar of Russian literature; Ruth Fecych, my editor at Times

Books; Deborah Foley, the helpful and ever-cheerful copyright and permissions associate of Times Books; the dedicated, underappreciated staff of the various branches of the New York Public Library; and, of course, my everlastingly patient and supportive wife, Carol Hochberg.

I. Chess Itself

To the ignorant outside world, two men over a chessboard look like a pair of dummies. And yet, inside the pale automata, dynamos pound incessantly. Here is nothing less than a silent duel between two human engines using and abusing all the faculties of the mind—the will, the imagination, logic, memory, caution, cunning, daring, foresight, hindsight, perspective, detail, unity and courage—in an effort to outwit, corner and demolish the not-less-than-hateful opponent. It is warfare in the most mysterious jungles of the human character.

This excerpt from Alfred Kreymborg's memoir "Chess Reclaims a Devotee" (given in full later in this volume) perfectly sets the stage for the explorations of those "mysterious jungles" undertaken by Charles Krauthammer and Andrew Waterman, and by the only great writer who was also a recognized composer of chess problems, Vladimir Nabokov.

Warfare is what Ezra Pound sees on the chessboard; with slashing images he depicts a world of endlessly recycling violence. Lord Dunsany (Edward John Moreton Drax Plunkett), a novelist, poet, and playwright, and an active chessplayer until his death in 1957, takes a philosophic view. His poem "The Sea and Chess" was composed for the opening of the 1950–51 Hastings Christmas Congress, an international chess tournament that has been held almost annually at that seaside resort in the south of England since 1895.

Charles Krauthammer

The Romance of Chess

"An art appearing in the form of a game"
—entry on chess in the *Great Soviet Encyclopedia.*

"You have, let us say, a promising politician, a rising artist that you wish to destroy. Dagger or bomb are archaic, clumsy, and unreliable—but teach him, inoculate him with chess." Anyone who has ever played chess all night only to curse the sunrise for marking a return to real life, will recognize—and resent—the hint of truth in H. G. Wells's malicious little indictment of chess. Wells went a bit further. For him chess was not just an addiction, its continuing popularity constituted a kind of heresy. "The passion for playing chess is one of the most unaccountable in the world. It slaps the theory of natural selection in the face. It is the most absorbing of occupations, the least satisfying of desires. . . . It annihilates a man." Now, counter-evolutionary is the ultimate epithet in the Wellsian lexicon. Why the animus? I suspect that at an impressionable age he left a rook hanging somewhere, and never quite recovered.

I have been careful to begin this essay on chess with a gratuitous ad hominem, because I want to be true to the spirit of my subject. It is drenched in polemics. It is curious that an activity (you mustn't call it a game unless you are prepared to join the fray on one side of the debate) as silent, cerebral, and apparently neutral as chess should engender such passion. Yet that passion animates not just life at the board, but the life of the mind, i.e., chess literature, that overgrown garden of theory, analysis, speculation, and argument.

To be sure, there are two kinds of chess literature, though most serious players extend diplomatic recognition only to one, the technical literature. And by that they don't just mean *The New York Times* column where one might learn that last fall the Swedish international master Schneider, playing former world champion Tal, overlooked a magnificent queen sacrifice on the 30th move that would have assured him both a win and a place in chess history; that's color. They mean the latest *Shakhmatni Byulleten* (in Russian), *64* (in German), and *Informant* (entirely in symbolic notation—chess's answer to Esperanto), where you must go if you want to learn the latest on, say, the Semi-Slav Defense; that's literature. And it is to be taken seriously, a lesson I learned the hard way. At clubs I used to play the Wilkes-Barre Variation of the Four Knights Defense, a very complicated opening which I had thoroughly studied and in which most opponents tended to get lost. Once, deep into opening play, an opponent (wearing a Chess City T-shirt—that should have tipped me off) sprung on me a move I'd never seen before, and the rest was commentary. When it was over, I looked up from the rubble and asked him about that move. Fixing me with the slightly disapproving look that professionals everywhere reserve for dilettantes, he replied that he had recently written an article proposing it in a Yugoslavian journal.

One would think that the technical literature, a vast labyrinth of mirror and memory, would not be conducive to polemic. Not so. There is much disputation in the corridors. The early Romantic play of dashing combinations and sacrifices fought a losing battle in the late nineteenth century with what is now known as Classical theory, which emphasized position, structure, and a strategy of methodical incrementalism. After World War I, an even more bitter struggle was waged by the Hypermodern revolutionaries who, consciously allying themselves with the avant-garde in music and art, challenged every article of the Classical canon, championing flank play over the center, force over mass, indirect control over frontal assault. The Classicists called their moves ugly. The Hypermoderns replied, to quote Breyer's sardonic comment on the most solid, classical, and perhaps perfect opening move, "1. P-K4 [and] White's game is in the last throes." The great Nimzovitch once went many years without talking to the

Polish master Przepiorka. At Liège in 1930 Nimzovitch finally broke his silence. Przepiorka asked him what happened. Nimzovitch replied, "I thought you were a member of the Tarrasch school."

Chess, however, has a second literature. The technical literature, elegant and forbidding, asks whether or not to exchange bishop for knight on the fourth move of the Ruy Lopez. The other literature—the moral literature—asks whether it matters. It questions what the technical literature assumes: the value of the entire enterprise. The debate on that question is no less passionate than on the other. Benjamin Franklin, one of the later entrants to the discussion, thought that chess promoted the prudential, utilitarian virtues he treasured. "Several very valuable qualities of mind, useful in the course of human life," he wrote, "are to be acquired and strengthened" by chess, including "foresight," "circumspection," and "caution." Franklin practiced what he preached. While ambassador to France, he was a habitué of the Café de la Régence, where the immortal Philidor played. "I rarely go to the operas at Paris," said Franklin, "I call this my opera." To the opposition, that sounded like pure rationalization. "A foolish expedient for making idle people believe they are doing something very clever, when they are only wasting their time." That's how George Bernard Shaw dispatched chess and its partisans. The most recent response to Shaw was delivered by my friend José Zalaquett, a Chilean human rights lawyer, who, when arrested by the Pinochet regime, was allowed to take three books with him to prison. He chose the Bible, the dialogues of Plato, and the thickest chess book he could find on his shelf. I once asked him about his choices. "I didn't know if I'd be in for a week or a lifetime," he replied, "so I looked for things that would last."

Whom to believe? I am tempted to say that it depends on whether you've ever walked into a chess club in a strange city, played the Yugoslav Attack on the Sicilian Dragon, and won in an avalanche of pawns in the twenty-third move. (Krauthammer-amateur, Washington, 1978; in the very next game, to be sure, she reduced me and my Nimzo-Indian Defense to a fine powder.) If you don't play—and most who don't have an opinion anyway—it depends on whom you read. The moral literature on chess is extensive, and its terms keep changing with the times. In Franklin's day the charge was that chess is a vice. The modern charge is that it challenges not virtue but more contemporary ideals: meaning and health. The double indictment against chess is that it is both pointless and an incubator of psychopathology. Empty and crazy. The two charges are interrelated, the existential one being used to explain the psychological one. "A chess genius," writes George Steiner in his incisive and often original *Fields of Force*, "is a human being who focuses vast, little-understood mental gifts and labors on an ultimately trivial human enterprise. Almost inevitably, this focus produces pathological symptoms and nervous stress and unreality."

I don't intend a total defense of chess. I have spent—wasted—too many hours at the board for that. The existential attack, however, strikes me as a feint on the flank that cannot withstand a simple probe or two. The psychological claim seems more menacing and leads to complications. Since both charges shape the modern conception of chess, I propose to examine them both.

Start with the pointlessness. What does it mean? In his classic chess novella, *The Royal Game,* Stefan Zweig describes chess as "thought that leads nowhere, mathematics that add up to nothing, art without an end product, architecture without substance." Without product: at the end of the game the players have nothing to show. Or, as Steiner says, "a radically sterile form of play."

But to indict chess for not producing monuments is to indict all play and many of the arts. To say that all that is left after the curtain falls on a symphony is the memory and the score is to judge music by the most perversely narrow utilitarian standards. It is in the nature of beauty to have no use and few products. Why turn somersaults on a four-inch (not three, not five) balance beam? Because it is difficult and demands perfection of certain human faculties, the exercise and apprehension of which are beautiful. There is no other answer.

The more subtle version of the existential charge is that chess shares a *special* pointlessness with those other totally abstract arts: music and (pure) mathematics. It has long been noted that these three activities—uniquely—are able to produce the truly original child prodigy. They can be mastered by someone innocent of experience because they are outside of language, indeed their terms are utterly without referent in reality. Consequently, the kinds of problems they generate are so radically abstract, so endlessly regressive, and ultimately so arbitrary and unreal that they possess only illusory, what Steiner calls "trivial," depth.

Scientists usually reserve the term "trivial" for those questions that have self-evidently simple answers. Here the charge is the opposite: they are too deep, too complex, too infinite, too self-referential. His own logic requires Steiner to indict not only chess but music (he does: "Though most of us would abhor the suggestion, this 'nonsignificance' may extend even to music") and mathematics (he doesn't). Thus the analysis breaks down at its conclusion: it is true that chess, like mathematics and music, is characterized by a bottomless and regressive abstractness, but that does not make for pointlessness. It does make for vertigo. And that brings us to the second charge, because vertigo is a perfectly adequate route to madness.

Madness is the great theme of chess literature and vertigo the great metaphor. In Nabokov's novel *The Defense,* the chess master Luzhin plays a climactic game with his arch-rival Turati, during which Luzhin suddenly apprehends "something unbearably awesome, the full horror of the abysmal depths of chess"—into which he falls, and goes mad. Of course, Luzhin is no paradigm of mental health to begin with; he is the prototype, and now the stereotype, of the autistic, inept genius. It is Zweig who pushes the vertiginous powers of chess to the extreme. *The Royal Game* has a Luzhin, too—Mirko Czentovic, the ignorant, illiterate, uncouth, almost aphasic Yugoslavian peasant, now (naturally) world champion. But Zweig doesn't drive him mad because he believes that Czentovic's atrophied mind, where only a stolid chess center survives, is incapable of such an exquisite fate. In *The Royal Game* it is the normal man, the man of culture, who is conquered by chess. Zweig's hero, Dr. B., is a Viennese intellectual imprisoned by the Gestapo in the most horrible sensory deprivation. He manages to steal a book, which turns out to contain only chess master games. Forced into the terrible mirror world of pure and endless reason that is chess, Dr. B., like Luzhin, falls into the void and wakes in the hospital.

A reader who relied solely on Nabokov and Zweig might conclude that chess sets should carry a warning label from the surgeon general. Which is what makes the most recent piece of first-rate chess fiction, Walter Tevis's *The Queen's Gambit,* such a refreshing dissent. Tevis, a gifted storyteller who understands the fascination of play (his first novel, *The Hustler,* is about a pool shark), has produced a taut narrative of tournament life, not a study of the boundary between genius and madness. Alone among chess novels, *The Queen's Gambit* is not a tragedy nor is its hero (in this case, heroine: the young Beth Harmon, who learns the game in the basement of her orphanage and rises to the world championship) an object of pity. She is a sympathetic character; *patzers* of the world may even envy her. And most interesting, she doesn't go mad. Quite the contrary. Emanuel Lasker once said that "on the chessboard lies and hypocrisy do not survive long." Harmon finds comfort in that kind of truth; it proves her salvation. Others, like Dr. B., feel only its mercilessness, and it proves their undoing.

Tevis's novel is valuable not just because it brilliantly evokes the rhythms of the game, but because it reminds us that on the question of the psychopathology of chess there are no pat answers. Regarding the move from clarity to madness, Tevis provides annotation that is not a refutation of Nabokov and Zweig, but an alternate line of analysis.

There is yet another line of analysis, however, that prizes patness. It is the view of "the Viennese delegation" that the "chess player sees Mom in his Queen and Pop in his opponent's King," to use Nabokov's unkind—and accurate—formulation. The most recent epic of this genre is Alexander Cockburn's *Idle Passion: Chess and the Dance of Death,* which, like Steiner's book, was provoked by the [1972] Fischer-Spassky match. Cockburn appears to have discovered the existence of Sigmund Freud and Bobby Fischer at about the same time. The result is a hilariously reductionist interpretation of chess, based on excruciatingly reverent quotes from two previous speculations, one by psychoanalyst Ernest Jones and the other by grandmaster and psychoanalyst Reuben Fine. Cockburn swallows everything whole. He relies on Jones to inform us that "the unconscious motive activating the players is . . . father murder," which accounts for the game's "anal-sadistic" features, and on Fine to inform us that the king "stands for the boy's penis in the phallic stage, and hence rearouses the castration anxiety characteristic of that period." Which explains, among other things, chess etiquette, like the "taboo" (i.e., rule) against touching the opponent's pieces, or one's own pieces except for the purpose of making a move. "It is 'explaining' or dismissing two suspicions," writes Cockburn relying on Fine, "that the player is masturbating, by touching his piece; or making a homosexual overture, by proposing physical contact between the players, or mutual masturbation." That's the sophisticated analysis. Cockburn uses these tools to go further, to probe the character of former world champions, particularly those whose reputations for emotional equilibrium tend to defy Freudian theory. Of Lasker he notes: "The two opening variations that bear his name involve an early exchange of queens—that is, to clarify the situation (his constant ambition in chess), he gets rid of women." On Capablanca: "[O]ne can see evidence for [his] narcissism and oral fixation (his keenness on cooking)." On Spassky: "He displays enthusiasm for the writings of Dostoevsky, which is not usually a passion for anyone with a perfectly balanced psyche." Psychohistory, apparently, fares no better at the chessboard than elsewhere.

And leaves us still with the question: What is the connection between chess and madness? That there is such a connection there is little doubt. It is not just a literary creation. (Though writers have long had fun with the idea: Stephen Leacock could not resist saying of his Dr. Allard, head of the Criminal Lunatic Asylum, "He goes back and forth between [the chess club] and the asylum. He says he is making comparative studies.") There is Fischer, who once said "chess is life," and at the peak of his powers recoiled from both, disappeared into a fundamentalist religious sect, and has not played a single game of chess that we know of since. There is Morphy, the only other American champion, whose genius, paranoia, and renunciation of chess anticipated Fischer by a century. There is Steinitz, who claimed to have played God at pawn odds and won. (Unfortunately, he left no record of the game.) And there is Alekhine, who probably was enjoying one of his more lucid moments when he declared to the Polish border police, who stopped him because he didn't have any papers: "I am Alekhine, chess champion of the world. This is my cat. Her name is Chess. I need no passport."

There is something mysterious about the psychopathology of genius, and it is the creators of Luzhin, Czentovic, and Dr. B. who have done the most to illuminate the problem. Most people imagine that what distinguishes the great chess player is his capacity for mechanical combination. But he plays the game at an entirely different level. Nabokov, a fine player and a renowned composer of chess problems, chose another metaphor. His Luzhin felt each square "occupied by a definite, concentrated force," and "envisioned the movement of a piece as a discharge, a shock, a stroke of lightning . . . the whole chess field quivered with tension, and over this tension he was sovereign, here gathering in and there releasing electric power." Luzhin preferred to play with his eyes closed. That way he

> did not have to deal with visible, audible, palpable pieces whose quaint shape and wooden materiality always disturbed him and always seemed to him but the crude, mortal shell of exquisite,

invisible chess forces. When playing blind he was able to sense these diverse forces in their original purity.

The amateur sees pieces and movement; the expert, additionally, sees sixty-four squares with holes and lines and spheres of influence; the genius apprehends a unified field within which space and force and mass are interacting valences—a bishop tears the board in half and a pawn bends the space around it the way mass can reshape space in the Einsteinian universe. To enter this fearsome universe one blinds oneself, so the pieces may evaporate and be replaced by whorls of energy and space.

And there lies danger. Tarrasch once said that "chess, like love, like music, has the power to make men happy." That is only half the story. The Luzhins, fictional and real, transfixed by the beauty of the game, are drawn into its vertiginous depths, where another fate awaits them. The rest of us are safe, however. We will never see that far. For me that is a source of reassurance, and some regret.

Andrew Waterman

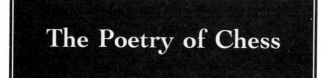

The Poetry of Chess

Almost inexhaustibly profound, chess is also an activity trivial and barren in being wholly self-contained and leading to nothing beyond itself. In the terms of Wordsworth's distinction, it is most extremely "a personal and individual acquisition" rather than "a necessary part of our existence." And if the pure sciences are also in that sense optional human enterprises, not in themselves engaging with the problems of identity, emotion, morality and relationship we all unavoidably experience simply through being human, they have an obvious validity as such in enlarging our understanding of the physical universe which is the conditioning context for our humanity. Chess is wholly sterile. Its play and pieces may supply symbols and metaphors for life; the way in which moves and combinations *not* played, latent hypotheses, contribute as crucially to what evolves as what *is* done, offers paradigms for human affairs. But any relationship between chess and life beyond it is entirely abstract and figurative. Whereas the supreme point of literature is that it explores, mediates and clarifies life itself, emerges from and takes as its ingredients man's "natural and unalienable inheritance"; and in the great poets and novelists achieves our most profound and searching articulation of the human spirit.

Now, as C. H. O'D. Alexander observed,

Chess Itself

◆

Social chess is played for fun; competitive chess is work and very hard work indeed—and while it can give very deep satisfaction, it is the kind of satisfaction and fulfilment one gets from work, not play.*

Also, like poetry, chess for the serious practitioner is exceptionally taxing work not accredited as such by society generally. Compound with this stress the crucial difference that chess does not engage with life, and the serious player becomes a freak prone to extreme pressures indeed. G. K. Chesterton's remark, "Poets do not go mad; but chess players do," if historically inaccurate in its first clause, embodies a true perception. The great poets seem on the whole a well-balanced orderly bunch compared to the great chess players. Five who would make anyone's list of the all-time top dozen players could fairly be described as, intermittently or terminally, mad. Paul Morphy, the original "pride and sorrow of chess," after demonstrating in 1859 that at twenty-one he was overwhelmingly the world's best, resentful of his fame as "a mere chess player" renounced the game and receded into reclusive decades of melancholic paranoia. Wilhelm Steinitz, World Champion from 1866 to 1894, ended his days convinced he could move chess pieces by impulses from his brain and defeat God at odds of pawn and move. Akiba Rubinstein, unlucky to be denied by Lasker a world title match he would probably have won, was paranoiac eventually to a point where he supposed other players and officials were intent on poisoning him, or would flee rooms others entered; incapacitated for formal play, he survived for decades shunning all social contacts. Alexander Alekhine, World Champion—except for two years—from 1927 until his death in 1946, the most single-minded and aggressive chess genius prior to Fischer, was outside his wonderfully creative play a monster of selfishness and crassness. After mysterious double-dealings he extricated himself from post-revolutionary Russia by a marriage of convenience, jettisoning his wife when he was safe. Two of his four subsequent wives were decades older than himself. Alekhine's chess manners included hurling pieces, smashing furniture, and once drunkenly urinating on the floor. He was an alcoholic. His last years were clouded by the appearance over his name in Nazi-occupied France of crazed ideo-

---

* C. H. O'D. Alexander, *Fischer v Spassky, Reykjavik 1972*, 1972.

logical articles extolling "Aryan" as opposed to morally depraved "Jewish" chess (many of the world's greatest players have been Jews). Bobby Fischer, the most recent notable chess eccentric, recalls his American predecessor Morphy in that, precisely as he had established a dominance over his contemporaries unparalleled since Morphy, he tragically withdrew from play. Brought up by a mother with whom in adolescence he definitively quarrelled, thereafter a social isolate living in hotel rooms, Fischer is the most lopsided of all chess champions, appearing to remain humanly undeveloped outside a passion for the game which more totally absorbed his life than any other player's. He loved crushing opponents, remarking "I like to see their egos crumble"; his rhetoric consisted of terms such as *smash, crunch, bam.* His egotistical fantasizing was extreme:

> This little thing between me and Spassky, it's a microcosm of the whole world political situation. They always suggest that the two world leaders should fight it out hand to hand, and this is the kind of thing we are doing.

(Compare Lowell's poem "The Winner," which non-chessplaying poetry-readers may not realize is an amalgam of Fischerisms.) Yet Fischer's lifelong extraordinary excess of temperament and behaviour, his demands, protests and walk-outs, far from furthering his own chess cause first perversely delayed for perhaps a decade his becoming World Champion, then subsequently prevented him from capitalizing on his pre-eminence: despite his financial demands Fischer never collected the huge rewards possible after his defeat of Spassky. That triumph led only to the closure of his chess career at twenty-nine because the international chess world would not allow him arrogantly to dictate all terms.

How did characters so weird play such powerfully lucid chess? As Joseph Conrad notes in *The Shadow Line,* a mad carpenter will still make a sane box. In the 1920s the precocious Mexican chessgenius Torre flipped suddenly, removing all his clothes on a New York bus, and never recovered sanity. Visitors years later found his chess unimpaired. Ability at chess, or carpentry, in contrast to poetic achievement, is unaffected by the sanity of one's human attitudes, so long as one's state of mind or behaviour allows the activity at all.

Unsurprisingly, chess and its players have attracted psychoanalytical comment. In 1930 Freud's eminent follower Ernest Jones read to the British Psychoanalytical Society a paper, "The Problem of Paul Morphy," in the course of which Jones found much material for comment in the game itself, seizing upon the crucial importance and vulnerability of the king to conclude that chess is "adapted to gratify at the same time both the homosexual and antagonistic aspects of the father-son contest."*

Reuben Fine, a candidate for Alekhine's title when the Second World War disrupted international chess, who subsequently forsook serious play for the profession of psychoanalysis, is uniquely placed to bring experience of play at the highest level to clinical discussion of chess. His book *The Psychology of the Chess Player* has small comfort for those of us who might prefer to believe the game's satisfactions innocent:

> Chess is a contest between two men in which there is considerable ego involvement. In some ways it certainly touches upon the conflicts surrounding aggression, homosexuality, masturbation and narcissism.†

And, again, "father-son rivalry." The king's special status as a piece, its loss deciding the game regardless of other considerations, is a feature making chess unique among board games. The king therefore becomes "the central figure in the symbolism of the game," deriving its meanings from its combination of all-importance and weakness: "The King stands for: the boy's penis in the phallic stage, the self-image of the man, and the father cut down to boy's size." Under the first head it "rearouses the castration anxiety characteristic of that period." The player prone to touch or fondle his own or captured pieces is subconsciously enacting masturbation or making a homosexual advance. Infantile omnipotence is another impulse offered huge scope by the nature of chess; and the role of the powerful queen attracts a further complex of psychoanalytical comment. Altogether chess is seen as enacting deeply repressed aggression, centred in and sublimating the Oedipal conflict: underlying the overt quest for checkmate is a basic ambition to expose as weak, castrate and destroy the father. Fine notes that the intense aggressiveness inherent in

---

* Ernest Jones, *Essays in Applied Psychoanalysis*, vol. I, 1951.
† Reuben Fine, *The Psychology of the Chess Player*, New York, 1967.

the game is controlled and repressed by its procedures and etiquette: here is no physical aggression or even contact; the rules of serious play virtually exclude dialogue; and only at novice-level are games pursued until checkmate, itself a position short of actual capture of the king. As for any homosexual ingredients, "overt homosexuality is almost unknown among chess players. . . . This is all the more striking in that artists, with whom chess masters like to compare themselves, are so frequently homosexual." Fine observes that where chess players' characteristically strong ego-control disintegrates before the underlying pressures, the symptoms tend to be "paranoia, megalomania and exhibitionism." A caricature-anticipation of Fischer's extravagant statement about playing Spassky occurs in a case Fine cites of psychotic breakdown in a chess player who in 1947, the year before the Soviet player Botvinnik in fact won the world title vacated by Alekhine's death, insisted: "The real ruler of Russia is not Stalin but Botvinnik. . . . I am going to go to Russia and beat Botvinnik. In this way I will conquer the world for America."

Fine's later book on the Fischer-Spassky match* naturally finds the American genius, with whom Fine was early acquainted, whose sublimation in chess of all other gratifications was so total, rich material for clinical comment. Fischer's expressed desire "to live the rest of my life in a house built exactly like a rook" moves Fine to offer "a typical double symbolic meaning: first of all it is the strong penis for which he apparently finds so little use in real life; second, it is a castle in which he can live in grandiose fantasy, like the kings of old, shutting out the real world."

Most of us woodpushers will not worry about the sinister proclivities psychoanalysts find lurking within our activity. Such interpretations of chess may, however, partly explain the decidedly inferior interest and ability in chess shown by women, who may be glad to be spared some of the necessary motivations. Certainly, as (in Fine's words) "an intellectual aggression, a successful sublimation," chess is crucially a *contest*; and so affords special outlets for intellectual abilities whether or not a man also develops these in other areas. Compounding the game's innate aggressiveness is the tension generated by such factors as its behavioural restraints; the slowness of play

---

* Reuben Fine, *Bobby Fischer's Conquest of the World's Chess Championship*, New York, 1973; London, 1975.

yet inexorableness of the chess clock ticking away one's time; the fact that unlike a scientist who if one hypothesis fails in practice can try another, or the poet who can redraft endlessly, the chess player has to commit himself irrevocably to a single over-the-board move among the many he will have considered; the absoluteness of defeat or victory and the certainty that in a game devoid of chance one has only oneself to blame for the former. The etherealized aggression and constant nervous strain produce a players' rhetoric vehement beyond the simply military nature of some of the game's terminology. Fischer's style of verbal exultation is characteristic of many players at all levels. Defeat stings, and is rarely acknowledged with grace, explanations offered being usually in terms of one's own "stupid" play or "blunders" rather than the opponent's excellence. During play, the "enemy" position is, with luck, "ruined," until he is "dead"; a passed pawn becomes "enormous," a captured one is "chopped," and so forth. I write this late on an evening in which I have won a ferocious game in my club championship, about which I admit to feeling exhilarating floods of satisfaction; but my polite inclination at the moment of victory to temper my real delight was reinforced by the taut silent fury on my opponent's face, as he swept immediately out looking as though he wanted to knife me. All he lacked was knives. Chess victory sweetens a day however troubled in other ways; while losing preys on one's sleep. The egotism of writers, which certainly exists, is less stark and more diffused; and mixed with a humbling sense of the complex intractability of life itself, which writing unlike chess engages and, if any good, has to acknowledge with exceptional openness.

Chess is certainly addictive, capable of becoming an obsession retarding or excluding achievement in other areas, as H. G. Wells understood:

> The passion for playing chess is one of the most unaccountable in the world. It slaps the theory of natural selection in the face. . . . It annihilates a man. You have, let us say, a promising politician, a rising artist, that you wish to destroy. Dagger or bomb are archaic, clumsy and unreliable—but teach him, inoculate him with chess.*

---

* H. G. Wells, *Certain Personal Matters*, 1898.

Anyone who has seen the serious chess scene from inside will have encountered lives observably deformed by enslavement to the game. It is perhaps surprising that any among the really committed, their mental faculties weirdly subverted into the insulated, fascinating yet sterile depths and harmonies of struggle within the sixty-four-square world, has accomplished anything outside the game at all. As, last century, Henry James Byron succinctly put it, "Life's too short for chess."

I should perhaps here outline my own credentials for more than hearsay comment. Learning the moves at six, I really caught chess at about ten, and for three years was an addictive casual player against anyone chancing my way. I read chess books and played through games of the masters, and whiled away school lessons with a pocket-set concealed on the desk-seat between myself and my opponent. At eleven I wonderfully enjoyed beating a nineteen-year-old to top my school chess club ladder. It is characteristic of chess players' psychology that the sixth-formers running the club, loath to print in that term's school magazine a first-year pupil above them, listed me seventh. I abandoned the club and reverted to casual play. Of course chess at English schools now, partly because of stimulus given by the 1972 Fischer-Spassky publicity, is vastly stronger and more organized than in the early 1950s. From age thirteen, when puberty ambushed me, until thirty-five, my chess-bug was dormant, though I knew it was there: I was a chess player the way an alcoholic who has stopped drinking is an alcoholic. Years elapsed between casual games; I followed only superficially even world title matches. My tertiary, though I hope not terminal, phase of reactivation, began when in 1976 a sort of chess epidemic broke out around the social areas of the New University of Ulster where I work. Since then my high-frequency casual chess has ranged from the carefully fought, through lunch-hour chess-fixes, to lightning games late on at some party when to the astonishment of those remaining I and a like-minded soul start shoving wood about. And, at long last, I have succumbed to joining clubs. This discovers the more consuming, intensified and satisfying world of formal play with the chess clock adding an extra dimension. Fortunately, at forty, after my years of abstinence, I know that most of any chess future I might have had is safely behind me. Playing for a club team, or very occasionally in a weekend congress where one is obsessively at it morning, afternoon and evening, is exhilarating but controllable; I switch off, and turn to other things. I am a moderate

club player, with at my level a certain talent for combative, compli-
cating middle-game resourcefulness; and that is all.

Observing some of the chess-junkies I now meet, I am glad my
own chess history precludes more serious temptation. But I know
enough about that freakish phenomenon the serious chess mind to be
impressed that, among the all-time greats, as well as the pure obses-
sives and madmen, any at all have developed other abilities. Philidor,
the eighteenth century's greatest player, was also a composer of note.
Staunton, the only Englishman so far with any claim to be, at his
brief peak in the 1840s, the world's best, was a prominent Shakespear-
ian scholar. Emanuel Lasker contributed to mathematics. Staunton
and Lasker, however, withdrew from chess for sustained periods,
and the Englishman was notoriously prickly, as when dishonourably
avoiding a match against and certain defeat by Morphy during the
latter's meteoric European visit, about any suggestion that he was
other than a literary gentleman and chess amateur. Such a rôle is
scarcely tenable since, over the past fifty years, the colossal prolifer-
ation of theory to be mastered for success at the highest levels. Reuben Fine had to abandon chess for another career. Top players
nowadays are effectively full-time professionals, often supplementing
their income from actual play by chess journalism, any other accom-
plishment a sideline.

There is, however, one twentieth-century example of a man who
forsook exceptional achievement in another field for the obsessive
pursuit of chess: the artist Marcel Duchamp, whose unique experience of success in both areas enabled him to make enlightening comments on similarities and differences between the creative processes
and temperaments of art and chess. He is also, for discussion of the
psychology of creativity in chess and in contrastingly life-orientated
areas, an interestingly illuminating "case." It is significant, in the
light of my general discussion so far, that Duchamp as an artist was
at the furthest remove from any tradition of naturalism or conception
of art as socially useful or in any normal sense for life's sake; from the
Lawrencean conviction that "the primary purpose of art is moral."
Born in 1887, Duchamp was an artistic ironist of the absurd, a Da-
daist and surrealist associated with André Breton. He was notorious
for painting moustaches on the Mona Lisa and exhibiting a urinal.
His painting, after his earliest work, dehumanizes people in the interests of geometric or conceptual pattern and movement. His *Nude
Descending a Staircase* is one of the archetypal "modern" paintings.

Painting itself Duchamp came to find an unsatisfactory medium for his particular bent: "It should have to do with the grey matter of our understanding instead of being purely visual."* For his final major work, unfinished after several years, *The Bride Stripped Bare by Her Bachelors, Even* (generally known for convenience as *The Large Glass*), he abandoned traditional painter's materials altogether in striving to achieve, on glass, a wholly abstract rendering of his extremely complex conception. By this time he was turning increasingly to the wholly conceptual world of chess: in a letter of 1919 to the three Stettheimer sisters apologizing for failure to write earlier, Duchamp explains: "My attention is so completely absorbed by chess. I play night and day and nothing in the world interests me more than finding the right move. . . . I like painting less and less."

He had always known the game; some of his paintings, such as *Portrait of Chess Players,* took it for a theme. For an artist eager to eliminate the "retinal" or "visual" aspects of painting and translate it to a world of ideas and movement, committed to an ideology of art's social non-utility and to subversion through art of social and community values, and a corresponding personal life-style, the attraction of chess is evident. It was not, as for artists of a different philosophy, a contrastingly abstract realm of creativity, but virtually a consummation of his whole artistic enterprise, his desire for the profoundly useless. So too, for this particular artist,

> The milieu of chess players is far more sympathetic than that of artists. These people are completely cloudy, completely blind, wearing blinkers . . . madmen of a certain quality, the way an artist is supposed to be, and isn't, in general.†

From his early thirties, Duchamp abandoned art for chess as a truly obsessive addict. Man Ray commented on Duchamp's marriage to Lydie Levassor-Sarrazin in 1927:

> Duchamp spent most of the one week they lived together studying chess problems, and his bride, in desperate retaliation, got up

---

* Duchamp quotations, except where otherwise indicated, are from Arturo Schwarz, *The Complete Works of Marcel Duchamp,* 1969.
† Pierre Cabanne, *Dialogues with Marcel Duchamp,* tr. Ron Padgett, 1971.

one night when he was asleep and glued the chess pieces to the board. They were divorced three months later.*

Another friend, Roché, remarked: "He needed a good chess game just as a baby needs his bottle."

One notices that Duchamp's excess of interest coincided with the advent of chess equivalents to Dadaism and surrealism, the "hypermodernism" of Réti and others, who revolutionized chess theory and practice by showing that all the accepted orthodox principles—advancing centre pawns, not moving a piece twice in the opening, or the queen early—could be successfully flouted in the interests of more devious strategies. Predictably, he greatly admired Nimzowitsch. Duchamp's serious chess career began with his return to France from the USA in 1923. He finished high in the French Championship several times; played for France in Chess Olympiads, alongside the naturalized Frenchman Alekhine; and won, for example, the Paris tournament of 1932 ahead of Znosko-Borovsky. He was essentially a profound positional player, with a predilection for the endgame where with the board uncluttered the logical element in chess creativity predominates. His one chess book, *Opposition and Sister Squares Are Reconciled,*† studies king and pawn endings, the most pared-down of all. It is also characteristic of Duchamp in its artistic perversity: he commented, "Chess champions never read this book, because the problem it poses never really turns up more than once in a lifetime. There are possible endgame problems, but they're so rare that they're almost Utopian."

As an artist so intent upon purities of introverted abstraction that he more or less resented the necessity for the painter's creativity to end in something so crassly external as an actual picture, Duchamp was pleased that "in chess there are some extremely beautiful things in the domain of movement, but not in the visual domain. It is the imagining of the movement or of the gesture that makes the beauty, in this case. It's completely in one's grey matter."**

---

* Man Ray, quoted in Pierre Cabanne, *op. cit.*
† Marcel Duchamp and Vitaly Halberstadt, *Opposition and Sister Squares Are Reconciled,* Brussels, 1932.
** Pierre Cabanne, *op. cit.*

In these terms, he finds that chess creativity has greater affinities with musical composition and poetry, where the external visual element—ink marks on paper—is the sketchiest notation of created beauty:

> Objectively, a game of chess looks very much like a pen-and-ink drawing, with the difference, however, that the chess player paints with black and white forms already prepared instead of inventing forms as does the artist. The design thus formed on the chessboard has apparently no visual aesthetic value, and is more like a score for music which can be played again and again. Beauty in chess does not seem to be a visual experience as in painting. Beauty in chess is closer to beauty in poetry; the chess pieces are the block alphabet which shapes thoughts, and these thoughts, although making a visual design on the chessboard, express their beauty *abstractly*, like a poem. Actually, I believe that every chess player experiences a mixture of two aesthetic pleasures: first, the abstract image akin to the poetic idea of writing; secondly, the sensuous pleasure of the ideographic execution of that image on the chessboard. From my close contact with artists and chess players I have come to the conclusion that while all artists are not chess players, all chess players are artists.

Of course, the analogy of creative conception and execution in chess and in poetry is confined to the aesthetic level, and ignores the crucial distinguishing features of chess as a contest for victory, poetry as engagement with life beyond the poem. In his conversations with Pierre Cabanne, Duchamp typically not so much acknowledges, as rejoices in, the fact that in chess "there is no social purpose. That above all is important."

Duchamp, exemplifying creativity in the two areas, emerges as an illustration of much that I have suggested both about the disparate psychological motivations of chess and the humane arts, and of their connection within the purely aesthetic realm of creative delight. Artists of a different stamp from Duchamp, working within the central tradition of painting as exploration and illumination of experience, would by no means have found addiction to chess so consonant with their artistic principles and quests. Yet, in concluding this discussion, it must be insisted too that, more than any other sport or game chess resembles writing, painting and music in being an obsessional mental activity preoccupied with exploring tension and complication to resolve them to triumphant harmony, eliciting unified pattern from diversity; so that in the greatest chess creations, as in art or poetry, beauty and truth are felt to become cathartically one.

Vladimir Nabokov

In the course of my twenty years in exile I devoted a prodigious amount of time to the composing of chess problems. A certain position is elaborated on the board, and the problem to be solved is how to mate Black in a given number of moves, generally two or three. It is a beautiful, complex and sterile art related to the ordinary form of the game only insofar as, say, the properties of a sphere are made use of both by a juggler in weaving a new act and by a tennis player in winning a tournament. Most chess players, in fact, amateurs and masters alike, are only mildly interested in these highly specialized, fanciful, stylish riddles, and though appreciative of a catchy problem would be utterly baffled if asked to compose one.

Inspiration of a quasi-musical, quasi-poetical, or to be quite exact, poetico-mathematical type, attends the process of thinking up a chess composition of that sort. Frequently, in the friendly middle of the day, on the fringe of some trivial occupation, in the idle wake of a passing thought, I would experience, without warning, a twinge of mental pleasure as the bud of a chess problem burst open in my brain, promising me a night of labor and felicity. It might be a new way of blending an unusual strategic device with an unusual line of defense; it might be a glimpse of the actual configuration of men that would render at last, with humor and grace, a difficult theme that I had despaired of expressing before; or it might be a mere gesture made in the mist of my mind by the various units of force represented by chessmen—a kind of swift dumb show, suggesting new harmonies and new conflicts; whatever it was, it belonged to an especially exhilarating order of sensation, and my only quarrel with it today is that the maniacal manipulation of carved figures, or of their mental counterparts, during my most ebullient and prolific years engulfed so much of the time I could have devoted to verbal adventure.

Experts distinguish several schools of the chess-problem art: the Anglo-American one that combines accurate construction with dazzling thematic patterns, and refuses to be bound by any conventional rules; the rugged splendor of the Teutonic school; the highly finished but unpleasantly slick and insipid products of the Czech style with its strict adherence to certain artificial conditions; the old Russian endgame studies, which attain the sparkling summits of the art, and the mechanical Soviet problem of the so-called "task" type, which replaces artistic strategy by the ponderous working of themes to their utmost capacity. Themes in chess, it may be explained, are such devices as forelaying, withdrawing, pinning, unpinning and so forth; but it is only when they are combined in a certain way that a problem is satisfying. Deceit, to the point of diabolism, and originality, verging upon the grotesque, were my notions of strategy; and although in matters of construction I tried to conform, whenever possible, to classical rules, such as economy of force, unity, weeding out of loose ends, I was always ready to sacrifice purity of form to the exigencies of fantastic content, causing form to bulge and burst like a spongebag containing a small furious devil.

It is one thing to conceive the main play of a composition and another to construct it. The strain on the mind is formidable; the element of time drops out of one's consciousness altogether: the building hand gropes for a pawn in the box, holds it, while the mind still ponders the need for a foil or a stopgap, and when the first opens, a whole hour, perhaps, has gone by, has burned to ashes in the incandescent cerebration of the schemer. The chessboard before him is a magnetic field, a system of stresses and abysses, a starry firmament. The bishops move over it like searchlights. This or that knight is a lever adjusted and tried, and readjusted and tried again, till the problem is tuned up to the necessary level of beauty and surprise. How often I have struggled to bind the terrible force of White's queen so as to avoid a dual solution! It should be understood that competition in chess problems is not really between White and Black, but between the composer and the hypothetical solver (just as in a first-rate work of fiction the real clash is not between the characters but between the author and the world), so that a great part of a problem's value is due to the number of "tries"—delusive opening moves, false scents, specious lines of play, astutely and lovingly prepared to lead the would-be solver astray. But whatever I can say about this matter of problem composing, I do not seem to convey sufficiently the ecstatic core of the process and its points of connection with various other, more overt and fruitful, operations of the creative mind, from the charting of dangerous seas to the writing of one of those incredible novels where the author, in a fit of lucid madness, has set himself certain unique rules that he observes, certain nightmare obstacles that he surmounts, with the zest of a deity building a live world from the most unlikely ingredients—rocks, and carbon, and blind throbbings. In the case of problem composition, the event is accompanied by a mellow physical satisfaction, especially when the chessmen are beginning to enact adequately, in a penultimate rehearsal, the composer's dream. There is a feeling of snugness (which goes back to one's childhood, to play-planning in bed, with parts of toys fitting into corners of one's brain); there is the nice way one piece is ambushed behind another, within the comfort and warmth of an out-of-the-way square; and there is the smooth motion of a well-oiled and polished machine that runs sweetly at the touch of two forked fingers lightly lifting and lightly lowering a piece.

I remember one particular problem I had been trying to compose for months. There came a night when I managed at last to express that particular theme. It was meant for the delectation of the very expert solver. The unsophisticated might miss the point of the problem entirely, and discover its fairly simple, "thetic" solution without having passed through the pleasurable torments prepared for the sophisticated one. The latter would start by falling for an illusory pattern of play based on a fashionable avant-garde theme (exposing White's king to checks), which the composer had taken the greatest pains to "plant" (with only one obscure little move by an inconspicuous pawn to upset it). Having passed through this "antithetic" inferno the by now ultrasophisticated solver would reach the simple key move (bishop to c2) as somebody on a wild goose chase might go from Albany to New York by way of Vancouver, Eurasia and the Azores. The pleasant experience of the roundabout route (strange landscapes, gongs, tigers, exotic customs, the thrice-repeated circuit of a newly married couple around the sacred fire of an earthen brazier) would amply reward him for the misery of the deceit, and after that, his arrival at the simple key move would provide him with a synthesis of poignant artistic delight.

I remember slowly emerging from a swoon of concentrated chess thought, and there, on a great English board of cream and cardinal leather, the flawless position was at last balanced like a constellation. It worked. It lived. My Staunton chessmen (a twenty-year-old set given to me by my father's Englished brother, Konstantin), splendidly massive pieces, of tawny or black wood, up to four and a quarter inches tall, displayed their shiny contours as if conscious of the part they played. Alas, if examined closely, some of the men were seen to be chipped (after traveling in their box through the fifty or sixty lodgings I had changed during those years); but the top of the king's rook and the brow of the king's knight still showed a small crimson crown painted upon them, recalling the round mark on a happy Hindu's forehead.

A brooklet of time in comparison to its frozen lake on the chessboard, my watch showed half-past three. The season was May—mid-May, 1940. The day before, after months of soliciting and cursing, the emetic of a bribe had been administered to the right rat at the right office and had resulted finally in a *visa de sortie* which, in its turn, conditioned the permission to cross the Atlantic. All of a sudden, I felt that with the completion of my chess problem a whole period of my life had come to a satisfactory close. Everything around was very quiet; faintly dimpled, as it were, by the quality of my relief. Sleeping in the next room were you and our child. The lamp on my table was bonneted with blue sugarloaf paper (an amusing military precaution) and the resulting light lent a lunar tinge to the voluted air heavy with tobacco smoke. Opaque curtains separated me from blacked-out Paris. The headline of a newspaper drooping from the seat of a chair spoke of Hitler's striking at the Low Countries.

I have before me the sheet of paper upon which, that night in Paris, I drew the diagram of the problem's position. White: King on a7 (meaning first file, seventh rank), Queen on b6, Rooks on f4 and h5, Bishops on e4 and h8, Knights on d8 and e6, Pawns on b7 and g3; Black: King on e5, Rook on g7, Bishop on h6, Knights on e2 and g5, Pawns on c3, c6 and d7. White begins and mates in two moves. The false scent, the irresistible "try" is: Pawn to b8, becoming a knight, with three beautiful mates following in answer to disclosed checks by Black; but Black can defeat the whole brilliant affair by not checking White and making instead a modest dilatory move elsewhere on the board. In one corner of the sheet with the diagram, I notice a certain stamped mark that also adorns other papers and books I took out of France to America in May 1940. It is a circular imprint, in the ultimate tint of the spectrum—*violet de bureau*. In its center there are two capital letters of pica size, *R.F.*, meaning of course *République Française*. Other letters in lesser type, running peripherally, spell *Contrôle des Informations*. However, it is only now, many years later, that the information concealed in my chess symbols, which that control permitted to pass, may be, and in fact is, divulged.

Ezra Pound

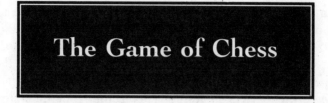

The Game of Chess

DOGMATIC STATEMENT CONCERNING THE
GAME OF CHESS: THEME FOR A SERIES
OF PICTURES

Red knights, brown bishops, bright queens,
Striking the board, falling in strong 'L's' of colour.
Reaching and striking in angles,
*   holding lines in one colour.*
This board is alive with light;
*   these pieces are living in form,*
Their moves break and reform the pattern:
*   luminous green from the rooks,*
Clashing with 'X's' of queen,
*   looped with the knight-leaps.*

'Y' pawns, cleaving, embanking!
Whirl! Centripetal! Mate! King down in the vortex,
Clash, leaping of bands, straight strips of hard colour,
Blocked lights working in. Escapes. Renewal of contest.

Lord Dunsany

The Sea and Chess

Silence. And silence still.
Then one long roller breaks,
And Hastings' houses fill
With the wild sound it makes.

Silence again. The sea,
Though it may seem to sleep,
Is still the vast and free
Inscrutable old deep.

Who shall entirely scan
All its mysteriousness?
Even the mind of man
Has deeps beyond our guess.

So, when a move has brought
Some strategy in sight,
We cannot plumb the thought
That brought that move to light.

And, small although it be,
And missed by careless eyes,
A chessboard, like the sea,
Has unplumbed mysteries.

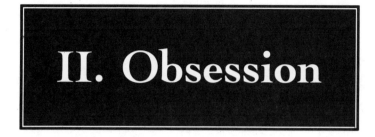

II. Obsession

Chess, according to one version of an old Indian proverb, is "a sea in which a gnat may drink and an elephant may bathe." And in which, one might add, a human may drown.

The two full-length masterpieces of literature that are wholly about chess—there are only two—are both about chess obsession. Vladimir Nabokov's novel *The Defense*, first published in Russian in 1929, is the story of Luzhin, a lethargic, neurotic boy with a genius for chess who grows into a lethargic, neurotic, world-renowned grandmaster and comes to believe, insanely, that his life is a chess game and that he is in danger of being defeated by some conspiracy of fate.

Luzhin was modeled in part, Nabokov said, on the Polish grandmaster Akiba Rubinstein (1882–1961), one of the world's leading players during the first three decades of this century. Rubinstein, like Luzhin, was uncomely, chess-obsessed, renowned for the elegance of his combinations, and, at the pinnacle of his career, deranged. But although Rubinstein spent his last thirty years in a mental institution, Luzhin's ultimate "defense" is to throw himself from a window. Nabokov, a chessplayer himself, must have been aware that in 1924 the well-known German master Curt von Bardeleben had killed himself in a similar manner.

Vladimir Nabokov

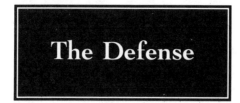

The Defense

In Grandfather's former study, which even on the hottest days was the dampest room in their country house no matter how much they opened the windows that looked straight out on grim dark fir trees, whose foliage was so thick and intricate that it was impossible to say where one tree ended and another began—in this uninhabited room where a bronze boy with violin stood on the bare desk—there was an unlocked bookcase containing the thick volumes of an extinct illustrated magazine. Luzhin would swiftly leaf through them until he reached the page where between a poem by Korinfski, crowned with a harp-shaped vignette, and the miscellany section containing information about shifting swamps, American eccentrics and the length of the human intestine, there was the woodcut of a chessboard. Not a single picture could arrest Luzhin's hand as it leafed through the volumes—neither the celebrated Niagara Falls nor starving Indian children (potbellied little skeletons) nor an attempted assassination of the King of Spain. The life of the world passed by with a hasty rustle, and suddenly stopped—the treasured diagram, problems, openings, entire games.

At the beginning of the summer holidays he had sorely missed his aunt and the old gentleman with the bunch of flowers—especially that fragrant old man smelling at times of violets and at times of lilies of the valley, depending upon what flowers he had brought to Luzhin's aunt. Usually he would arrive just right—a few minutes after Luzhin's aunt had glanced at her watch and left the house. "Never mind, let's wait a while," the old man would say, removing the damp paper from his bouquet, and Luzhin would draw up an armchair for him to the table where the chessmen had already been set out. The appearance of the old gentleman with the flowers had provided him with a way out of a rather awkward situation. After three or four truancies from school it became apparent that his aunt had really no aptitude for chess. As the game proceeded, her pieces would conglomerate in an unseemly jumble, out of which there would suddenly dash an exposed helpless King. But the old gentleman played divinely. The first time his aunt, pulling on her gloves, had said rapidly, "Unfortunately I must leave but you stay on and play chess with my nephew, thank you for the wonderful lilies of the valley," the first time the old man had sat down and sighed: "It's a long time since I touched . . . now, young man—left or right?"—this first time when after a few moves Luzhin's ears were burning and there was nowhere to advance, it seemed to Luzhin he was playing a completely different game from the one his aunt had taught him. The board was bathed in fragrance. The old man called the Officer a Bishop and the Tower, a Rook, and whenever he made a move that was fatal for his opponent he would immediately take it back, and as if disclosing the mechanism of an expensive instrument he would show the way his opponent should have played in order to avert disaster. He won the first fifteen games without the slightest effort, not pondering his moves for a moment, but during the sixteenth game he suddenly began to think and won with difficulty, while on the last day, the day he drove up with a whole bush of lilac for which no place could be found, and the boy's aunt darted about on tiptoe in her bedroom and then, presumably, left by the back door—on this last day, after a long exciting struggle during which the old man revealed a capacity for breathing hard through the nose—Luzhin perceived something, something was set free within him, something cleared up, and the mental myopia that had been painfully beclouding his chess vision disappeared. "Well, well, it's a draw," said the old man. He moved his Queen back and forth a few times the way you move the lever of a broken machine and repeated: "A draw, Perpetual check." Luzhin also tried the lever to see if it would work, wiggled it, and then sat still, staring stiffly at the board. "You'll go far," said the old man. "You'll go far if you continue on the same lines. Tremendous progress! Never saw anything like it before. . . . Yes, you'll go very, very far. . . ."

It was this old man who explained to Luzhin the simple method of notation in chess, and Luzhin, replaying the games given in the magazine, soon discovered in himself a quality he had once envied when his father used to tell somebody at table that he personally was unable to understand how his father-in-law could read a score for hours and hear in his mind all the movements of the music as he ran his eye over the notes, now smiling, now frowning, and sometimes turning back like a reader checking a detail in a novel—a name, the time of the year. "It must be a great pleasure," his father had said, "to assimilate music in its natural state." It was a similar pleasure that Luzhin himself now began to experience as he skimmed fluently over the letters and numbers representing moves. At first he learned to replay the immortal games that remained from former tournaments—he would rapidly glance over the notes of chess and silently move the pieces on his board. Now and then this or that move, provided in the text with an exclamation or a question mark (depending upon whether it had been beautifully or wretchedly played), would be followed by several series of moves in parentheses, since that remarkable move branched out like a river and every branch had to be traced to its conclusion before one returned to the main channel. These possible continuations that explained the essence of blunder or foresight Luzhin gradually ceased to reconstruct actually on the board and contented himself with perceiving their melody mentally through the sequence of symbols and signs. Similarly he was able to "read" a game already perused once without using the board at all; and this was all the more pleasant in that he did not have to fiddle about with chessmen while constantly listening for someone coming; the door, it is true, was locked, and he would open it unwillingly, after the brass handle had been jiggled many times—and Luzhin senior, coming to see what his son was doing in that damp uninhabited room, would find his son restless and sullen with red ears; on the desk lay the bound volumes of the magazine and Luzhin senior would be seized by the suspicion that his son might have been looking for pictures of naked women. "Why do you lock yourself up?" he would ask (and little Luzhin would draw his head into his shoulders and with hideous clarity imagine his father looking under the sofa and finding the chess set). "The air in here's really icy. And what's so interesting about these old magazines? Let's go and see if there are any red mushrooms under the fir trees."

Yes, they were there, those edible red boletes. Green needles adhered to their delicately brick-colored caps and sometimes a blade of grass would leave on one of them a long narrow trace. Their undersides might be holey, and occasionally a yellow slug would be sitting there—and Luzhin senior would use his pocketknife to clean moss and soil from the thick speckled-gray root of each mushroom before placing it in the basket. His son followed behind him at a few paces' distance, with his hands behind his back like a little old man, and not only did he not look for mushrooms but even refused to admire those his father, with little quacks of pleasure, unearthed himself. And sometimes, plump and pale in a dreary white dress that did not become her, Mrs. Luzhin would appear at the end of the avenue and hurry toward him, passing alternately through sunlight and shadow, and the dry leaves that never cease to occur in northern woods would rustle beneath the slightly skewed high heels of her white slippers. One July day, she slipped on the veranda steps and sprained her foot, and for a long time afterwards she lay in bed— either in her darkened bedroom or on the veranda—wearing a pink negligee, her face heavily powdered, and there would always be a small silver bowl with *boules-de-gomme*—balls of hard candy standing on a little table beside her. The foot was soon better but she continued to recline as if having made up her mind that this was to be her lot, that this precisely was her destiny in life. Summer was unusually hot, the mosquitoes gave no peace, all day long the shrieks of peasant girls bathing could be heard from the river, and on one such oppressive and voluptuous day, early in the morning before the gadflies had yet begun to torment the black horse daubed with pungent ointment, Luzhin senior stepped into the calash and was taken to the station to spend the day in town. "At least be reasonable, it's essential for me to see Silvestrov," he had said to his wife the night before, pacing about the bedroom in his mouse-colored dressing gown. "Really, how queer you are. Can't you see this is important? I myself would prefer not to go." But his wife continued to lie with her face thrust into the pillow, and her fat helpless back shook with sobs. Nonetheless, in the morning he left—and his son standing in the garden saw the top part of the coachman and his father's hat skim along the serrated line of young firs that fenced off the garden from the road.

That day Luzhin junior was in low spirits. All the games in the old magazine had been studied, all the problems solved, and he was forced to play with himself, but this ended inevitably in an exchange of all the pieces and a dull draw. And it was unbearably hot. The veranda cast a black triangular shadow on the bright sand. The avenue was paved with sunflecks, and these spots, if you slitted your eyes, took on the aspect of regular light and dark squares. An intense latticelike shadow lay flat beneath a garden bench. The urns that stood on stone pedestals at the four corners of the terrace threatened one another across their diagonals. Swallows soared: their flight recalled the motion of scissors swiftly cutting out some design. Not knowing what to do with himself he wandered down the footpath by the river, and from the opposite bank came ecstatic squeals and glimpses of naked bodies. He stole behind a tree trunk and with beating heart peered at these flashes of white. A bird rustled in the branches, and taking fright he quickly left the river and went back. He had lunch alone with the housekeeper, a taciturn sallow-faced old woman who always gave off a slight smell of coffee. Afterwards, lolling on the drawing room couch, he drowsily listened to all manner of slight sounds, to an oriole's cry in the garden, to the buzzing of a bumblebee that had flown in the window, to the tinkle of dishes on a tray being carried down from his mother's bedroom—and these limpid sounds were strangely transformed in his reverie and assumed the shape of bright intricate patterns on a dark background; and in trying to unravel them he fell asleep. He was wakened by the steps of the maid dispatched by his mother. . . . It was dim and cheerless in the bedroom; his mother drew him to her but he braced himself and turned away so stubbornly that she had to let him go. "Come, tell me something," she said softly. He shrugged his shoulders and picked at his knee with one finger. "Don't you want to tell me anything?" she asked still more softly. He looked at the bedside table, put a *boule-de-gomme* in his mouth and began to suck—he took a second, a third, another and another until his mouth was full of sweet-thudding and bumping balls. "Take some more, take as many as you wish," she murmured, and stretching one hand from under the bedclothes she tried to touch him, to stroke him. "You haven't got tanned at all this year," she said after a pause. "But perhaps I simply can't see, the light here is so dead, everything looks blue. Raise the Venetian blinds, please. Or no, wait, stay. Later." Having sucked his *boules-de-gomme* to the end he inquired if he could leave. She asked him what he would do now and would he not like to drive to the station and meet his father off the seven o'clock train? "Let me go," he said. "It smells of medicine in here."

He tried to slide down the stairs the way they did at school—the way he himself never did it there; but the steps were too high. Beneath the staircase, in a cupboard that had still not been thoroughly explored, he looked for magazines. He dug out one and found a checkers section in it, diagrams of stupid clumsy round blobs on their boards, but there was no chess. As he rummaged on, he kept coming across a bothersome herbarium album with dried edelweiss and purple leaves in it and with inscriptions in pale violet ink, in a childish, thin-spun hand that was so different from his mother's present handwriting: *Davos 1885; Gatchina 1886.* Wrathfully he began to tear out the leaves and flowers, sneezing from the fine dust as he squatted on his haunches amid the scattered books. Then it got so dark beneath the stairs that the pages of the magazine he was again leafing through began to merge into a gray blur and sometimes a small picture would trick him, because it looked like a chess problem in the diffuse darkness. He thrust the books back anyhow into the drawers and wandered into the drawing room, thinking listlessly that it must be well past seven o'clock since the butler was lighting the kerosene lamps. Leaning on a cane and holding on to the banisters, his mother in mauve peignoir came heavily down the stairs, a frightened look on her face. "I don't understand why your father isn't here yet," she said, and moving with difficulty she went out onto the veranda and began to peer down the road between the fir trunks that the setting sun banded with bright copper.

He came only around ten, said he had missed the train, had been extremely busy, had dined with his publisher—no, no soup, thank you. He laughed and spoke very loudly and ate noisily, and Luzhin was struck by the feeling that his father was looking at him all the time as if staggered by his presence. Dinner graded into late evening tea. Mother, her elbow propped on the table, silently slitted her eyes at her plate of raspberries, and the gayer her husband's stories became the narrower her eyes grew. Then she got up and quietly left and it seemed to Luzhin that all this had happened once before. He remained alone on the veranda with his father and was afraid to raise his head, feeling that strange searching stare on him the whole time.

"How have you been passing the time?" asked his father suddenly. "What have you been doing?" "Nothing," replied Luzhin.

"And what are you planning to do now?" asked Luzhin senior in the same tone of forced jollity, imitating his son's manner of using the formal plural for "you." "Do you want to go to bed or do you want to sit here with me?" Luzhin killed a mosquito and very cautiously stole a glance upwards and sideways at his father. There was a crumb on his father's beard and an unpleasantly mocking expression gleamed in his eyes. "Do you know what?" his father said and the crumb jumped off. "Do you know what? Let's play some game. For instance, how about me teaching you chess?"

He saw his son slowly blush and taking pity on him immediately added: "Or cabala—there is a pack of cards over there in the table drawer." "But no chess set, we have no chess set," said Luzhin huskily and again stole a cautious look at his father. "The good ones remained in town," said his father placidly, "but I think there are some old ones in the attic. Let's go take a look."

And indeed, by the light of the lamp that his father held aloft, among all sorts of rubbish in a case Luzhin found a chessboard, and again he had the feeling that all this had happened before—that open case with a nail sticking out of its side, those dust-powdered books, that wooden chessboard with a crack down the middle. A small box with a sliding lid also came to light; it contained puny chessmen. And the whole time he was looking for the chess set and then carrying it down to the veranda, Luzhin tried to figure out whether it was by accident his father had mentioned chess or whether he had noticed something—and the most obvious explanation did not occur to him, just as sometimes in solving a problem its key turns out to be a move that seemed barred, impossible, excluded quite naturally from the range of possible moves.

And now when the board had been placed on the illuminated table between the lamp and the raspberries, and its dust wiped off with a bit of newspaper, his father's face was no longer mocking, and Luzhin, forgetting his fear, forgetting his secret, felt permeated all at once with proud excitement at the thought that he could, if he wanted, display his art. His father began to set out the pieces. One of the Pawns was replaced by an absurd purple-colored affair in the shape of a tiny bottle; in place of one Rook there was a checker; the Knights were headless and the one horse's head that remained after the box had been emptied (leaving a small die and a red counter) turned out not to fit any of them. When everything had been set out, Luzhin suddenly made up his mind and muttered: "I already can play a little." "Who taught you?" asked his father without lifting his head. "I learned it at school," replied Luzhin. "Some of the boys could play." "Oh! Fine," said his father, and added (quoting Pushkin's doomed duelist): "Let's start, if you are willing."

He had played chess since his youth, but only seldom and sloppily, with haphazard opponents—on serene evenings aboard a Volga steamer in the foreign sanatorium where his brother was dying years ago, here, in the country, with the village doctor, an unsociable man who periodically ceased calling on them—and all these chance games, full of oversights and sterile meditations, were for him little more than a moment of relaxation or simply a means of decently preserving silence in the company of a person with whom conversation kept petering out—brief, uncomplicated games, remarkable neither for ambition nor inspiration, which he always began in the same way, paying little attention to his adversary's moves. Although he made no fuss about losing, he secretly considered himself to be not at all a bad player, and told himself that if ever he lost it was through absentmindedness, good nature or a desire to enliven the game with daring sallies, and he considered that with a little application it was possible, without theoretic knowledge, to refute any gambit out of the textbook. His son's passion for chess had so astounded him, seemed so unexpected—and at the same time so fateful and inescapable—so strange and awesome was it to sit on this bright veranda amid the black summer night, across from this boy whose tensed forehead seemed to expand and swell as soon as he bent over the pieces—all this was so strange and awesome that Luzhin senior was incapable of thinking of the game, and while he feigned concentration, his attention wandered from vague recollections of his illicit day in St. Petersburg, that left a residue of shame it was better not to investigate, to the casual, easy gestures with which his son moved this or that piece. The game had lasted but a few minutes when his son said: "If you do this it's mate and if you do that you lose your Queen," and he, confused, took his move back and began to think properly, inclining his head first to the left and then to the right, slowly stretching out his fingers toward the Queen and quickly snatching them away again, as if burned, while in the meantime his son calmly, and with uncharacteristic tidiness, put the taken pieces into their box. Finally Luzhin senior made his move, whereupon there started a devastation of his positions, and then he laughed unnaturally and knocked his King over in sign of surrender. In this way he lost three games and realized that should he play ten more the result would be just the same, and yet he was unable to stop. At the very beginning of the fourth game Luzhin pushed back the piece moved by his father and with a shake of his head said in a confident unchildlike voice: "The worst reply. Chigorin suggests taking the Pawn." And when with incomprehensible, hopeless speed he had lost this game as well, Luzhin senior again laughed, and with trembling hand began to pour milk into a cut-glass tumbler, on the bottom of which lay a raspberry core, which now floated to the surface and circled, unwilling to be extracted. His son put away the board and the box on a wicker table in the corner and having blurted a phlegmatic "good night" softly closed the door behind him.

"Oh well, I should have expected something like this," said Luzhin senior, wiping the tips of his fingers with a handkerchief. "He's not just amusing himself with chess, he's performing a sacred rite."

A fat-bodied, fluffy moth with glowing eyes fell on the table after colliding with the lamp. A breeze stirred lightly through the garden. The clock in the drawing room started to chime daintily and struck twelve.

"Nonsense," he said, "stupid imagination. Many youngsters are excellent chess players. Nothing surprising in that. The whole affair is getting on my nerves, that's all. Bad of her—she shouldn't have encouraged him. Well, no matter. . . ."

He thought drearily that in a moment he would have to lie, to remonstrate, to soothe, and it was midnight already. . . .

"I want to sleep," he said, but remained sitting in the armchair.

And early next morning in the darkest and mossiest corner of the dense coppice behind the garden little Luzhin buried his father's precious box of chessmen, assuming this to be the simplest way of avoiding any kind of complications, for now there were other chessmen that he could use openly. His father, unable to suppress his interest in the matter, went off to see the gloomy country doctor, who was a far better chess player than he, and in the evening after dinner, laughing and rubbing his hands, doing his best to ignore the fact that all this was wrong—but why wrong he could not say—he sat his son down with the doctor at the wicker table on the veranda, himself set out the pieces (apologizing for the purple thingum), sat down beside the players and began avidly following the game. Twitching his bushy eyebrows and tormenting his fleshy nose with a large hairy fist, the doctor thought long over every move and from time to time would lean back in his chair as if able to see better from a distance, and make big eyes, and then lurch heavily forward, his hands braced against his knees. He lost—and grunted so loudly that his wicker armchair creaked in response. "But look, look!" exclaimed Luzhin senior. "You should go this way and everything is saved— you even have the better position." "Don't you see I'm in check?" growled the doctor in a bass voice and began to set out the pieces anew. And when Luzhin senior went out into the dark garden to accompany the doctor as far as the footpath with its border of glow-worms leading down to the bridge, he heard the words he had so thirsted to hear once, but now these words weighed heavy upon him—he would rather not have heard them at all.

The doctor started coming every night and since he was really a first-rate player he derived enormous pleasure from these incessant defeats. He brought Luzhin a chess handbook, advising him, how-ever, not to get too carried away by it, not to tire himself, and to read in the open air. He spoke about the grand masters he had had the occasion to see, about a recent tournament, and also about the past of chess, about a somewhat doubtful rajah and about the great Philidor, who was also an accomplished musician. At times, grinning gloom-ily, he would bring what he termed "a sugarplum"—an ingenious problem cut out of some periodical. Luzhin would pore over it a while, find finally the solution and with an extraordinary expression on his face and radiant bliss in his eyes would exclaim, burring his r's: "How glorious, how glorious!" But the notion of composing prob-lems himself did not entice him. He dimly felt that they would be a pointless waste of the militant, charging, bright force he sensed within him whenever the doctor, with strokes of his hairy finger, removed his King farther and farther, and finally, nodded his head and sat there quite still, looking at the board, while Luzhin senior, who was always present, always craving a miracle—his son's defeat—and was both frightened and overjoyed when his son won (and suffered from this complicated mixture of feelings), would seize a Knight or a Rook, crying that everything was not lost and would himself some-times play to the end of a hopelessly compromised game.

And thus it began. Between this sequence of evenings on the veranda and the day when Luzhin's photograph appeared in a St. Petersburg magazine it was as if nothing had been, neither the coun-try autumn drizzling on the asters, nor the journey back to town, nor the return to school. The photograph appeared on an October day soon after his first, unforgettable performance in a chess club. And everything else that took place between the return to town and the photograph—two months after all—was so blurry and so mixed up that later, in recalling this time, Luzhin was unable to say exactly when, for instance, that social evening had taken place at school—where in a corner, almost unnoticed by his schoolfellows, he had quietly beaten the geography teacher, a well-known amateur—or when on his father's invitation a gray-haired Jew came to dinner, a senile chess genius who had been victorious in all the cities of the world but now lived in idleness and poverty, purblind, with a sick heart, having lost forever his fire, his grip, his luck. . . . But one thing Luzhin remembered quite clearly—the fear he experienced in school, the fear they would learn of his gift and ridicule him—and consequently, guided by this infallible recollection, he judged that after the game played at the social evening he must not have gone to school any more, for remembering all the shudders of his childhood he was unable to imagine the horrible sensation he would have experienced upon entering the classroom on the following morning and meeting those inquisitive, all-knowing eyes. He remembered, on the other hand, that after his picture appeared he refused to go to school and it was impossible to untangle in his memory the knot in which the social evening and the photograph were joined, it was impossible to say which came first and which second. It was his father who brought him the magazine, and the photograph was one taken the previous year, in the country: a tree in the garden and he next to it, a pattern of foliage on his forehead, a sullen expression on his slightly inclined face, and those narrow white shorts that always used to come unbuttoned in front. Instead of the joy expected by his father, he expressed nothing—but he did feel a secret joy: now this would put an end to school. They pleaded with him during the course of a week. His mother, of course, cried. His father threatened to take away his new chess set—enormous pieces on a morocco board. And suddenly everything was decided by itself. He ran away from home—in his autumn coat, since his winter one had been hidden after one unsuccessful attempt to run away—and not knowing where to go (a stinging snow was falling and settling on the cornices, and the wind would blow it off, endlessly reenacting this miniature blizzard), he wandered finally to his aunt's place, not having seen her since spring. He met her as she was leaving. She was wearing a black hat and holding flowers wrapped in paper, on her way to a funeral. "Your old partner is dead," she said. "Come with me." Angry at not being allowed to warm himself, angry at the snow falling, and at the sentimental tears shining behind his aunt's veil, he turned sharply and walked away, and after walking about for an hour set off for home. He did not remember the actual return—and even more curiously, was never sure whether things had happened thus or differently; perhaps his memory later added much that was taken from his delirium—for he was delirious for a whole week, and since he was extremely delicate and high-strung, the doctors presumed he would not pull through. It was not the first time he had been ill and when later reconstructing the sensation of this particular illness, he involuntarily recalled others, of which his childhood had been full: he remembered especially the time when he was quite small, playing all alone, and wrapping himself up in the tiger rug, to represent, rather forlornly, a king—it was nicest of all to represent a king since the imaginary mantle protected him against the chills of fever, and he wanted to postpone for as long as possible that inevitable moment when they would feel his forehead, take his temperature and then bundle him into bed. Actually, there had been nothing quite comparable to his October chess-permeated illness. The gray-haired Jew who used to beat Chigorin, the corpse of his aunt's admirer muffled in flowers, the sly, gay countenance of his father bringing a magazine, and the geography teacher petrified with the suddenness of the mate, and the tobacco-smoke-filled room at the chess club where he was closely surrounded by a crowd of university students, and the clean-shaven face of the musician holding for some reason the telephone receiver like a violin, between shoulder and cheek—all this participated in his delirium and took on the semblance of a kind of monstrous game on a spectral, wobbly, and endlessly disintegrating board.

Upon his recovery, a tall and thinner boy, he was taken abroad, at first to the Adriatic coast where he lay on the garden terrace in the sun and played games in his head, which nobody could forbid him, and then to a German resort where his father took him for walks along footpaths fenced off with twisted beech railings. Sixteen years later when he revisited this resort he recognized the bearded earthenware dwarfs between the flower beds, and the garden paths of colored gravel before the hotel that had grown bigger and handsomer, and also the dark damp wood on the hill and the motley daubs of oil paint (each hue marking the direction of a given walk) with which a beech trunk or a rock would be equipped at an intersection, so that the stroller should not lose his way. The same paperweights bearing emerald-blue views touched up with mother-of-pearl beneath convex glass were on sale in the shops near the spring and no doubt the same orchestra on the stand in the park was playing potpourris of opera, and the same maples were casting their lively shade over small tables where people drank coffee and ate wedge-shaped slices of apple tart with whipped cream.

"Look, do you see those windows?" he said, pointing with his cane at the wing of the hotel. "It was there we had that pretty little tournament. Some of the most respectable German players took part. I was a boy of fourteen. Third prize, yes, third prize."

He replaced both hands on the crook of his thick cane with that sad, slightly old-mannish gesture that was natural to him now, and bent his head as if listening to distant music.

"What? Put on my hat? The sun is scorching, you say? I'd say it is ineffective. Why should you fuss about it? We are sitting in the shade."

Nevertheless he took the straw hat extended to him across the little table, drummed on the bottom where there was a blurred dark spot over the hatmaker's name, and donned it with a wry smile—wry in the precise sense: his right cheek and the corner of his mouth went up slightly, exposing bad, tobacco-stained teeth; he had no other smile. And one would never have said that he was only beginning his fourth decade: from the wings of his nose there descended two deep, flabby furrows, his shoulders were bent; in the whole of his body one remarked an unhealthy heaviness; and when he rose abruptly, with raised elbow defending himself from a wasp, one saw he was rather stout—nothing in the little Luzhin had foreshadowed this lazy, unhealthy fleshiness. "But why does it pester me?" he cried in a thin, querulous voice, continuing to lift his elbow and endeavoring with his other hand to get out his handkerchief. The wasp, having described one last circle, flew away, and he followed it with his eyes for a long time, mechanically shaking out his handkerchief; then he set his metal chair more firmly on the gravel, picked up his fallen cane and sat down again, breathing heavily.

"Why are you laughing? Wasps are extremely unpleasant insects." Frowning, he looked down at the table. Beside his cigarette case lay a handbag, semicircular, made of black silk. He reached out for it absently and began to click the lock.

"Shuts badly," he said without looking up. "One fine day you'll spill everything out."

He sighed, laid the handbag aside and added in the same tone of voice: "Yes, the most respectable German players. And one Austrian. My late papa was unlucky. He hoped there would be no real interest in chess here and we landed right in a tournament."

Things had been rebuilt and jumbled, the wing of the house now looked different. They had lived over there, on the second floor. It had been decided to stay until the end of the year and then return to Russia—and the ghost of school, which his father dared not mention, again loomed into view. His mother went back much earlier, at the beginning of summer. She said she was *insanely* homesick for the Russian countryside, and that protracted "insanely" with such a plaintive, aching middle syllable was practically the sole intonation of hers that Luzhin retained in his memory. She left reluctantly, however, not really knowing whether to go or stay. It was already some time since she had begun to experience a strange feeling of estrangement from her son, as if he had drifted away somewhere, and the one she loved was not this grown-up boy, not the chess prodigy that the newspapers were writing about, but that little warm, insupportable child who at the slightest provocation would throw himself flat on the floor, screaming and drumming his feet. And everything was so sad and so unnecessary—that sparse un-Russian lilac in the station garden, those tulip-shaped lamps in the sleeping car of the Nord Express, and those sinking sensations in the chest, a feeling of suffocation, perhaps angina pectoris and perhaps, as her husband said, simply nerves. She went away and did not write; his father grew gayer and moved to a smaller room; and then one July day when little Luzhin was on his way home from another hotel—in which lived one of those morose elderly men who were his playmates—accidentally, in the bright low sun, he caught sight of his father by the wooden railings of a hillside path. His father was with a lady, and since that lady was certainly his young red-haired aunt from St. Petersburg, he was very surprised and somehow ashamed and he did not say anything to his father. Early one morning a few days after this he heard his father swiftly approach his room along the corridor, apparently laughing loudly. The door was burst open and his father entered holding out a slip of paper as if thrusting it away. Tears rolled down his cheeks and along his nose as if he had splashed his face with water and he kept repeating with sobs and gasps: "What's this? What's this? It's a mistake, they've got it wrong"—and continued to thrust away the telegram. . . .

The whole time, however, now feebly, now sharply, shadows of his real chess life would show through this dream and finally it broke through and it was simply night in the hotel, chess thoughts, chess insomnia and meditations on the drastic defense he had invented to counter Turati's opening. He was wide-awake and his mind worked clearly, purged of all dross and aware that everything apart from chess was only an enchanting dream, in which, like the golden haze of the moon, the image of a sweet, clear-eyed maiden with bare arms dissolved and melted. The rays of his consciousness, which were wont to disperse when they came into contact with the incompletely intelligible world surrounding him, thereby losing one half of their force, had grown stronger and more concentrated now that this world had dissolved into a mirage and there was no longer any need to worry about it. Real life, chess life, was orderly, clear-cut and rich in adventure, and Luzhin noted with pride how easy it was for him to reign in this life, and the way everything obeyed his will and bowed to his schemes. Some of his games at the Berlin tournament had been even then termed immortal by connoiseurs. He had won one after sacrificing in succession his Queen, a Rook and a Knight; in another he had placed a Pawn in such a dynamic position that it had acquired an absolutely monstrous force and had continued to grow and swell, balefully for his opponent, like a furuncle in the tenderest part of the board; and finally in a third game, by means of an apparently absurd move that provoked a murmuring among the spectators, Luzhin constructed an elaborate trap for his opponent that the latter divined too late. In these games and in all the others that he played at this unforgettable tournament, he manifested a stunning clarity of thought, a merciless logic. But Turati also played brilliantly, Turati also scored point after point, somewhat hypnotizing his opponents with the boldness of his imagination and trusting too much, perhaps, to the chess luck that till now had never deserted him. His meeting with Luzhin was to decide who would get first prize and there were those who said that the limpidity and lightness of Luzhin's thought would prevail over the Italian's tumultuous fantasy, and there were

those who forecast that the fiery, swift-swooping Turati would defeat the far-sighted Russian player. And the day of their meeting
arrived.

Luzhin awoke fully dressed, even wearing his overcoat; he
looked at his watch, rose hastily and put on his hat, which had been
lying in the middle of the room. At this point he recollected himself
and looked round the room, trying to understand what exactly he
had slept on. His bed was unrumpled and the velvet of the couch was
completely smooth. The only thing he knew for sure was that from
time immemorial he had been playing chess—and in the darkness of
his memory, as in two mirrors reflecting a candle, there was only a
vista of converging lights with Luzhin sitting at a chessboard, and
again Luzhin at a chessboard, only smaller, and then smaller still, and
so on an infinity of times. But he was late, he was late, and he had to
hurry. He swiftly opened the door and stopped in bewilderment.
According to his concept of things, the chess hall, and his table, and
the waiting Turati should have been right here. Instead of this he saw
an empty corridor and a staircase beyond it. Suddenly from that
direction, from the stairs, appeared a swiftly running little man who
caught sight of Luzhin and spread out his hands. "Maestro," he
exclaimed, "what is this? They are waiting for you, they are waiting
for you, Maestro. . . . I telephoned you three times and they said
you didn't answer their knocks. Signor Turati has been at his post a
long time." "They removed it," said Luzhin sourly, pointing to the
empty corridor with his cane. "How was I to know that everything
would be removed?" "If you don't feel well . . ." began the little
man, looking sadly at Luzhin's pale, glistening face. "Well, take me
there!" cried Luzhin in a shrill voice and banged his cane on the floor.
"With pleasure, with pleasure," muttered the other distractedly. His
gaze concentrated on the little overcoat with its raised collar running
in front of him, Luzhin began to conquer the incomprehensible space.
"We'll go on foot," said his guide, "it's exactly a minute's walk."
With a feeling of relief Luzhin recognized the revolving doors of the
café and then the staircase, and finally he saw what he had been
looking for in the hotel corridor. Upon entering he immediately felt
fullness of life, calm, clarity, and confidence. "There's a big victory
coming," he said loudly, and a crowd of dim people parted in order
to let him through. "*Tard, tard, très tard,*" jabbered Turati, materi-
alizing suddenly and shaking his head. "*Avanti,*" said Luzhin and
laughed. A table appeared between them and upon it was a board

with pieces set out ready for battle. Luzhin took a cigarette from his waistcoat pocket and unconsciously lit up.

At this point a strange thing happened. Turati, although having white, did not launch his famous opening and the defense Luzhin had worked out proved an utter waste. Whether because Turati had anticipated possible complications or else had simply decided to play warily, knowing the calm strength which Luzhin had revealed at this tournament, he began in the most banal way. Luzhin momentarily regretted the work done in vain, but nevertheless he was glad: this gave him more freedom. Moreover, Turati was evidently afraid of him. On the other hand there was undoubtedly some trick concealed in the innocent, jejune opening proposed by Turati, and Luzhin settled down to play with particular care. At first it went softly, softly, like muted violins. The players occupied their positions cautiously, moving this and that up but doing it politely, without the slightest sign of a threat—and if there was any threat it was entirely conventional—more like a hint to one's opponent that over there he would do well to build a cover, and the opponent would smile, as if all this were an insignificant joke, and strengthen the proper place and himself move forward a fraction. Then, without the least warning, a chord sang out tenderly. This was one of Turati's forces occupying a diagonal line. But forthwith a trace of melody very softly manifested itself on Luzhin's side also. For a moment mysterious possibilities were quivering, and then all was quiet again: Turati retreated, drew in. And once more for a while both opponents, as if having no intention of advancing, occupied themselves with sprucing up their own squares—nursing, shifting, smoothing things down at home— and then there was another sudden flare-up, a swift combination of sounds: two small forces collided and both were immediately swept away: a momentary, masterly motion of the fingers and Luzhin removed and placed on the table beside him what was no longer an incorporeal force but a heavy, yellow Pawn; Turati's fingers flashed in the air and an inert, black Pawn with a gleam of light on its head was in turn lowered onto the table. And having got rid of these two chess quantities that had so suddenly turned into wood the players seemed to calm down and forget the momentary flare-up: the vibration in this part of the board, however, had not yet quite died down, something was still endeavoring to take shape. . . . But these sounds did not succeed in establishing the desired relationship—some other deep, dark note chimed elsewhere and both players abandoned the still quivering square and became interested in another part of the board. But here too everything ended abortively. The weightiest elements on the board called to one another several times with trumpet voices and again there was an exchange, and again two chess forces were transformed into carved, brightly lacquered dummies. And then there was a long, long interval of thought, during which Luzhin bred from one spot on the board and lost a dozen illusionary games in succession, and then his fingers groped for and found a bewitching, brittle, crystalline combination—which with a gentle tinkle disintegrated at Turati's first reply. But neither was Turati able to do anything after that and playing for time (time is merciless in the universe of chess), both opponents repeated the same two moves, threat and defense, threat and defense—but meanwhile both kept thinking of the most tricky conceit that had nothing in common with these mechanical moves. And Turati finally decided on this combination—and immediately a kind of musical tempest overwhelmed the board and Luzhin searched stubbornly in it for the tiny, clear note that he needed in order in his turn to swell it out into a thunderous harmony. Now everything on the board breathed with life, everything was concentrated on a single idea, was rolled up tighter and tighter; for a moment the disappearance of two pieces eased the situation and then again—*agitato*. Luzhin's thought roamed through entrancing and terrible labyrinths, meeting there now and then the anxious thought of Turati, who sought the same things as he. Both realized simultaneously that white was not destined to develop his scheme any further, that he was on the brink of losing rhythm. Turati hastened to propose an exchange and the number of forces on the board was again reduced. New possibilities appeared, but still no one could say which side had the advantage. Luzhin, preparing an attack for which it was first necessary to explore a maze of variations, where his every step aroused a perilous echo, began a long meditation: he needed, it seemed, to make one last prodigious effort and he would find the secret move leading to victory. Suddenly, something occurred outside his being, a scorching pain—and he let out a loud cry, shaking his hand stung by the flame of a match, which he had lit and forgotten to apply to his cigarette. The pain immediately passed, but in the fiery gap he had seen something unbearably awesome, the full horror of the abysmal depths of chess. He glanced at the chessboard and his brain wilted from hitherto unprecedented weariness. But the chessmen were pitiless, they held and absorbed him. There was horror in this, but in this also was the sole harmony, for what else exists in the world besides chess? Fog, the unknown, non-being . . . He noticed that Turati was no longer sitting; he stood stretching himself. "Adjournment, Maestro," said a voice from behind. "Note down your next move." "No, no, not yet," said Luzhin pleadingly, his eyes searching for the person who spoke. "That's all for today," the same voice went on, again from behind, a gyratory kind of voice. Luzhin wanted to stand up but was unable to. He saw that he had moved backwards somewhere together with his chair and that people had hurled themselves rapaciously upon the position on the chessboard, where the whole of his life had just been, and were wrangling and shouting as they nimbly moved the pieces this way and that. He again tried to stand up and again was unable to. "Why, why?" he said plaintively, trying to distinguish the board between the narrow, black backs bent over it. They dwindled completely away and disappeared. On the board the pieces were mixed up now and stood about in disorderly groups. A phantom went by, stopped and began swiftly to stow the pieces away in a tiny coffin. "It's all over," said Luzhin and groaning from the effort, wrenched himself out of the chair. A few phantoms still stood about discussing something. It was cold and fairly dark. Phantoms were carrying off the boards and chairs. Tortuous and transparent chess images roamed about in the air, wherever you looked—and Luzhin, realizing that he had got stuck, that he had lost his way in one of the combinations he had so recently pondered, made a desperate attempt to free himself, to break out somewhere— even if into nonexistence. "Let's go, let's go," cried someone and disappeared with a bang. He remained alone. His vision became darker and darker and in relation to every vague object in the hall he stood in check. He had to escape; he moved, the whole of his fat body shaking, and was completely unable to imagine what people did in order to get out of a room—and yet there should be a simple method—abruptly a black shade with a white breast began to hover about him, offering him his coat and hat. "Why is this necessary?" he muttered, getting into the sleeves and revolving together with the obliging ghost. "This way," said the ghost briskly and Luzhin stepped forward and out of the terrible hall. Catching sight of the stairs he began to creep upward, but then changed his mind and went down, since it was easier to descend than to climb up. He found himself in a smoky establishment where noisy phantoms were sitting. An attack was developing in every corner—and pushing aside tables, a bucket with a gold-necked glass Pawn sticking out of it and a drum that was being beaten by an arched, thick-maned chess Knight, he made his way to a gently revolving glass radiance and stopped, not knowing where to go next. People surrounded him and wanted to do something with him. "Go away, go away," a gruff voice kept repeating. "But where?" said Luzhin, weeping. "Go home," whispered another voice insinuatingly and something pushed against Luzhin's shoulder. "What did you say?" he asked again, suddenly ceasing to sob. "Home, home," repeated the voice, and the glass radiance, taking hold of Luzhin, threw him out into the cool dusk. Luzhin smiled. "Home," he said softly. "So that's the key to the combination."

Stefan Zweig

The Royal Game

Stefan Zweig's novella The Royal Game *was his last work, completed in 1942. In the first excerpt, the unnamed narrator's discovery that the ship on which he is a passenger is also carrying world chess champion Czentovic elicits a brilliant and often quoted rumination on the nature of chess.*

The second excerpt is the final scene of the novella. Another passenger, Dr. B., befriended by the narrator, has told him of his recent imprisonment and isolation torture by the Gestapo. After stealing a book of chess games from a guard, Dr. B. tried to keep his mental balance by teaching himself chess and playing against an imaginary alter ego, but the strain drove him to a mental breakdown anyway—"chess-poisoning," he calls it. Now, tempted by the presence of Czentovic to play against an actual person using a real chessboard and tangible pieces, he engages the champion in a game that is meant to be casual but turns out to be something altogether different.

I had never yet in my life had the opportunity of actually meeting a chess champion, and the more concerned I became about fitting a label to this specific type of man, so the thought processes involved seemed to me the more incredible—that a man could spend his whole life revolving exclusively round a space consisting of sixty-four black-and-white squares. I knew well enough from my own experience the mysterious attraction of "the royal game," that game among games devised by man, which rises majestically above every tyranny of chance, which grants its victor's laurels only to a great intellect, or rather, to a particular form of mental ability.

But are we not already guilty of an insulting limitation in calling chess a game? Isn't it also a science, an art, hovering between these two categories as Muhammad's coffin hovered between heaven and earth? Isn't it a unique bond between every pair of opponents, ancient and yet eternally new; mechanical in its framework and yet only functioning through use of the imagination; confined in geometrically fixed space and at the same time released from confinement by its permutations; continuously evolving yet sterile; thought that leads nowhere, mathematics that add up to nothing, art without an end product, architecture without substance, and nevertheless demonstrably more durable in its true nature and existence than any books or creative works? Isn't it the only game that belongs to all peoples and all times? And who knows whether God put it on earth to kill boredom, to sharpen the wits or to lift the spirits? Where is its beginning and where its end?

Every child can lean its basic rules, every bungler can try it; and yet it requires, within those unchanging small squares, the production of a special species of master, not comparable to any other kind, men who have a singular gift for chess, geniuses of a particular kind, in whom vision, patience and technique function in just as precise divisions as they do in mathematicians, poets and musicians, only on different levels and in different conjunctions.

At an earlier stage of the great interest in research into physiognomy, someone like Gall would have dissected the brains of chess champions to establish if such geniuses had a unique coil in their grey matter, a kind of chess muscle or chess bump which was more intensively inscribed there than in other skulls. And how a case like Czentovic's would have excited such a physiognomist, where this precise type of genius appears to be deposited in intellectually totally inert matter, like a single vein of gold in a hundredweight of dead rock!

In principle I understood the time-honoured fact that such a unique, such an ingenious game must produce its own special matadors. But how difficult it is, how impossible even, to visualise the life of an alert, intelligent man who reduces the world to the narrow linear traffic between black and white, who looks for his life's apogee in the mere toing and froing, back and forth, of thirty-two pieces. How hard it is to understand a man who, through using a new opening, moving the Knight instead of the pawn, achieves a feat, and his tiny little scrap of immortality tucked away in a chess book reference—a man, an intelligent man, who without losing his reason, for ten, twenty, thirty, forty years, concentrates all his mental energy over and over again on the ludicrous exercise of manoeuvring into a corner a wooden king on a wooden board! . . .

The next day we gathered in the smoking-room punctually at the agreed time of three o'clock. Our circle had increased by two more lovers of the royal game, two ship's officers who had sought leave from their duties to watch the match. Even Czentovic didn't keep us waiting as he had done the day before. After the necessary choice of colours the memorable game between this *homo obscurissimus* and the famous world champion began. I regret it was played before such thoroughly incompetent spectators as we were, and that its course is as lost to the annals of chess as Beethoven's piano impromptus are to music. True, we tried the next afternoon between us to reconstruct the game from memory, but without success. Quite possibly we had all concentrated too much on the two players during the game instead of taking note of its progress. For in the course of the game the intellectual contrast between the two opponents became more and more physically apparent in their manner. Czentovic, the man of routine, remained as immovably solid as a rock the whole time, his eyes fixed unwaveringly on the board. Thinking seemed almost to cause him actual physical effort, as though he had to engage all his senses with the utmost concentration. Dr. B., on the other hand, was completely relaxed and unconstrained. Like the true dilettante in the best sense of the word, who plays for the pure joy—the *diletto*—of playing, he was physically relaxed and chatted to us during the early pauses, explaining the moves. He lit a cigarette with a steady hand and when it was his move looked at the board only for a minute. Each time it seemed as though he had expected the move his opponent made.

The routine opening moves were made quite quickly. It was only at about the seventh or eighth move that a definite plan seemed to emerge. Czentovic was taking longer over his pauses for thought; from that we sensed the real battle for domination had begun. But to tell you the truth the gradual unfolding of the positional play was something of a disappointment for us non-specialists—as in every true tournament game. For the more the pieces wove in and out in a strange design the more impenetrable the actual position seemed to us. We couldn't perceive what either opponent had in mind or which of the two really had the upper hand. We noticed only that individual pieces were being moved like levers to breach the enemy front, but we were unable to grasp the strategic objective behind these ma-noeuvres. For with these two experienced players every move was combined in advance with other projected moves.

We were gradually overtaken by mild fatigue, principally be-cause of Czentovic's interminable pauses for reflection. These began visibly to annoy our friend as well. I noticed uneasily how the longer the game went on the more restlessly he began to fidget about on his chair. Soon he was so tense he began to light one cigarette after another. Then he grabbed a pencil to make a note of something. Then he ordered mineral water, which he gulped down quickly, one glass after another. It was obvious that he could plan his moves a hundred times faster than Czentovic. Every time the latter, after endless re-flection, decided to move a piece forward with his heavy hand, our friend smiled like someone who had seen something he had long expected, and made his counter-move immediately. With his agile mind he must have worked out in advance all the possibilities open to his opponent. The longer Czentovic delayed his decision the more Dr. B.'s impatience grew, and as he waited his lips were pressed together in an angry and almost hostile line. But Czentovic didn't allow himself to be hurried. He studied the board stubbornly and silently and his pauses became longer the more the field was emptied of chessmen. By the forty-second move, after two and three-quarter hours had gone by, we were all sitting wearily round the tournament table, almost indifferent to it. One of the ship's officers had already gone, the other had taken out a book to read and looked up for a moment only when a move was made. But then suddenly the unex-pected happened, following a move by Czentovic. As soon as Dr. B. saw Czentovic touch his Knight to move it forward he gathered himself together like a cat about to pounce. His whole body began to tremble, and scarcely had Czentovic moved his Knight than Dr. B. pushed his Queen forward with a flourish, and said loudly and triumphantly: "There! That settles it!" He leaned back, folded his arms on his chest and looked challengingly at Czentovic. His eyes were suddenly aglow with a burning light.

Instinctively we bent over the board to try to understand this move that had been proclaimed so triumphantly. At first sight no direct threat was visible. Our friend's exclamation must therefore have referred to a development we, as amateurs who couldn't think far ahead, were unable to calculate as yet. Czentovic was the only one among us who hadn't stirred when the challenging statement was made. He sat quite unmoved as though he had completely missed the insulting "That settles it!" Nothing happened. You could hear us all involuntarily draw in our breath and also the ticking of the clock that had been placed on the table to measure the time for each move. Three minutes, seven, eight passed—Czentovic didn't stir, but it seemed to me that his thick nostrils were flaring as a result of inner tension.

Our friend found this silent waiting just as unbearable as we did. He stood up suddenly in one movement, and began to pace up and down the smoking-room. At first he walked slowly, but then faster and faster. Everyone looked at him in surprise but none as uneasily as I did. For it struck me that in spite of the vigour of the way he paced up and down his steps covered only a precisely measured area: it was as though in the middle of this spacious room he ran up against an invisible cupboard which forced him to turn back every time. And I recognised with a shudder that without his being aware of it this reproduced the limits of the area of his former cell. He must have paced rapidly up and down like a caged animal in exactly this way during the months of his incarceration, with his hands clenched and his shoulders hunched. He must have rushed up and down exactly like this a thousand times, with the glowing light of madness in his staring expression.

His thought processes seemed completely unimpaired, however, for occasionally he would turn to the table impatiently to see if Czentovic had made a decision yet. But nine minutes, ten minutes went by. Then what no one had expected finally happened. Czentovic slowly lifted his heavy hand, which until then had rested motionless on the table. Intently we all hung on his decision. But Czentovic didn't move a piece; with a sweep of the back of his hand he pushed all the pieces slowly off the board. It took us a moment to grasp the situation: Czentovic had conceded the match. He had given in to avoid our seeing him being checkmated. The improbable had happened. The world champion, winner of countless tournaments, had struck his colours in the face of an unknown player—and one who hadn't touched a chessboard for twenty or twenty-five years. Our friend—anonymous, unknown—had beaten the strongest chess player on earth in open battle!

Without thinking, one after another of us jumped up, we were so excited. We all felt we had to say or do something to release our pent-up joy. The only one who remained calmly unmoved was Czentovic. After a measured interval he raised his head and looked stonily at our friend.

"Another game?" he asked.

"Of course," Dr. B. answered with an eagerness that made me apprehensive. He sat down again before I could remind him of his intention of being satisfied with one game only, and began to set up the pieces with desperate haste. He assembled them with such passionate intensity that twice a pawn slipped to the floor through his shaking fingers. My earlier embarrassed unease in the face of his abnormal agitation grew to something approaching alarm. This hitherto calm, quiet man was now visibly over-excited. The nervous tic at the corner of his mouth was more frequent, and his body was quivering as though racked with fever.

"No!" I whispered to him softly. "Not now! That's enough for one day! It's too much of a strain for you."

"Strain! Ha!" He laughed loudly and with contempt. "I could have played seventeen games in the time instead of dawdling like that. The only strain I have, playing at that speed, is to stop myself falling asleep! Well! Go on, begin!"

He addressed these last remarks to Czentovic in a vehement, almost churlish, tone. Czentovic looked at him calmly and evenly but his stony expression had something of the clenched fist in it. All at once a new element had sprung up between the two players: a dangerous tension, a violent hatred. They were no longer two opponents wanting to test each other's playing skill, but two enemies who had sworn to annihilate each other. Czentovic hesitated a long time before he made the first move, and I had a definite feeling his delay was deliberate. Clearly this trained tactician had already noted that he wearied and annoyed his opponent by playing slowly. So he sat for at least four minutes before he made the most normal and simplest of all openings, pushing the King's pawn the customary two squares forward. Our friend immediately followed by advancing his own King's pawn, but again Czentovic created an almost unbearably long pause. It was like seeing a fierce flash of lightning and waiting with bated breath for the thunder—and then the thunder not happening. Czentovic didn't move. He thought silently and slowly, and I was increasingly certain his slowness was malicious. However, he gave me ample time to observe Dr. B., who had just gulped down a third glass of water. I recalled involuntarily how he had told me about the feverish thirst he had had in his cell. He was showing clearly all the symptoms of abnormal excitement. I saw the perspiration on his forehead, and the scar on his hand growing redder and standing out more distinctly than it had done before. But he was still self-controlled. It was not until the fourth move, when Czentovic again went on thinking interminably, that he could no longer restrain himself.

"For heaven's sake make a move, will you!"

Czentovic looked up coldly. "As I recall, we agreed ten minutes per move. I don't play to a shorter limit on principle."

Dr. B. bit his lip. I noticed how he was moving his foot up and down under the table more and more restlessly and I became uncontrollably more nervous myself. I had an awful premonition that some kind of madness was working itself up inside him. In fact there was a further incident at the eighth move. Dr. B. had been growing increasingly impatient while he waited and couldn't contain his tension any further. He shifted about on his chair and started involuntarily to drum on the table with his fingers. Once again Czentovic lifted his heavy, peasant's head.

"Would you mind not drumming, please? It disturbs me. I can't play if you do that."

"Ha!" Dr. B. gave a curt laugh. "That's obvious."

Czentovic went red in the face. "What do you mean by that?" His question was sharp and angry.

Dr. B. gave another tight and malicious laugh. "Nothing. Only that you are obviously feeling the strain."

Czentovic was silent and lowered his head again.

It was seven minutes before he made his next move, and the game dragged on at this funereal pace. Czentovic became more like a block of stone than ever, in the end always taking the maximum of agreed time for thought before deciding on a move. And from one interval to the next our friend's behaviour grew stranger. It seemed as though he was no longer interested in the game but was occupied with something quite different. He stopped walking up and down and remained motionless on his chair. He had a fixed and almost crazed expression as he stared into space, ceaselessly muttering unintelligible words to himself. Either he was lost in endless combinations or—as I suspected deep down—he was working through completely different games. For whenever Czentovic eventually moved Dr. B. had to be brought back from his private reverie. Then he always needed a whole minute to find out exactly how the game stood. The suspicion was borne in on me more and more that he had long since quite forgotten Czentovic and the rest of us in this chilling form of madness, which could suddenly explode in violence of some kind. And indeed the crisis came at the nineteenth move. Czentovic had scarcely made his move before Dr. B. suddenly, without looking at the board properly, pushed his Bishop forward three squares and shouted out so loudly that we all jumped.

"Check! The King's in check!"

We looked at the board at once in expectation of a particularly significant move. But after a minute what happened was not what any of us had anticipated. Czentovic raised his head very, very slowly towards our circle—something he hadn't done before—and looked from one man to the next. He seemed to be relishing something immensely, because slowly a satisfied and clearly sarcastic smile began to play about his lips. Only after he had savoured to the full the triumph that we still didn't understand, did he turn with pretended courtesy to our group.

"I'm sorry—but I see no check. Do any of you gentlemen see a check against my King, by any chance?"

We looked at the board and then uneasily at Dr. B. The square Czentovic's King occupied was in fact—a child could see it—fully protected from the Bishop by a pawn, so the King couldn't possibly be in check. We were uneasy. Had our friend in his excitement mistakenly pushed a piece one square too far or too short? Roused by our silence Dr. B. now gazed at the board and began to stammer and protest.

"But the King should be on KB7 . . . its position is wrong, quite wrong. You've moved incorrectly! Everything is quite wrong on this board . . . the pawn should be on KKt5, not on KKt4. That is a completely different game . . . That's . . ."

He stopped abruptly. I had grabbed him fiercely by the arm, or rather had gripped his arm so tightly that even in his fevered and confused state he must have felt my hold on him. He turned around and stared at me like a sleep-walker.

"What do you want?"

All I said was "Remember!" and lightly drew my finger at the same time over the scar on his hand. Involuntarily he followed my movement, his eyes staring glassily at the inflamed line. Then he began to shiver suddenly and his whole body shook.

"For God's sake," he whispered, his lips pale. "Have I said or done anything untoward? Has it really happened again?"

"No," I whispered gently. "But you must stop playing at once. It's high time you did. Remember what the doctor told you!"

Dr. B. stood up quickly. "Please excuse me for my stupid mistake," he said in his earlier polite voice. He bowed to Czentovic. "What I said was of course complete nonsense. Clearly, it's your game." Then he turned to us. "I must also ask you to forgive me. But I did warn you at the outset not to expect too much. Excuse me for making a fool of myself—that's the last time I shall try my hand at chess." He bowed and left us, in the same modest and mysterious way as he had first appeared. I alone knew why this man would never again touch a chessboard. The others remained silently bewildered. They had a vague feeling they had only just escaped something unpleasant and dangerous. "Damned fool!" McConnor growled with disappointment. The last person to stand up was Czentovic. He glanced at the half-finished game.

"Pity," he said generously. "The attack was quite well conceived. That gentleman is really exceptionally able. For an amateur."

Walter Tevis

The Queen's Gambit

An obsession with chess is not automatically to be equated with insanity, of course. In Walter Tevis's The Queen's Gambit, *Beth Harmon, condemned to a bitterly unhappy childhood in an orphanage, becomes addicted both to chess and to narcotic drugs. The seed of insanity is not present in young Beth, however, and she escapes her childhood to become one of the world's best chessplayers—lonely and not free of her chemical dependency, granted, but self-reliant and reasonably well adjusted.*

    The idea that a girl—with the additional disadvantages of being drug-dependent, emotionally scarred, and virtually alone—could reach the highest levels of a sport as male-dominated as international chess was greeted with some dubiousness by Walter Tevis's editors. But in 1992, less than ten years after publication of The Queen's Gambit, *a fifteen-year-old girl, Judit Polgar of Hungary, became the youngest person in history—male or female—to earn the title of international grandmaster.*

"Will you teach me?"

Mr. Shaibel said nothing, did not even register the question with a movement of his head. Distant voices from above were singing "Bringing in the Sheaves."

She waited for several minutes. Her voice almost broke with the effort of her words, but she pushed them out anyway: "I want to learn to play chess."

Mr. Shaibel reached out a fat hand to one of the larger black pieces, picked it up deftly by its head and set it down on a square at the other side of the board. He brought the hand back and folded his arms across his chest. He still did not look at Beth. "I don't play strangers."

The flat voice had the effect of a slap in the face. Beth turned and left, walking upstairs with the bad taste in her mouth.

"I'm not a stranger," she said to him two days later. "I live here." Behind her head a small moth circled the bare bulb, and its pale shadow crossed the board at regular intervals. "You can teach me. I already know some of it, from watching."

"Girls don't play chess." Mr. Shaibel's voice was flat.

She steeled herself and took a step closer, pointing at, but not touching, one of the cylindrical pieces that she had already labeled a cannon in her imagination. "This one moves up and down or back and forth. All the way, if there's space to move in."

Mr. Shaibel was silent for a while. Then he pointed at the one with what looked like a slashed lemon on top. "And this one?"

Her heart leapt. "On the diagonals."

You could save up pills by taking only one at night and keeping the other. Beth put the extras in her toothbrush holder, where nobody would ever look. She just had to make sure to dry the toothbrush as much as she could with a paper towel after she used it, or else not use it at all and rub her teeth clean with a finger.

That night for the first time she took three pills, one after the other. Little prickles went across the hairs on the back of her neck; she had discovered something important. She let the glow spread all over her, lying on her cot in her faded blue pajamas in the worst place in the Girls' Ward, near the door to the corridor and across from the bathroom. Something in her life was solved: she knew about the chess pieces and how they moved and captured, and she knew how to make herself feel good in the stomach and in the tense joints of her arms and legs, with the pills the orphanage gave her.

"Okay, child," Mr. Shaibel said. "We can play chess now. I play White."

She had the erasers. It was after Arithmetic, and Geography was in ten minutes. "I don't have much time," she said. She had learned all the moves last Sunday, during the hour that chapel allowed her to be in the basement. No one ever missed her at chapel, as long as she checked in, because of the group of girls that came from Children's, across town. But Geography was different. She was terrified of Mr. Schell, even thought she was at the top of the class.

The janitor's voice was flat. "Now or never," he said.

"I have Geography . . ."

"Now or never."

She thought only a second before deciding. She had seen an old milk crate behind the furnace. She dragged it to the other end of the board, seated herself and said, "Move."

He beat her with what she was to learn later was called the Scholar's Mate, after four moves. It was quick, but not quick enough to keep her from being fifteen minutes late for Geography. She said she'd been in the bathroom.

Mr. Schell stood at the desk with his hands on his hips. He surveyed the class. "Have any of you young ladies seen this young lady in the ladies'?"

There were subdued giggles. No hands were raised, not even Jolene's, although Beth had lied for her twice.

"And how many of you ladies were in the ladies' before class?"

There were more giggles and three hands.

"And did any of you see Beth there? Washing her pretty little hands, perhaps?"

There was no response. Mr. Schell turned back to the board, where he had been listing the exports of Argentina, and added the word "silver." For a moment Beth thought it was done with. But then he spoke, with his back to the class. "Five demerits," he said.

With ten demerits you were whipped on the behind with a leather strap. Beth had felt that strap only in her imagination, but her imagination expanded for a moment with a vision of pain like fire on the soft parts of her. She put a hand to her heart, feeling in the bottom of the breast pocket of her blouse for that morning's pill. The fear reduced itself perceptibly. She visualized her toothbrush holder, the long rectangular plastic container; it had four more pills in it now, there in the drawer of the little metal stand by her cot.

That night she lay on her back in bed. She had not yet taken the pill in her hand. She listened to the night noises and noticed how they seemed to get louder as her eyes grew accustomed to the darkness. Down the hallway Mr. Byrne began talking to Mrs. Holland, at the desk. Beth's body grew taut at the sound. She blinked and looked at the dark ceiling overhead and forced herself to see the chessboard with its green and white squares. Then she put the pieces on their home squares: rook, knight, bishop, queen, king, and the row of pawns in front of them. Then she moved White's king pawn up to the fourth row. She pushed Black's up. She could do this! It was simple. She went on, beginning to replay the game she had lost.

She brought Mr. Shaibel's knight up to the third row. It stood there clearly in her mind on the green-and-white board on the ceiling of the ward.

The noises had already faded into a white, harmonious background. Beth lay happily in bed, playing chess.

The next Sunday she blocked the Scholar's Mate with her king's knight. She had gone over the game in her mind a hundred times, until the anger and humiliation were purged from it, leaving the pieces and the board clear in her nighttime vision. When she came to play Mr. Shaibel on Sunday, it was all worked out, and she moved the knight as if in a dream. She loved the feel of the piece, the miniature horse's head in her hand. When she set down the knight on the square, the janitor scowled at it. He took his queen by the head and checked Beth's king with it. But Beth was ready for that too; she had seen it in bed the night before.

It took him fourteen moves to trap her queen. She tried to play on, queenless, to ignore the mortal loss, but he reached out and stopped her hand from touching the pawn she was about to move. "You resign now," he said. His voice was rough.

"Resign?"

"That's right, child. When you lose the queen that way, you resign."

She stared at him, not comprehending. He let go of her hand, picked up her black king, and set it on its side on the board. It rolled back and forth for a moment and then lay still.

"*No,*" she said.

"Yes. You have resigned the game."

She wanted to hit him with something. "You didn't tell me that in the rules."

"It's not a rule. It's sportsmanship."

She knew now what he meant, but she did not like it. "I want to finish," she said. She picked up the king and set it back on its square.

"No."

"You've got to finish," she said.

He raised his eyebrows and got up. She had never seen him stand in the basement—only out in the halls when he was sweeping or in the classrooms when he washed the blackboards. He had to stoop a bit now to keep his head from hitting the rafters on the low ceiling. "No," he said. "You lost."

It wasn't fair. She had no interest in sportsmanship. She wanted to play and to win. She wanted to win more than she had ever wanted anything. She said a word she had not said since her mother died: "Please."

"Game's over," he said.

She stared at him in fury. "You greedy . . ."

He let his arms drop straight at his sides and said slowly, "No more chess. Get out."

If only she were bigger. But she wasn't. She got up from the board and walked to the stairs while the janitor watched her in silence.

On Tuesday when she went down the hall to the basement door carrying the erasers, she found that the door was locked. She pushed against it twice with her hip, but it wouldn't budge. She knocked, softly at first and then loudly, but there was no sound from the other side. It was horrible. She knew he was in there sitting at the board, that he was just being angry at her for the last time, but there was nothing she could do about it. When she brought back the erasers, Miss Graham didn't even notice they hadn't been cleaned or that Beth was back sooner than usual.

On Thursday she was certain it would be the same, but it wasn't. The door was open, and when she went down the stairs, Mr. Shaibel acted as though nothing had happened. The pieces were set up. She cleaned the erasers hurriedly and seated herself at the board. Mr.

Shaibel had moved his king's pawn by the time she got there. She played her king's pawn, moving it two squares forward. She would not make any mistakes this time.

He responded to her move quickly, and she immediately replied. They said nothing to each other, but kept moving. Beth could feel the tension, and she liked it.

On the twentieth move Mr. Shaibel advanced a knight when he shouldn't have and Beth was able to get a pawn to the sixth rank. He brought the knight back. It was a wasted move and she felt a thrill when she saw him do it. She traded her bishop for the knight. Then, on the next move, she pushed the pawn again. It would become a queen on the next move.

He looked at it sitting there and then reached out angrily and toppled his king. Neither of them said anything. It was her first win. All of the tension was gone, and what Beth felt inside herself was as wonderful as anything she had ever felt in her life.

Alan Sharp

Night Moves

An obsession of another kind is the subtext of Alan Sharp's moody detective novel Night Moves. *Harry Moseby, a private investigator, carries with him a pocket chess set on which he repeatedly replays a combination that could have occurred in an actual game from a tournament at Bad Oeynhausen, Germany, in 1922. Moritz (Black) had an opportunity to checkmate his opponent Emmrich ("Emmerich" in the novel and elsewhere, but "Emmrich" in the contemporaneous account of the tournament and in Jeremy Gaige's authoritative* Chess Personalia—A Biobibliography *[McFarland, 1987]) in four moves, beginning with a surprising queen sacrifice and continuing with three knight moves. It would have been a memorable brilliancy. But Moritz missed it and played something else, and two moves later he resigned. To Moseby, the game represents the missed opportunities in his own life.*

Here are the moves of the game: 1 d4 d5 2 c4 e5 3 dxe5 d4 4 Nf3 Nc6 5 Nbd2 f6 6 exf6 Qxf6 7 g3 Bg4 8 Bg2 0-0-0 9 0-0 Nge7 10 Qb3 Ng6 11 a4 Bb4 12 a5 Bxa5 13 Qa4 Rhe8 14 Nb3 Rxe2 15 Nxa5 Bxf3 16 Bh3+ Rd7 17 Qb5 Nce5 18 Bxd7+ Nxd7 19 Ra3 Re5 20 Qb3 Nh4 21 Bf4 Qg6 22 Bxe5 Nxe5 23 Qb5 Qh5 24 Qc5 Nhg6 25 Qb5 Nf4 26 Re1

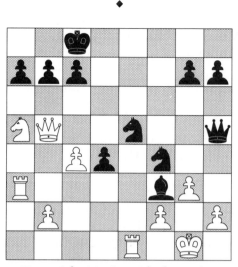

Emmrich–Moritz; Black to play

    *Moritz now played 26 . . . Bd5, and after 27 cxd5 Nh3 +
28 Kf1 he resigned. The combination he missed was 26 . . .
Qxh2 + 27 Kxh2 Ng4 + 28 Kg1 Nh3 + 29 Kf1 5 Nh2 mate.
Pity.*

    *The opening of the novel introduces Moseby and his chess
set while he prepares to resolve a minor matter for his client
Mr. Steegmeyer.*

The old man stood occasionally on tiptoes as though the inch gained
would reveal new horizons. Bonnie Brae Street remained empty, save
for the black-and-white terrier dog that described multiple sniffing
loops back and forth across the road and sidewalk and who at frequent
intervals checked with the old man to see if everything was all right.

    Moseby also checked, not as frequently as the dog, whose name
was Sam, but regularly enough. The rest of his attention he gave to a
point in history long past, but crystallized on his traveling set, a
remote, trivial moment of truth that had once engaged two men he
had never met just as intensely as it now did him. Emmerich and
Moritz had, it appeared, played chess together in 1922 at a place
called Bad Oeynhausen and Moritz, playing Black, had severely
fucked up. Moseby, with a considerable sensitivity to the art of fucking up, studied this particular instance with a pained delight.

    The Los Angeles day inclined to the gauzy, the sun filtered

heavily through the thin cloud and the smog, sounds rubbed smooth by the gentle abrasion of the atmosphere. Somewhere, implying drama, a police car yowled. Nearer, a tune spun a long strand of melody and once or twice Sam barked, causing Moseby to look up, each time to see the old man, who was called Mr. Steegmeyer, beckon the dog to him.

Sitting in his car on Bonnie Brae Street at eleven-thirty on a Tuesday morning looking at Mr. Moritz's mistake, Moseby had a strong sense of the meaninglessness of things. He had allowed four phone calls from Mr. Steegmeyer to badger him into a visit and the visit had led, on the promise of a ten-dollar retainer, to what Mr. Steegmeyer called a stakeout. They were waiting—Moseby, Mr. Steegmeyer, and Sam—for a lady called Rubicheck who had been for some time past trying to poison Sam with doctored chocolate chip cookies. Mr. Steegmeyer was incensed by the woman's cunning in having hit upon chocolate chip cookies—Sam's favorite kind.

Moseby knew he should have gone away, pleaded a downtown appointment, been rude, whatever, but he hadn't. Partially because under his long-nosed, quavery craziness the man actually cared about the dog, and because in his distorted, pathetic old way he was fascinating, with his head full of plots and police parlance and prejudice and paranoia, and because there was something relaxing about sitting in his car looking at the position from that long gone game and anyway he didn't have anything else to do.

Moritz had had that most flamboyant of possibilities for a chess player. Back to the wall, in danger of defeat, he had a Queen sacrifice leading to an exquisite mate by means of three little knight moves, prancing in interlocking checks, driving the King into the pit. Moritz, in the heat of something now cold, had missed it, played defensively, and lost. If he were still alive he would be about Mr. Steegmeyer's age; another elliptic reason for being here.

"She's coming."

Moseby wound down the window to meet the gazes of Steegmeyer and Sam. Glancing down Bonnie Brae Street, he could see a woman pulling a shopping cart along behind her. This discomforted him for some reason. He had expected her to arrive in a car.

"You ready then?"

Moseby closed over the chess case, nodded. "I'm ready."

*   *   *

Night Moves

◆

[*Moseby, hired by an aging actress to locate her sexually precocious sixteen-year-old daughter, Delly, has found the girl living with her stepfather and a woman named Paula Hirsch in the Florida Keys.*]

Delly sat cross-legged on the bed with the contents of Moseby's suitcase spread out in front of her. She looked up at him and smiled. "Hi. I'm getting your stuff sorted out." The traveling chess set was open beside her, the men set in random positions. Moseby picked it up, irked in a trivial, old-mannish way about the illogic of both bishops being on the same diagonal, and started to rearrange the pieces. Delly watched him for a moment, then picked up a pair of his underpants. "Hey, why don't you get some of those little jockey shorts, these things are a real turn-off."

Moseby glanced at her, uncertain whether to be amused or irritated by the flagrancy of the child. "They keep selling them to all those little jockeys."

Delly didn't know how to take that. She dropped the shorts and in order to refrain from sucking her thumb got up from the bed. "Is chess hard to learn?"

"It ain't easy," hearing as he said it Joey Zeigler's voice and being oddly comforted by the recall. He looked at Delly and smiled. There was a knock at the door and then it opened and Paula came in, carrying a bowl of ice.

"Brought you some ice."

"Thanks."

He was aware of Delly starting to tighten up beside him and he looked at Paula to see if she had noticed. She put the ice on the table and sat down in a chair.

Delly moved toward the bathroom. "You don't mind if I use your shower, do you? Mine doesn't work so good."

"Be my guest."

Delly went in with a little flounce, and closed the door firmly behind her.

Paula crossed her legs. "Did she offer you the key to the city?"

"It was more of a guided tour."

"How did you resist?"

"I thought of good clean things like Thanksgiving and George Washington's teeth." And Paula laughed, a low, quick sound but unmistakably a laugh. She reached up for the board. Moseby moved another piece and gave it to her.

She looked at it for a moment. "You beating yourself?"

"It's a position from a game played in nineteen twenty-two . . . do you play?"

A shrug, still looking at the board. "I know the moves."

Moseby came around behind her. "Black had a mate and he didn't see it . . ." and for the first time he caught her scent, faintest odor of skin and its chemistry with the elements of air and salt and soap, ". . . Queen sacrifice in the corner . . ." moving the piece and the inside of his wrist near enough to sense her shoulder, its exhalation through the soft fabric of the shirt, ". . . then three little knight moves, check, check, check . . ." and with the dance complete, ". . . mate."

Paula nodded, twice, put the pieces back in position. "That's nice."

The bathroom door opened and released a waft of steam into the room. Delly reached out through it and picked up one of Moseby's shirts, went in again. Paula looked up at him and winked her left eye, her face otherwise expressionless. The door opened again and Delly came out, wearing the shirt, damp in patches from her body.

"I'll give you your shirt back in the morning. Okay?"

"Sure."

Delly paused for a moment and looked at Paula, who winked at her, her right eye this time. Delly went without a response, padding off down the porch.

"You didn't know we had a laundry service."

"Are you protecting me from something?"

Paula smiled, then looked back at the board. "Show me that again." Moseby played the moves again. "It's a beauty."

"He didn't see it. Name was Moritz. He played something else and lost." The sadness of it touched him again, faint, like a twinge of pain remembered. "He must have regretted it every day of his life—well, I know I would . . ." then, lest that sound unduly portentous, he smiled, ". . . fact is I do, and I wasn't even born."

Paula stood up, gave him back the set.

"That's no excuse."

"No, I guess not," and she went, almost abruptly, without further word, leaving Moseby with the chess board like a little graveyard in his hand and his mind full of lost opportunities and frail fragrances.

Miguel de Unamuno

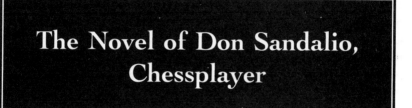

The Novel of Don Sandalio, Chessplayer

Miguel de Unamuno (1864–1936) was a Spanish philoso-
pher, scholar, teacher, political activist, and writer in various
forms. In The Novel of Don Sandalio, Chessplayer, *he uses*
chess to explore themes of isolation.

14 SEPTEMBER

I'm beginning to know the members of the club, my fellow members—for I have joined up, become a member, though transient. Of
course, it's only a matter of knowing them by sight. And I amuse
myself in speculating on what they might be thinking—as long as
they say nothing, that is, for as soon as they open their mouths I can
no longer imagine what might really be taking place in their minds.
And thus it is that I have certain preferences among the games when
it comes time to play my role of spectator. In the game of *mus*, for
example, all the verbal fireworks amuse me for a time, but I quickly
tire of the yells of *envido!* and *quiero!* or *cinco más!* or *diez más!* or
órdago! The last cry amuses me the most; the word *órdago* itself is
apparently a Basque word meaning "There you are!" and when it is

hurled at one player by another it sounds as if one fighting cock were challenging the other.

I am more attracted, in the end, by the chess games. Even in my youth, as you know, I fell into this solitary vice of two men together in company. If one can call that company. Although here in this Casino not all the chess games are silent, not even are they the solitude of two men together in company. Instead, what usually happens is that a circle of spectators forms and they argue out the moves with the players and they even go so far as to move the pieces. There is the continuing game, for instance, played between a forestry engineer and a retired judge, and it is absolutely hilarious. Yesterday, the judge, who must have a weak bladder, was squirming about and, when someone suggested he go relieve himself, he vowed he would not go alone, but insisted the engineer go with him, for he was afraid that otherwise his opponent would shift the pieces. So they went together, the judge to urinate and the engineer as escort, and while they were gone the spectators slyly altered the composition of the game.

But there is one poor devil who has so far drawn my attention more than anyone else. The few who venture to address him at all—for he does not speak to anyone himself—call him Don Sandalio, and his sole activity seems to be that of chessplayer. I have not been able to ascertain a single detail of his life—though in all truth I am not much interested in finding out any of the details. I'd rather imagine them for myself. He goes to the Casino only to play chess, and he plays with scarcely a word and with the avid concentration of a sick man. Outside the world of chess there seems no world at all for him. The other members respect his silence, or perhaps merely ignore him, although I think I detect a certain measure of pity in their attitude. Or perhaps they think him a maniac, a monomaniac. Still, he always seems to find someone for a game, even if it be only from motives of compassion.

One thing he doesn't have is a circle of spectators. Everyone is aware that such a group only serves to annoy him and they keep their distance. Even I haven't ventured to go near his table, though he certainly does interest me. He seems so alone, so isolated in the midst of all the others! He's so withdrawn into himself! Or rather, withdrawn into the game, which seems like a sacred rite for him, a religious function. And I wonder to myself: what does he do when he's not playing chess? How does he make a living? What's his profession? Does he have a family? Does he love anyone? Has he known sorrow and disillusion? Is he the victim of some tragedy?

I've even ventured to follow him when he left the Casino for home. And I've watched to see whether, as he walked across the center of the town's Plaza, he would jump from square to square like a chesspiece. But shame forced me to cut short my pursuit. . . .

20 SEPTEMBER

Yesterday I finally couldn't stand it any longer! Don Sandalio arrived at the Casino at his usual hour, which is exactly the same time, chronometrically, every day, very early in the morning. He drank his coffee down and hurried over to his chess table, ordered the pieces to be brought to him, set them up, and awaited his opponent. And the opponent did not put in his appearance. Don Sandalio stared into the void with an anguished face. I felt sorry for him. So much so that I could not contain myself and went up to ask:

"Apparently your opponent is not coming today," I ventured.

"Apparently not," he answered.

"Well, if you like, until he comes, I could substitute for him. I am not a great player but, although I have not seen you play, I don't think you would find my game boring. . . ."

"Thank you," he said.

I thought that he meant to turn down my offer, in expectation that the other player would actually show up. But instead he accepted. He did not, of course, even ask who I might be. It was as if I did not exist in reality, exist as someone apart from himself, exist except for him. He, nevertheless, certainly existed for me. . . . That is, I think he did. He scarcely deigned to look at me, but stared instead at the board. In his eyes, obviously, the pawns and bishops and knights and castles and kings and queens have more soul than the people who manipulate them. And perhaps he's right.

He plays quite well, with assurance, not too slow, never arguing or changing his moves, and the only word he utters is "Check!" As I wrote the other day, he plays as if he were taking part in a religious service. Or better, like one composing some unheard religious music. Yes, his play is musical. He picks at the pieces as if he were picking a harp. One can almost hear his knight's horse musically breathing— not neighing, no—as he moves in to checkmate. A winged horse, a

Pegasus. Or more like a Clavileño, since both of them are wood. This horse doesn't jump on the table, it lands flying! And when Don Sandalio picks at the queen, it's pure music! . . .

12 OCTOBER

I don't know what idiot devil tempted me today to suggest the solving of a chess problem to Don Sandalio.

"A problem?" he inquired. "I'm not interested in problems. The ones the game itself presents are enough for me. I don't mean to go looking for others."

Now that was the longest string of words I've ever heard from Don Sandalio. And what words! No other member of the Casino could have understood them as well as I did. And yet I later repaired to the seashore once again to look for whatever problems the waves of the sea might suggest to me.

14 OCTOBER

I'm incorrigible, Felipe, incorrigible. As if the lesson Don Sandalio gave me the day before yesterday were not quite enough, today I tried out on him a dissertation on the nature of the bishop, a chesspiece I do not handle well at all.

I told him that our Spanish *alfil*—which the French call *fou*, crazy—the bishop, in English, struck me as being a sort of crazy bishop, with something elephantine in its advance, for it proceeds obliquely, sideways, and never straight ahead, and from white to white or from black to black, never changing the color of its ground whatever its own color. And I went on and on about such things as a white bishop on a white ground and a white on black ground and a black bishop on black ground and a black on white ground! And in short I created a mountain of shavings from so much wood-turning! Don Sandalio looked at me as he might a mad bishop, rather taken aback, and then he looked as if he might bolt, as from a wild elephant. I told him as much, that later part, too, as we exchanged sets, black for white and white for black, the whites beginning the play as always. Don Sandalio's look made me shut up.

When finally I quit the Casino, I hurried along wondering if Don Sandalio's look did not prove that I had, indeed, taken leave of my senses. Had I gone mad? Was I crazy? I thought it probable. In my headlong flight from human stupidity I had doubtless fallen into madness. In my terror of stumbling upon the naked footprint of a fellow human's soul, was I not moving sidewise like a mad bishop? Black or white?

Don Sandalio is driving me mad, Felipe.

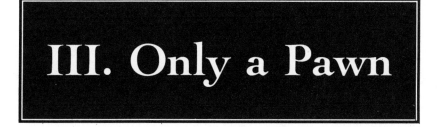

III. Only a Pawn

The chess position that serves as the frontispiece of Lewis Carroll's *Through the Looking-Glass* has perplexed chess-playing readers since the book was published in 1871. Although it appears to be a normal chess problem and poses a typical task—"White Pawn [Alice] to play, and win in eleven moves"—the solution provided by Carroll conforms to neither the laws nor the logic of chess. Among other transgressions:

- White's first, third, ninth, and tenth numbered "moves" (listed in the left column), and Red's ninth (in the right column), are not actual moves and are not played on the board.
- The two sides do not alternate turns as required by the laws of chess: Counting actual moves, White makes thirteen and Red three.
- White illegally ignores a check (Red's eighth move attacks the White king).
- White overlooks two forced checkmates: On the first move, White can play N-N3ch, forcing the Red queen to its K4 (if it goes to Q5 or Q6, White mates with Q-B3), and now White mates in two moves with Q-B5ch followed by Q-Q6; and on the second move, although technically it should not be White's turn (the White pawn [Alice] has just moved to Q4), Carroll has the White queen going to QB4—but were it to go to K3 instead, the Black king would be checkmated.
- Queens do not castle in chess (Red's ninth and White's tenth).
- The first actual move is made by the Red queen, not the White pawn as the task specifies.

Many years later, Carroll, who knew chess well, acknowledged that his solution did not adhere strictly to the rules, but his attempt to clear up the confusion left most questions unanswered. In the hundred years since then, many interpretations of Carroll's use of chess in *Through the Looking-Glass* have been suggested, most of them either wrongheaded or silly (readers wishing to investigate this fascinating subject should begin with Martin Gardner's *The Annotated Alice* [Clarkson N. Potter, 1960] and *More Annotated Alice* [Random House, 1990]). Only A. L. Taylor, in his book *The White Knight,* gets it exactly right.

Lewis Carroll

Through the Looking-Glass

RED

WHITE

White Pawn (Alice) to play, and win in eleven moves

1. Alice meets R.Q.
2. Alice through Q.'s 3d (*by railway*) to Q.'s 4th (*Tweedledum and Tweedledee*)
3. Alice meets W.Q. (*with shawl*)
4. Alice to Q.'s 5th (*shop, river, shop*)

1. R.Q. to K.R.'s 4th
2. W.Q. to Q.B.'s 4th (*after shawl*)

3. W.Q. to Q.B.'s 5th (*becomes sheep*)
4. W.Q. to K.B.'s 8th (*leaves egg on shelf*)

5. Alice to Q.'s 6th (*Humpty Dumpty*)	5. W.Q. to Q.B.'s 8th (*flying from R.Kt.*)
6. Alice to Q.'s 7th (*forest*)	6. R.Kt. to K.'s 2nd (ch.)
7. W.Kt. takes R.Kt.	7. W.Kt. to K.B.'s 5th
8. Alice to Q.'s 8th (*coronation*)	8. R.Q. to K.'s sq. (*examination*)
9. Alice becomes Queen	9. Queens castle
10. Alice castles (*feast*)	10. W.Q. to Q.R.'s 6th (*soup*)
11. Alice takes R.Q. and wins	

"Are there any more people in the garden besides me?" Alice said, not choosing to notice the Rose's last remark.

"There's one other flower in the garden that can move about like you," said the Rose. "I wonder how you do it—" ("You're always wondering," said the Tiger-lily), "but she's more bushy than you are."

"Is she like me?" Alice asked eagerly, for the thought crossed her mind, "There's another little girl in the garden, somewhere!"

"Well, she has the same awkward shape as you," the Rose said: "but she's redder—and her petals are shorter, I think."

"They're done up close, like a dahlia," said the Tiger-lily: "not tumbled about, like yours."

"But that's not *your* fault," the Rose added kindly. "You're beginning to fade, you know—and then one can't help one's petals getting a little untidy."

Alice didn't like this idea at all: so, to change the subject, she asked, "Does she ever come out here?"

"I daresay you'll see her soon," said the Rose. "She's one of the kind that has nine spikes, you know."

"Where does she wear them?" Alice asked with some curiosity.

"Why, all round her head, of course," the Rose replied. "I was wondering *you* hadn't got some too. I thought it was the regular rule."

"She's coming!" cried the Larkspur. "I hear her footstep, thump, thump, along the gravel-walk."

Alice looked round eagerly and found that it was the Red Queen. "She's grown a good deal!" was her first remark. She had indeed:

when Alice first found her in the ashes, she had been only three inches high—and here she was, half a head taller than Alice herself!

"It's the fresh air that does it," said the Rose: "wonderfully fine air it is, out here."

"I think I'll go and meet her," said Alice, for, though the flowers were interesting enough, she felt that it would be far grander to have a talk with a real Queen.

"You can't possibly do that," said the Rose: "*I* should advise you to walk the other way."

This sounded nonsense to Alice, so she said nothing, but set off at once toward the Red Queen. To her surprise she lost sight of her in a moment, and found herself walking in at the front-door again.

A little provoked, she drew back, and, after looking everywhere for the Queen (whom she spied out at last, a long way off), she thought she would try the plan, this time, of walking in the opposite direction.

It succeeded beautifully. She had not been walking a minute before she found herself face to face with the Red Queen, and full in sight of the hill she had been so long aiming at.

"Where do you come from?" said the Red Queen. "And where are you going? Look up, speak nicely, and don't twiddle your fingers all the time."

Alice attended to all these directions, and explained, as well as she could, that she had lost her way.

"I don't know what you mean by *your* way," said the Queen: "all the ways about here belong to *me*—but why did you come out here at all?" she added in a kinder tone. "Curtsey while you're think-ing what to say. It saves time."

Alice wondered a little at this, but she was too much in awe of the Queen to disbelieve it. "I'll try it when I go home," she thought to herself, "the next time I'm a little late for dinner."

"It's time for you to answer now," the Queen said, looking at her watch: "open your mouth a *little* wider when you speak, and always say 'your Majesty.' "

"I only wanted to see what the garden was like, your Majesty—"

"That's right," said the Queen, patting her on the head, which Alice didn't like at all: "though, when you said 'garden'—*I've* seen gardens, compared with which this would be a wilderness."

Alice didn't dare to argue the point, but went on: "—and I thought I'd try and find my way to the top of that hill—"

"When you say 'hill,' " the Queen interrupted, "*I* could show you hills, in comparison with which you'd call that a valley."

"No, I shouldn't," said Alice, surprised into contradicting her at last: "a hill *can't* be a valley, you know. That would be nonsense—"

The Red Queen shook her head. "You may call it 'nonsense' if you like," she said, "but *I've* heard nonsense, compared with which that would be as sensible as a dictionary!"

Alice curtseyed again, as she was afraid from the Queen's tone that she was a *little* offended: and they walked on in silence till they got to the top of the little hill.

For some minutes Alice stood without speaking, looking out in all directions over the country—and a most curious country it was. There were a number of tiny little brooks running straight across it from side to side, and the ground between was divided up into squares by a number of little green hedges, that reached from brook to brook.

"I declare it's marked out just like a large chess-board!" Alice said at last. "There ought to be some men moving about some-where—and so there are!" she added in a tone of delight, and her heart began to beat quick with excitement as she went on. "It's a great huge game of chess that's being played—all over the world—if this *is* the world at all, you know. Oh, what fun it is! How I *wish* I was one of them! I wouldn't mind being a Pawn, if only I might join—though of course I should *like* to be a Queen, best."

She glanced rather shyly at the real Queen as she said this, but her companion only smiled pleasantly, and said, "That's easily man-aged. You can be the White Queen's Pawn, if you like, as Lily's too young to play; and you're in the Second Square to begin with: when you get to the Eighth Square you'll be a Queen—" Just at this mo-ment, somehow or other, they began to run.

Alice never could quite make out, in thinking it over afterwards, how it was that they began: all she remembers is, that they were running hand in hand, and the Queen went so fast that it was all she could do to keep up with her: and still the Queen kept crying "Faster! Faster!" but Alice felt she *could not* go faster, though she had no breath left to say so.

The most curious part of the thing was, that the trees and the other things round them never changed their places at all: however fast they went, they never seemed to pass anything. "I wonder if all the things move along with us?" thought poor puzzled Alice. And the Queen seemed to guess her thoughts, for she cried "Faster! Don't try to talk!"

Not that Alice had any idea of doing *that*. She felt as if she would never be able to talk again, she was getting so much out of breath: and still the Queen cried "Faster! Faster!" and dragged her along. "Are we nearly there?" Alice managed to pant out at last.

"Nearly there!" the Queen repeated. "Why, we passed it ten minutes ago! Faster!" And they ran on for a time in silence, with the wind whistling in Alice's ears, and almost blowing her hair off her head, she fancied.

"Now! Now!" cried the Queen. "Faster! Faster!" And they went so fast that at last they seemed to skim through the air, hardly touching the ground with their feet, till suddenly, just as Alice was getting quite exhausted, they stopped, and she found herself sitting on the ground, breathless and giddy.

The Queen propped her up against a tree, and said kindly. "You may rest a little, now."

Alice looked round her in great surprise. "Why, I do believe we've been under this tree the whole time! Everything's just as it was!"

"Of course it is," said the Queen. "What would you have it?"

"Well, in *our* country," said Alice, still painting a little, "you'd generally get to somewhere else—if you ran very fast for a long time as we've been doing."

"A slow sort of country!" said the Queen. "Now, *here*, you see it takes all the running *you* can do, to keep in the same place. If you want to get somewhere else, you must run at least twice as fast as that."

"I'd rather not try, please!" said Alice. "I'm quite content to stay here—only I *am* so hot and thirsty!"

"I know what *you'd* like!" the Queen said good-naturedly, taking a little box out of her pocket. "Have a biscuit?"

Alice thought it would not be civil to say "No," though it wasn't at all what she wanted. So she took it, and ate it as well as she could: and it was *very* dry: and she thought she had never been so nearly choked in all her life.

"While you're refreshing yourself," said the Queen, "I'll just take the measurements." And she took a ribbon out of her pocket, marked in inches, and began measuring the ground, and sticking little pegs in here and there.

"At the end of two yards," she said, putting in a peg to mark the distance, "I shall give you your directions—have another biscuit?"

"No, thank you," said Alice: "one's *quite* enough!"

"Thirst quenched, I hope?" said the Queen.

Alice did not know what to say to this, but luckily the Queen did not wait for an answer, but went on. "At the end of *three* yards I shall repeat them—for fear of your forgetting them. At the end of *four*, I shall say good-bye. And at the end of *five*, I shall go!"

She had got all the pegs put in by this time, and Alice looked on with great interest as she returned to the tree, and then began slowly walking down the row.

At the two-yard peg she faced round, and said, "A pawn goes two squares in its first move, you know. So you'll go *very* quickly through the Third Square—by railway, I should think—and you'll find yourself in the Fourth Square in no time. Well, *that* square belongs to Tweedledum and Tweedledee—the Fifth is mostly water—the Sixth belongs to Humpty Dumpty—But you make no remark?"

"I—I didn't know I had to make one—just then," Alice faltered out.

"You *should* have said," the Queen went on in a tone of grave reproof, " 'It's extremely kind of you to tell me all this'—however, we'll suppose it said—the Seventh Square is all forest—however, one of the Knights will show you the way—and in the Eighth Square we shall be Queens together, and it's all feasting and fun!" Alice got up and curtseyed, and sat down again.

At the next peg the Queen turned again, and this time she said, "Speak in French when you can't think of the English for a thing—turn out your toes as you walk—and remember who you are!" She did not wait for Alice to curtsey, this time, but walked on quickly to the next peg, where she turned for a moment to say "Good-bye," and then hurried on to the last.

How it happened, Alice never knew, but exactly as she came to the last peg, she was gone. Whether she vanished into the air, or whether she ran quickly into the wood ("and she *can* run very fast!" thought Alice), there was no way of guessing, but she was gone, and Alice began to remember that she was a Pawn, and that it would soon be time for her to move.

A. L. Taylor

The White Knight

Alice when she is a pawn is continually meeting chess-men, red and white, and according to the key, they are always on the square next to her on one side or the other. To the right, she meets the Red Queen, the Red King, the Red Knight, the White Knight and, at the end of the board, the Red Queen again. To the left, she meets the White Queen, the White King and, at the end of the board, the White Queen again. Of what is happening in the other parts of the board she has no knowledge. She sweeps a narrow track, and events more than one square distant to either side, or behind, or ahead of her, are out of her world. A certain lack of coherence in her picture of the game is understandable, particularly as it is in an advanced stage when she begins to move.

In the *Lewis Carroll Handbook*, Falconer Madan regrets that "the chess framework is full of absurdities and impossibilities" and considers it a pity that Dodgson did not bring the game, as a game, up to chess standard, as, says Mr. Madan, he could easily have done. He points out that among other absurdities the white side is allowed to make nine consecutive moves, the White King to be checked unnoticed; Queens castle, and the White Queen flies from the Red Knight when she could take it. "Hardly a move," he says, "has a sane purpose, from the point of view of chess" (pp. 48–49). There is also a mate for White at the fourth move (Dodgson's reckoning): W.Q. to

K.'s 3rd instead of Q.B.'s 4th. Alice and the Red Queen are both out of the way and the Red King could not move out of check.

Dodgson's own words, in a preface written in 1887, in reply to criticism of this kind, are as follows:

> As the chess problem given on the previous page has puzzled some of my readers, it may be well to explain that it is correctly worked out so far as the *moves* are concerned. The alternation of Red and White is perhaps not so strictly observed as it might be, and the "castling" of the three Queens is merely a way of saying that they entered the palace; but the "check" of the White King at move 6, the capture of the Red Knight at move 7, and the final "checkmate" of the Red King, will be found, by any one who will take the trouble to set the pieces and play the moves as directed, to be strictly in accordance with the laws of the game.

He was not interested in the game as a game, but in the implications of the moves. Dodgson could easily have "worked out a problem." He spent a considerable part of his life doing that kind of thing. But in *Through the Looking-Glass* he was otherwise engaged. In the first place it would be illogical to expect logic in a game of chess dreamed by a child. It would be still more illogical to expect a pawn which can see only a small patch of board to understand the meaning of its experiences. And there is a moral in that. This is a pawn's impression of chess, which is like a human being's impression of life.

Alice never grasps the purpose of the game at all and when she reaches the Eighth Square tries to find out from the two Queens if it is over. None of the pieces has the least idea what it is all about. The Red King is asleep. The White King has long ago abandoned any attempt to intervene. "You might as well try to catch a Bandersnatch." The Red Knight is quite justified in his battle-cry of "Ahoy! Ahoy! Check!" but the White Knight, too, leaps out of the wood, shouting "Ahoy! Ahoy! Check!" and he is not giving check at all but capturing the Red Knight. Neither of them has any control over the square on which Alice is situated, yet the Red Knight thinks he has captured her and the White Knight that he has rescued her. Alice cannot argue with either of them but is simply relieved to have the matter settled in a manner favourable to herself.

As for the Queens, they "see" so much of the board that they might be expected to know what is happening fairly well. But, as will appear, their manner of "seeing" is so peculiar that they know less about it than anybody. To understand one's part in a game of chess, one would have to be aware of the room and the unseen intelligence which is combining the pieces. Deprived of any such knowledge, the chess-men have to explain things as best they can. Nor is this a game between two players. To have made it that would have been tantamount to a confession that he believed in two separate and opposite Powers above us. Dodgson deliberately avoided any such implication.

He based his story, not on a game of chess, but on a chess lesson or demonstration of the moves such as he gave to Alice Liddell, a carefully worked-out sequence of moves designed to illustrate the queening of a pawn, the relative powers of the pieces—the feeble king, the eccentric knight and the formidable queen whose powers include those of rook and bishop—and finally a checkmate. That is to say, he abstracted from the game exactly what he wanted for his design, and expressed that as a game between a child of seven-and-a-half who was to "be" a White Pawn and an older player (himself) who was to manipulate the other pieces.

Only the other day, it will be remembered, Alice had had a long argument with her sister about playing kings and queens. Alice had been reduced at last to saying, "Well *you* can be one of them, then, and *I'll* be all the rest." Through the Looking-Glass she was "one of them" and the Other Player "all the rest." Perhaps that is how things are. Dodgson certainly hoped so.

Observe the Red Queen about to do her disappearing-trick:

"At the end of two yards," she said, putting in a peg to mark the distance, "I shall give you your directions—have another biscuit?"

The biscuit is deliberately used to distract our attention from the fact that these pegs mark out the stages of Alice's pawn-life.

"At the end of *three* yards I shall repeat them—for fear of your forgetting them. At the end of *four,* I shall say good-bye. And at the end of *five,* I shall go!"

She had got all the pegs put in by this time, and Alice looked on with great interest as she returned to the tree, and then began slowly walking down the row.

Only a Pawn

◆

At the two-yard peg she faced round, and said, "A pawn goes two squares in its first move."

To demonstrate that, she had walked two yards. As a pawn starts from the second square, that takes us to the fourth square on the board. The third peg marks the fifth square, the fourth the sixth and the fifth the seventh. There is still another square, the eighth, but on that Alice will no longer be a pawn. " 'In the Eighth Square we shall be Queens together, and it's all feasting and fun!' "

The Red Queen had begun "slowly walking down the row." At the two-yard peg she paused to give Alice her instructions. Alice got up and curtseyed, and sat down again. At the next peg the Queen jerked out some staccato remarks. She did not wait for Alice to curtsey this time, but "walked on quickly" to the next peg, where she turned to say good-bye and then "hurried" on to the last. She was getting up speed. "How it happened, Alice never knew, but exactly as she came to the last peg, she was gone."

What happened we can represent but not really imagine. According to the key, the Red Queen moved away from Alice at an angle across the board (R.Q. to K.R.'s 4th).

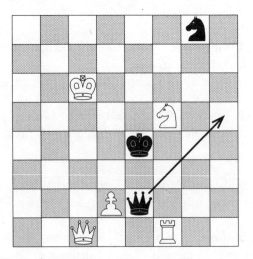

So long as the Red Queen was in the square next to her, Alice could see her and hear her, but when she steamed off in a direction which did not as yet exist for Alice, she simply vanished.

The White Knight

♦

Whether she vanished into the air, or ran quickly into the wood ("and she *can* run very fast!" thought Alice), there was no way of guessing, but she was gone, and Alice began to remember that she was a pawn, and that it would soon be time to move.

The moves of the two Queens are inexplicable to Alice because of the limitation in her powers. She is unable to conceive of such moves as R.Q. to K.R.'s 4th or W.Q. to Q.B.'s 4th. They can zig-zag about the board, sweep from end to end of it if they like, or from side to side. She must laboriously crawl from square to square, always in one direction, with a half-remembered promise to spur her on: " 'In the Eighth Square we shall be Queens together, and it's all feasting and fun!' "

But if the length of the board is time, the breadth of the board must be time also, a kind of time known only to mathematicians and mystics: the kind of time we call eternity.

> *For was and is, and will be are but is;*
> *And all creation is one act at once,*
> *The birth of light: but we that are not all*
> *As parts, can see but parts, now this now that,*
> *And live, perforce from thought to thought and make*
> *One act a phantom of succession; thus*
> *Our weakness somehow shapes the Shadow, Time.**

What Tennyson puts in poetry, Dodgson represented on his chess-board. Alice as she trotted along could see but parts, now the Red King to her right, now the White Queen to her left, but once she became a Queen there was a change:

Everything was happening so oddly that she didn't feel a bit surprised at finding the Red Queen and the White Queen sitting close to her, one on each side: she would have liked very much to ask them how they came there,

(we can follow their moves by the key)

but she feared it would not be quite civil.

---

*Tennyson, *The Princess* [Editor].

Only a Pawn

◆

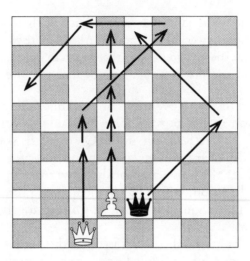

She could see them both at once; in the language of psychology, she could attend to a plurality of impressions to which formerly she would have attended in succession.

However, she was by no means sure of herself or her crown as yet, and the Queens put her through her paces:

"In *our* country," Alice remarked, "there's only one day at a time."

The Red Queen said, "That's a poor thin way of doing things. Now *here*, we mostly have days and nights two or three at a time, and sometimes in the winter we take as many as five nights together—for warmth, you know."

"Are five nights warmer than one night, then?" Alice ventured to ask.

"Five times as warm, of course."

"But they should be five times as *cold*, by the same rule—"

"Just so!" said the Red Queen. "Five times as warm, *and* five times as cold—just as I'm five times as rich as you are, *and* five times as clever!"

(Note clever and rich as opposites here.)

Alice sighed and gave it up. "It's exactly like a riddle with no answer!" she thought.

It is, however, the answer to the "chess-problem," or at any rate, one part of it, the checkmate which, Dodgson said in the 1887 Preface, was strictly in accordance with the laws of the game, while Mr. Madan in the *Handbook* gives him the lie direct: "whereas there is no attempt at one."

According to the key, the position would appear to be:

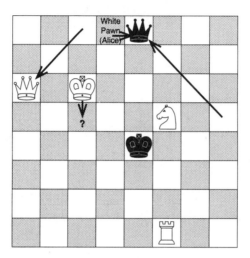

There is therefore something very like a checkmate and a fairly complicated one. The only objection is that the White King must have been in check while the White Queen moved to Q.R. 6th (soup) at Move 10. On the other hand, when Alice was on the Seventh Square she was still a pawn. The White King was behind her and if he had moved to Q.B. 5th she would not have known and he would not have been in check.

As to the succession of the moves, Dodgson admitted that was "perhaps not so strictly observed as it might be." When Alice reached the Eighth Square and became a Queen she naturally acquired new powers, but not all at once. She could now see from end to end of the board, but her sweep of vision from side to side was limited by the presence of the White Queen on one side and the Red Queen on the other. Whenever the White Queen moved to Q.R. 6th Alice had to wake up. " 'I can't stand this any longer!' she cried," and as the chess world collapsed in ruins she seized the Red Queen and accomplished the checkmate.

Jorge Luis Borges

Chess

Alice, with the limited viewpoint of a mere pawn, has no conception of the chess game of which she is a part—just as we, if we imagine ourselves as pawns in some cosmic chess game, could have no idea of the players or their purpose or the roles we are destined to play. The great Argentine writer Jorge Luis Borges says it best.

I

*In their serious corner, the players
move the gradual pieces. The board
detains them until dawn in its hard
compass: the hatred of two colors.*

*In the game, the forms give off a severe
magic: Homeric castle, gay
knight, warlike queen, king solitary,
oblique bishop, and pawns at war.*

Finally, when the players have gone in,

Chess

◆

and when time has eventually consumed them,
surely the rites then will not be done.

In the east, this war has taken fire.
Today, the whole earth is its provenance.
Like that other, this game is for ever.

II

Tenuous king, slant bishop, bitter queen,
straightforward castle and the crafty pawn—
over the checkered black and white terrain
they seek out and enjoin their armed campaign.

They do not realize the dominant
hand of the player rules their destiny.
They do not know an adamantine fate
governs their choices and controls their journey.

The player, too, is captive of caprice
(the sentence is Omar's) on another ground
crisscrossed with black nights and white days.

God moves the player, he, in turn, the piece.
But what god beyond God begins the round
of dust and time and dream and agonies?

—Translated by ALASTAIR REID

Ian Fleming

From Russia, With Love

A pawn of another kind altogether—a willing pawn who understands quite well the nature of the game his masters are playing—is depicted in Ian Fleming's entertaining espionage novel From Russia, With Love. *In the 1963 movie based on the book, the chess scene, which in the novel contains only a single move, is expanded to include the brilliant conclusion of a checkmating combination that was taken from an actual game won by Boris Spassky against David Bronstein in the 1959–60 USSR championship.*

The two faces of the double clock in the shiny, domed case looked out across the chess-board like the eyes of some huge sea monster that had peered over the edge of the table to watch the game.

The two faces of the chess clock showed different times. Kronsteen's showed twenty minutes to one. The long red pendulum that ticked off the seconds was moving in its staccato sweep across the bottom half of his clock's face, while the enemy clock was silent and its pendulum motionless down the face. But Makharov's clock said five minutes to one. He had wasted time in the middle of the game and he now had only five minutes to go. He was in bad "time-trouble" and unless Kronsteen made some lunatic mistake, which was unthinkable, he was beaten.

Kronsteen sat motionless and erect, as malevolently inscrutable as a parrot. His elbows were on the table and his big head rested on clenched fists that pressed into his cheeks, squashing the pursed lips into a pout of hauteur and disdain. Under the wide, bulging brow the rather slanting black eyes looked down with deadly calm on his winning board. But, behind the mask, the blood was throbbing in the dynamo of his brain, and a thick worm-like vein in his right temple pulsed at a beat of over ninety. He had sweated away a pound of weight in the last two hours and ten minutes, and the spectre of a false move still had one hand at his throat. But to Makharov, and to the spectators, he was still "The Wizard of Ice" whose game had been compared to a man eating fish. First he stripped off the skin, then he picked out the bones, then he ate the fish. Kronsteen had been Champion of Moscow two years running, was now in the final for the third time and, if he won this game, would be a contender for Grand Mastership.

In the pool of silence round the roped-off top table there was no sound except the loud tripping feet of Kronsteen's clock. The two umpires sat motionless in their raised chairs. They knew, as did Makharov, that this was certainly the kill. Kronsteen had introduced a brilliant twist into the Meran Variation of the Queen's Gambit Declined. Makharov had kept up with him until the 28th move. He had lost time on that move. Perhaps he had made a mistake there, and perhaps again on the 31st and 33rd moves. Who could say? It would be a game to be debated all over Russia for weeks to come.

There came a sigh from the crowded tiers opposite the Championship game. Kronsteen had slowly removed the right hand from his cheek and had stretched it across the board. Like the pincers of a pink crab, his thumb and forefinger had opened, then they had descended. The hand, holding a piece, moved up and sideways and down. Then the hand was slowly brought back to the face.

The spectators buzzed and whispered as they saw, on the great wall map, the 41st move duplicated with a shift of one of the three-foot placards. R-Kt8. That must be the kill!

Kronsteen reached deliberately over and pressed down the lever at the bottom of his clock. His red pendulum went dead. His clock showed a quarter to one. At the same instant, Makharov's pendulum came to life and started its loud, inexorable beat.

Kronsteen sat back. He placed his hands flat on the table and looked coldly across at the glistening, lowered face of the man whose guts he knew, for he too had suffered defeat in his time, would be writhing in agony like an eel pierced with a spear. Makharov, Champion of Georgia. Well, tomorrow Comrade Makharov could go back to Georgia and stay there. At any rate this year he would not be moving with his family up to Moscow.

A man in plain clothes slipped under the ropes and whispered to one of the umpires. He handed him a white envelope. The umpire shook his head, pointing at Makharov's clock, which now said three minutes to one. The man in plain clothes whispered one short sentence which made the umpire sullenly bow his head. He pinged a handbell.

"There is an urgent personal message for Comrade Kronsteen," he announced into the microphone. "There will be a three minutes' pause."

A mutter went round the hall. Even though Makharov now courteously raised his eyes from the board and sat immobile, gazing up into the recesses of the high, vaulted ceiling, the spectators knew that the position of the game was engraved on his brain. A three minutes' pause simply meant three extra minutes for Makharov.

Kronsteen felt the same stab of annoyance, but his face was expressionless as the umpire stepped down from his chair and handed him a plain, unaddressed envelope. Kronsteen ripped it open with his thumb and extracted the anonymous sheet of paper. It said, in the large typewritten characters he knew so well, "YOU ARE REQUIRED THIS INSTANT." No signature and no address.

Kronsteen folded the paper and carefully placed it in his inside breast pocket. Later it would be recovered from him and destroyed. He looked up at the face of the plain-clothes man standing beside the umpire. The eyes were watching him impatiently, commandingly. To hell with these people, thought Kronsteen. He would *not* resign with only three minutes to go. It was unthinkable. It was an insult to the People's Sport. But, as he made a gesture to the umpire that the game could continue, he trembled inside, and he avoided the eyes of the plain-clothes man who remained standing, in coiled immobility, inside the ropes.

The bell pinged. "The game proceeds."

Makharov slowly bent down his head. The hand of his clock slipped past the hour and he was still alive.

Kronsteen continued to tremble inside. What he had done was unheard of in an employee of SMERSH, or of any other State agency.

He would certainly be reported. Gross disobedience. Dereliction of duty. What might be the consequences? At the best a tongue-lashing from General G., and a black mark on his *zapiska*. At the worst? Kronsteen couldn't imagine. He didn't like to think. Whatever happened, the sweets of victory had turned bitter in his mouth.

But now it was the end. With five seconds to go on his clock, Makharov raised his whipped eyes no higher than the pouting lips of his opponent and bent his head in the brief, formal bow of surrender. At the double ping of the umpire's bell, the crowded hall rose to its feet with a thunder of applause.

Kronsteen stood up and bowed to his opponent, to the umpires, and finally, deeply, to the spectators. Then, with the plain-clothes man in his wake, he ducked under the ropes and fought his way coldly and rudely through the mass of his clamouring admirers towards the main exit.

Outside the Tournament Hall, in the middle of the wide Pushkin Ulitza, with its engine running, stood the usual anonymous black ZIK saloon. Kronsteen climbed into the back and shut the door. As the plain-clothes man jumped on to the running-board and squeezed into the front seat, the driver crashed his gears and the car tore off down the street.

Kronsteen knew it would be a waste of breath to apologize to the plain-clothes guard. It would also be contrary to discipline. After all, he was Head of the Planning Department of SMERSH, with the honorary rank of full Colonel. And his brain was worth diamonds to the organization. Perhaps he could argue his way out of the mess. He gazed out of the window at the dark streets, already wet with the work of the night cleaning squad, and bent his mind to his defence. Then there came a straight street at the end of which the moon rode fast between the onion spires of the Kremlin, and they were there.

When the guard handed Kronsteen over to the A.D.C., he also handed the A.D.C. a slip of paper. The A.D.C. glanced at it and looked coldly up at Kronsteen with half-raised eyebrows. Kronsteen looked calmly back without saying anything. The A.D.C. shrugged his shoulders and picked up the office telephone and announced him.

When they went into the big room and Kronsteen had been waved to a chair and had nodded acknowledgment of the brief pursed smile of Colonel Klebb, the A.D.C. went up to General G. and handed him the piece of paper. The General read it and looked hard across at Kronsteen. While the A.D.C. walked to the door and went out, the General went on looking at Kronsteen. When the door was shut, General G. opened his mouth and said softly, "Well, Comrade?"

Kronsteen was calm. He knew the story that would appeal. He spoke quietly and with authority. "To the public, Comrade General, I am a professional chess player. Tonight I became Champion of Moscow for the third year in succession. If, with only three minutes to go, I had received a message that my wife was being murdered outside the door of the Tournament Hall, I would not have raised a finger to save her. My public know that. They are as dedicated to the game as myself. Tonight, if I had resigned the game and had come immediately on receipt of that message, five thousand people would have known that it could only be on the orders of such a department as this. There would have been a storm of gossip. My future goings and comings would have been watched for clues. It would have been the end of my cover. In the interests of State Security, I waited three minutes before obeying the order. Even so, my hurried departure will be the subject of much comment. I shall have to say that one of my children is gravely ill. I shall have to put a child into hospital for a week to support the story. I deeply apologize for the delay in carrying out the order. But the decision was a difficult one. I did what I thought best in the interests of the Department."

General G. looked thoughtfully into the dark slanting eyes. The man was guilty, but the defence was good. He read the paper again as if weighing up the size of the offence, then he took out his lighter and burned it. He dropped the last burning corner on to the glass top of his desk and blew the ashes sideways on to the floor. He said nothing to reveal his thoughts, but the burning of the evidence was all that mattered to Kronsteen. Now nothing could go on his *zapiska*. He was deeply relieved and grateful. He would bend all his ingenuity to the matter on hand. The General had performed an act of great clemency. Kronsteen would repay him with the full coin of his mind.

Poul Anderson

The Immortal Game

*In his powerful fantasy "The Immortal Game," Poul Ander-
son, like Carroll, imagines life as it might be viewed by the
chess pieces themselves, who, obeying some mysterious compulsion, fight an endless series of battles for reasons none of
them comprehends.*

*The action of the story approximately re-creates the classic
"Immortal Game," a casual encounter played in London in
1851 between two of the best players of the time, Adolph
Anderssen (White) and Lionel Kieseritsky. Here are the
moves: 1 e4 e5 2 f4 exf4 3 Bc4 Qh4+ 4 Kf1 b5 5 Bxb5 Nf6
6 Nf3 Qh6 7 d3 Nh5 8 Nh4 Qg5 9 Nf5 c6 10 Rg1 cxb5 11
g4 Nf6 12 h4 Qg6 13 h5 Qg5 14 Qf3 Ng8 15 Bxf4 Qf6 16
Nc3 Bc5 17 Nd5 Qxb2 18 Bd6 Qxa1+ 19 Ke2 Bxg1 20 e5
Na6 21 Nxg7+ Kd8 22 Qf6+ Nxf6 23 Be7 mate.*

The first trumpet sounded far and clear and brazen cold, and Rogard
the Bishop stirred to wakefulness with it. Lifting his eyes, he looked
through the suddenly rustling, murmuring line of soldiers, out across
the broad plain of Cinnabar and the frontier, and over to the realm of
LEUKAS.

Away there, across the somehow unreal red-and-black distances of the steppe, he saw sunlight flash on armor and caught the remote wild flutter of lifted banners. *So it is war,* he thought. *So we must fight again.*

Again? He pulled his mind from the frightening dimness of that word. Had they ever fought before?

On his left, Sir Ocher laughed aloud and clanged down the vizard on his gay young face. It gave him a strange, inhuman look, he was suddenly a featureless thing of shining metal and nodding plumes, and the steel echoed in his voice: "Ha, a fight! Praise God, Bishop, for I had begun to fear I would rust here forever."

Slowly, Rogard's mind brought forth wonder. "Were you sitting and thinking—before now?" he asked.

"Why—" Sudden puzzlement in the reckless tones: "I think I was. . . . Was I?" Fear turning into defiance: "Who cares? I've got some LEUKANS to kill!" Ocher reared in his horse till the great metallic wings thundered.

On Rogard's right, Flambard the King stood, tall in crown and robes. He lifted an arm to shade his eyes against the blazing sunlight. "They are sending DIOMES, the royal guardsman, first," he murmured, "A good man." The coolness of his tone was not matched by the other hand, its nervous plucking at his beard.

Rogard turned back, facing over the lines of Cinnabar to the frontier. DIOMES, the LEUKAN King's own soldier, was running. The long spear flashed in his hand, his shield and helmet threw back the relentless light in a furious dazzle, and Rogard thought he could hear the clashing of iron. Then that noise was drowned in the trumpets and drums and yells from the ranks of Cinnabar, and he had only his eyes.

DIOMES leaped two squares before coming to a halt on the frontier. He stopped then, stamping and thrusting against the Barrier which suddenly held him, and cried challenge. A muttering rose among the cuirassed soldiers of Cinnabar, and spears lifted before the flowing banners.

King Flambard's voice was shrill as he leaned forward and touched his own guardsman with his scepter. "Go, Carlon! Go to stop him!"

"Aye, sire." Carlon's stocky form bowed, and then he wheeled about and ran, holding his spear aloft, until he reached the frontier. Now he and DIOMES stood face to face, snarling at each other across the Barrier, and for a sick moment Rogard wondered what those two had done, once in an evil and forgotten year, that there should be such hate between them.

"Let me go, sire!" Ocher's voice rang eerily from the slit-eyed mask of his helmet. The winged horse stamped on the hard red ground, and the long lance swept a flashing arc. "Let me go next."

"No, no, Sir Ocher." It was a woman's voice. "Not yet. There'll be enough for you and me to do, later in this day."

Looking beyond Flambard, the Bishop saw his Queen, Evyan the Fair, and there was something within him which stumbled and broke into fire. Very tall and lovely was the gray-eyed Queen of Cinnabar, where she stood in armor and looked out at the growing battle. Her sun-browned young face was coiffed in steel, but one rebellious lock blew forth in the wind, and she brushed at it with a gauntleted hand while the other drew her sword snaking from its sheath. "Now may God strengthen our arms," she said, and her voice was low and sweet. Rogard drew his cope tighter about him and turned his mitered head away with a sigh. But there was a bitter envy in him for Columbard, the Queen's Bishop of Cinnabar.

Drums thumped from the LEUKAN ranks, and another soldier ran forth. Rogard sucked his breath hissingly in, for this man came till he stood on DIOMES' right. And the newcomer's face was sharp and pale with fear. There was no Barrier between him and Carlon.

"To his death," muttered Flambard between his teeth. "They sent that fellow to his death."

Carlon snarled and advanced on the LEUKAN. He had little choice—if he waited, he would be slain, and his King had not commanded him to wait. He leaped, his spear gleamed, and the LEUKAN soldier toppled and lay emptily sprawled in the black square.

"First blood!" cried Evyan, lifting her sword and hurling sunbeams from it. "First blood for us!"

Aye so, thought Rogard bleakly, *but King* MIKILLATI *had a reason for sacrificing that man. Maybe we should have let Carlon die. Carlon the bold, Carlon the strong, Carlon the lover of laughter. Maybe we should have let him die.*

And now the Barrier was down for Bishop ASATOR of LEUKAS, and he came gliding down the red squares, high and cold in his glistening white robes, until he stood on the frontier. Rogard thought he could see ASATOR's eyes as they swept over Cinnabar. The LEUKAN Bishop was poised to rush in with his great mace should Flambard, for safety, seek to change with Earl Ferric as the Law permitted.

Law?

There was no time to wonder what the Law was, or why it must be obeyed, or what had gone before this moment of battle. Queen Evyan had turned and shouted to the soldier Raddic, guardsman of her own Knight Sir Cupran: "Go! Halt him!" And Raddic cast her his own look of love, and ran, ponderous in his mail, up to the frontier. There he and ASATOR stood, no Barrier between them if either used a flanking move.

Good! Oh, good, my Queen! thought Rogard wildly. For even if ASATOR did not withdraw, but slew Raddic, he would be in Raddic's square, and his threat would be against a wall of spears. *He will retreat, he will retreat—*

Iron roared as ASATOR's mace crashed through helm and skull and felled Raddic the guardsman.

Evyan screamed, once only. "And I sent him! I sent him!" Then she began to run.

"Lady!" Rogard hurled himself against the Barrier. He could not move, he was chained here in his square, locked and barred by a Law he did not understand, while his lady ran toward death. "O Evyan, Evyan!"

Straight as a flying javelin ran the Queen of Cinnabar. Turning, straining after her, Rogard saw her leap the frontier and come to a halt by the Barrier which marked the left-hand bound of the kingdoms, beyond which lay only dimness to the frightful edge of the world. There she wheeled to face the dismayed ranks of LEUKAS, and her cry drifted back like the shriek of a stooping hawk: "MIKILLATI! Defend yourself!"

The thunder-crack of cheering from Cinnabar drowned all answer, but Rogard saw, at the very limits of his sight, how hastily King MIKILLATI stepped from the line of her attack, into the stronghold of Bishop ASATOR. Now, thought Rogard fiercely, now the white-robed ruler could never seek shelter from one of his Earls. Evyan had stolen his greatest shield.

"Hola, my Queen!" With a sob of laughter, Ocher struck spurs into his horse. Wings threshed, blowing Rogard's cope about him, as the Knight hurled over the head of his own guardsman and came to rest two squares in front of the Bishop. Rogard fought down his own anger; he had wanted to be the one to follow Evyan. But Ocher was a better choice.

Oh, much better! Rogard gasped as his flittering eyes took in the broad battlefield. In the next leap, Ocher could cut down DIOMES, and then between them he and Evyan could trap MIKILLATI!

Briefly, that puzzlement nagged at the Bishop. Why should men die to catch someone else's King? What was there in the Law that said Kings should strive for mastery of the world and—

"Guard yourself, Queen!" Sir MERKON, King's Knight of LEUKAS, sprang in a move like Ocher's. Rogard's breath rattled in his throat with bitterness, and he thought there must be tears in Evyan's bright eyes. Slowly, then, the Queen withdrew two squares along the edge, until she stood in front of Earl Ferric's guardsman. It was still a good place to attack from, but not what the other had been.

BOAN, guardsman of the LEUKAN Queen DOLORA, moved one square forward, so that he protected great DIOMES from Ocher. Ocher snarled and sprang in front of Evyan, so that he stood between her and the frontier: clearing the way for her, and throwing his own protection over Carlon.

MERKON jumped likewise, landing to face Ocher with the frontier between them. Rogard clenched his mace and vision blurred from him; the LEUKANS were closing in on Evyan.

"Ulfar!" cried the King's Bishop. "Ulfar, can you help her?"

The stout old yeoman who was guardsman of the Queen's Bishop nodded wordlessly and ran one square forward. His spear menaced Bishop ASATOR, who growled at him—no Barrier between those two now!

MERKON of LEUKAS made another soaring leap, landing three squares in front of Rogard. "Guard yourself!" the voice belled from his faceless helmet. "Guard yourself, O Queen!"

No time now to let Ulfar slay ASATOR. Evyan's great eyes looked wildly about her; then, with swift decision, she stepped between MERKON and Ocher. Oh, a lovely move! Out of the fury in his breast, Rogard laughed.

The guardsman of the LEUKAN King's Knight clanked two squares ahead, lifting his spear against Ocher. It must have taken boldness thus to stand before Evyan herself; but the Queen of LEUKAS could slay her. "Get free, Ocher!" she cried. "Get away!" Ocher cursed and leaped from danger, landing in front of Rogard's guardsman.

The King's Bishop bit his lip and tried to halt the trembling in his limbs. How the sun blazed! Its light was a cataract of dry white fire over the barren red and black squares. It hung immobile, enormous in the vague sky, and men gasped in their armor. The noise of bugles

and iron, hoofs and wings and stamping feet, was loud under the
small wind that blew across the world. There had never been anything but this meaningless war, there would never be aught else, and
when Rogard tried to think beyond the moment when the fight had
begun, or the moment when it would end, there was only an abyss of
darkness.

Earl RAFAEON of LEUKAS took one ponderous step toward his
King, a towering figure of iron readying for combat. Evyan whooped.
"Ulfar!" she yelled. "Ulfar, your chance!"

Columbard's guardsman laughed aloud. Raising his spear, he
stepped over into the square held by ASATOR. The white-robed Bishop
lifted his mace, futile and feeble, and then he rolled in the dust at
Ulfar's feet. The men of Cinnabar howled and clanged sword on
shield.

Rogard held aloof from triumph. ASATOR, he thought grimly,
had been expendable anyway. King MIKILLATI had something else in
mind.

It was like a blow when he saw Earl RAFAEON's guardsman run
forward two squares and shout to Evyan to guard herself. Raging, the
Queen of Cinnabar withdrew a square to her rearward. Rogard saw
sickly how unprotected King Flambard was now, the soldiers scattered over the field and the hosts of LEUKAS marshaling. But Queen
DOLORA, he thought with a wild clutching hope, Queen DOLORA, her
tall cold beauty was just as open to a strong attack.

The soldier who had driven Evyan back took a leap across the
frontier. "Guard yourself, O Queen!" he cried again. He was a
small, hard-bitten, unkempt warrior in dusty helm and corselet.
Evyan cursed, a bouncing soldierly oath, and moved one square
forward to put a Barrier between her and him. He grinned impu-
dently in his beard.

It is ill for us, it is a bootless and evil day. Rogard tried once more
to get out of his square and go to Evyan's aid, but his will would not
carry him. The Barrier held, invisible and uncrossable, and the Law
held, the cruel and senseless Law which said a man must stand by and
watch his lady be slain, and he railed at the bitterness of it and lapsed
into a gray waiting.

Trumpets lifted brazen throats, drums boomed, and Queen DO-
LORA of LEUKAS stalked forth into battle. She came high and white and
icily fair, her face chiseled and immobile in its haughtiness under the
crowned helmet, and stood two squares in front of her husband,

looming over Carlon. Behind her, her own Bishop SORKAS poised in his stronghold, hefting his mace in armored hands. Carlon of Cinnabar spat at DOLORA's feet, and she looked at him from cool blue eyes and then looked away. The hot dry wind did not ruffle her long pale hair; she was like a statue, standing there and waiting.

"Ocher," said Evyan softly, "out of my way."

"I like not retreat, my lady," he answered in a thin tone.

"Nor I," said Evyan. "But I must have an escape route open. We will fight again."

Slowly, Ocher withdrew, back to his own home. Evyan chuckled once, and a wry grin twisted her young face.

Rogard was looking at her so tautly that he did not see what was happening until a great shout of iron slammed his head around. Then he saw Bishop SORKAS, standing in Carlon's square with a bloodied mace in his hands, and Carlon lay dead at his feet.

Carlon, your hands are empty, life has slipped from them and there is an unending darkness risen in you who loved the world. Goodnight, my Carlon, goodnight.

"Madame—" Bishop SORKAS spoke quietly, bowing a little, and there was a smile on his crafty face. "I regret, madame, that—ah—"

"Yes. I must leave you." Evyan shook her head, as if she had been struck, and moved a square backwards and sideways. Then, turning, she threw the glance of an eagle down the black squares to LEUKAS' Earl ARACLES. He looked away nervously, as if he would crouch behind the three soldiers who warded him. Evyan drew a deep breath sobbing into her lungs.

Sir THEUTAS, DOLORA's Knight, sprang from his stronghold, to place himself between Evyan and the Earl. Rogard wondered dully if he meant to kill Ulfar the soldier; he could do it now. Ulfar looked at the Knight who sat crouched, and hefted his spear and waited for his own weird.

"Rogard!"

The Bishop leaped, and for a moment there was fire-streaked darkness before his eyes.

"Rogard, to me! To me, and help sweep them from the world!"
Evyan's voice.

She stood in her scarred and dinted armor, holding her sword aloft, and on that smitten field she was laughing with a new-born hope. Rogard could not shout his reply. There were no words. But he raised his mace and ran.

The black squares slid beneath his feet, footfalls pounding, jarring his teeth, muscles stretching with a resurgent glory and all the world singing. At the frontier, he stopped, knowing it was Evyan's will though he could not have said how he knew. Then he faced about, and with clearing eyes looked back over that field of iron and ruin. Save for one soldier and a knight, Cinnabar was now cleared of LEUKAS forces, Evyan was safe, a counterblow was readying like the first whistle of hurricane. Before him were the proud banners of LEUKAS—now to throw them into the dust! Now to ride with Evyan into the home of MIKILLATI!

"Go to it, sir," rumbled Ulfar, standing on the Bishop's right and looking boldly at the white Knight who could slay him. "Give 'em hell from us."

Wings beat in the sky, and THEUTAS soared down to land on Rogard's left. In the hot light, the blue metal of his armor was like running water. His horse snorted, curveting and flapping its wings; he sat it easily, the lance swaying in his grasp, the black helmet turned to Flambard. One more such leap, reckoned Rogard wildly, and he would be able to assail the King of Cinnabar. Or—no—a single spring from here and he would spit Evyan on his lance.

And there is a Barrier between us!

"Watch yourself, Queen!" The arrogant LEUKAS voice boomed hollow out of the steel mask.

"Indeed I will, Sir Knight!" There was only laughter in Evyan's tone. Lightly, then, she sped up the row of black squares. She brushed by Rogard, smiling at him as she ran, and he tried to smile back but his face was stiffened. Evyan, Evyan, she was plunging alone into her enemy's homeland!

Iron belled and clamored. The white guardsman in her path toppled and sank at her feet. One fist lifted strengthlessly, and a dying shrillness was in the dust: "Curse you, curse you, MIKILLATI, curse you for a stupid fool, leaving me here to be slain—no, no, no—"

Evyan bestrode the body and laughed again in the very face of Earl ARACLES. He cowered back, licking his lips—he could not move against her, but she could annihilate him in one more step. Beside Rogard, Ulfar whooped, and the trumpet of Cinnabar howled in the rear.

Now the great attack was launched! Rogard cast a fleeting glance at Bishop SORKAS. The lean white-coped form was gliding forth, mace swinging loose in one hand, and there was a little sleepy smile on the pale face. No dismay—? SORKAS halted, facing Rogard, and smiled a little wider, skinning his teeth without humor. "You can kill me if you wish," he said softly. "But do you?"

For a moment Rogard wavered. To smash that head—!

"Rogard! Rogard, to me!"

Evyan's cry jerked the King's Bishop around. He saw now what her plan was, and it dazzled him so that he forgot all else. LEUKAS *is ours!*

Swiftly he ran, DIOMES and BOAN howled at him as he went between them, brushing impotent spears against the Barriers. He passed Queen DOLORA, and her lovely face was as if cast in steel, and her eyes followed him as he charged over the plain of LEUKAS. Then there was no time for thinking, Earl RAFAEON loomed before him, and he jumped the last boundary into the enemy's heartland.

The Earl lifted a meaningless ax. The Law read death for him, and Rogard brushed aside the feeble stroke. The blow of his mace shocked in his own body, slamming his jaws together. RAFAEON crumpled, falling slowly, his armor loud as he struck the ground. Briefly, his fingers clawed at the iron-hard black earth, and then he lay still.

They have slain Raddic and Carlon—we have three guardsmen, a Bishop, and an Earl—. Now we need only be butchers! Evyan, Evyan, warrior Queen, this is your victory!

DIOMES of LEUKAS roared and jumped across the frontier. Futile, futile, he was doomed to darkness. Evyan's lithe form moved up against ARACLES, her sword flamed and the Earl crashed at her feet. Her voice was another leaping brand: "Defend yourself, King!"

Turning, Rogard grew aware the MIKILLATI himself had been right beside him. There was a Barrier between the two men—but MIKILLATI had to retreat from Evyan, and he took one step forward and sideways. Peering into his face, Rogard felt a sudden coldness. There was no defeat there, it was craft and knowledge and an unbending steel will—*what was* LEUKAS *planning?*

Evyan tossed her head, and the wind fluttered the lock of hair like a rebel banner. "We have them, Rogard!" she cried.

Far and faint, through the noise and confusion of battle, Cinnabar's bugles sounded the command of her King. Peering into the haze, Rogard saw that Flambard was taking precautions. Sir THEUTAS was still a menace, where he stood beside SORKAS. Sir Cupran of Cinnabar flew heavily over to land in front of the Queen's Earl's guardsman, covering the route THEUTAS must follow to endanger Flambard.

Wise, but—Rogard looked again at MIKILLATI's chill white face, and it was as if a breath of cold blew through him. Suddenly he wondered why they fought. For victory, yes, for mastery over the world—but when the battle had been won, what then?

He couldn't think past that moment. His mind recoiled in horror he could not name. In that instant he knew icily that this was not the first war in the world, there had been others before, and there would be others again. *Victory is death.*

But Evyan, glorious Evyan, she could not die. She would reign over all the world and—

Steel blazed in Cinnabar. MERKON of LEUKAS came surging forth, one tigerish leap which brought him down on Ocher's guardsman. The soldier screamed, once, as he fell under the trampling, tearing hoofs, but it was lost in the shout of the LEUKAN Knight: "Defend yourself, Flambard! Defend youself!"

Rogard gasped. It was like a blow in the belly. He had stood triumphant over the world, and now all in one swoop it was brought toppling about him. THEUTAS shook his lance, SORKAS his mace, DIOMES raised a bull's bellow—somehow, incredibly somehow, the warriors of LEUKAS had entered Cinnabar and were thundering at the King's own citadel.

"No, no—" Looking down the long empty row of squares, Rogard saw that Evyan was weeping. He wanted to run to her, hold her close and shield her against the falling world, but the Barriers were around him. He could not stir from his square, he could only watch.

Flambard cursed lividly and retreated into his Queen's home. His men gave a shout and clashed their arms—there was still a chance!

No, not while the Law bound men, thought Rogard, not while the Barriers held. Victory was ashen, and victory and defeat alike were darkness.

Beyond her thinly smiling husband, Queen DOLORA swept forward. Evyan cried out as the tall white woman halted before Rogard's terrified guardsman, turned to face Flambard where he crouched, and called to him: "Defend yourself, King!"

"No—no—you fool!" Rogard reached out, trying to break the Barrier, clawing at MIKILLATI. "Can't you see, none of us can win, it's death for us all if the war ends. Call her back!"

The Immortal Game
◆

MIKILLATI ignored him. He seemed to be waiting.

And Ocher of Cinnabar raised a huge shout of laughter. It belled over the plain, dancing joyous mirth, and men lifted weary heads and turned to the young Knight where he sat in his own stronghold, for there was youth and triumph and glory in his laughing. Swiftly, then, a blur of steel, he sprang, and his winged horse rushed out of the sky on DOLORA herself. She turned to meet him, lifting her sword, and he knocked it from her hand and stabbed with his own lance. Slowly, too haughty to scream, the white Queen sank under his horse's hoofs.

And MIKILLATI smiled.

"I see," nodded the visitor. "Individual computers, each controlling its own robot piece by a tight beam, and all the computers on a given side linked to form a sort of group-mind constrained to obey the rules of chess and make the best possible moves. Very nice. And it's a pretty cute notion of yours, making the robots look like medieval armies." His glance studied the tiny figures where they moved on the oversized board under one glaring floodlight.

"Oh, that's pure frippery," said the scientist. "This is really a serious research project in multiple computer-linkages. By letting them play game after game, I'm getting some valuable data."

"It's a lovely setup," said the visitor admiringly. "Do you realize that in this particular contest the two sides are reproducing one of the great classic games?"'

"Why, no. Is that a fact?"

"Yes. It was a match between Anderssen and Kieseritsky, back in—I forget the year, but it was quite some time ago. Chess books often refer to it as the Immortal Game. . . . So your computers must share many of the properties of a human brain."

"Well, they're complex things, all right," admitted the scientist. "Not all their characteristics are known yet. Sometimes my chessmen surprise even me."

"Hm." The visitor stooped over the board. "Notice how they're jumping around inside their squares, waving their arms, batting at each other with their weapons?" He paused, then murmured slowly: "I wonder—I wonder if your computers may not have consciousness. If they might not have—minds."

"Don't get fantastic," snorted the scientist.

"But how do you know?" persisted the visitor. "Look, your feed-

back arrangement is closely analogous to a human nervous system. How do you know that your individual computers, even if they are constrained by the group linkage, don't have individual personalities? How do you know that their electronic senses don't interpret the game as, oh, as an interplay of free will and necessity; how do you know they don't receive the data of the moves as their own equivalent of blood, sweat and tears?" He shuddered a little.

"Nonsense," grunted the scientist. "They're only robots. Now— hey! Look there! Look at that move!"

Bishop SORKAS took one step ahead, into the black square adjoining Flambard's. He bowed and smiled. "The war is ended," he said.

Slowly, very slowly, Flambard looked about him. SORKAS, MERKON, THEUTAS, they were crouched to leap on him wherever he turned; his own men raged helpless against the Barriers; there was no place for him to go.

He bowed his head. "I surrender," he whispered.

Rogard looked across the red and black to Evyan. Their eyes met, and they stretched out their arms to each other.

"Checkmate," said the scientist. "That game's over."

He crossed the room to the switchboard and turned off the computers.

Slawomir Mrozek

In this allegorical story by the Polish satirist Slawomir Mrozek, humans play the roles of chess pieces in a living chess exhibition. The "pieces" have minds of their own, how-ever, and when it becomes clear to them that their masters are incompetent, their own hierarchy breaks down and an-archy rules.

The day was cloudy. I do not mind the weather myself, but I met a friend who seemed to be very worried about it.

"I'm developing rheumatism. Can't be helped. I wouldn't pay much attention to it, but what's worse, I caught a cold a few days ago. But all I need now is to get soaked through. I already have the beginnings of a flu. My bones are aching. And what next? Nobody can be sure that there will be no serious complications."

I pointed out that after all he did not have to get soaked through; all he had to do was to stay under cover when it rained. And thank God we were not short of roofs.

"It's easy for you to talk, you've no outdoor duties. But I have to work in the open day in day out. One has got to live."

I asked about his work. We had known each other for a long time. Together we had worked as extras in the theatre. We had had a succession of temporary jobs, always at the mercy of changing

119

circumstances: delivery men, part-time caretakers, fourth men at bridge or fourteenth at dinner, temporary comforters, birds of passage, bodyguards, baby-sitters and professional guests.

He explained that he had found relatively light work, which would have been entirely satisfactory if it were not for his inborn sensitivity to changes of temperature.

"Do you know what living chess is? It's exactly the same as normal chess, except that instead of a chessboard on a table one uses a much larger board marked out on the pavement of a square; instead of inanimate chessmen real men suitably dressed up take part in the game. The players themselves must, of course, be in raised positions at the opposite sides of the board so that they can see it all at a glance. Because of its value as a spectacle, live chess is organized as a part of celebrations and open-air festivals. The public likes it very much. After all, how many people can watch a game on a normal board? Three, five at the most, and they disturb the players. Now, any number can watch live chess, while the players, separated from the multitude, are able to concentrate on the problem of winning. Add to that the attraction of colourful costumes and you'll see why live chess is a popular spectacle. You will find it also in clubs which have a suitable courtyard or other space at their disposal.

"Apart from space you need, of course, the personnel. Sixteen men for white and sixteen for black, and a few reserve (men are only human), and also a wardrobe. The volunteers don't have to pass any exams. After the first few minutes of enjoyment the attractions of the game, which had made them offer their services, tend to evaporate. Soon they get tired and impatient and then withdraw under the slightest pretext (death in the family, an electric iron left on at home, an alleged headache), thus spoiling an interesting game. What's needed are regulars, men who having no interest in the game don't stand the risk of losing it and can be relied upon to stick it out to the end without any ups or downs. They get a regular salary, and as professionals they give the required standard of service.

"The work is relatively light. I say, relatively, because this depends on a number of variable factors. In the summer, when the sun shines, it can be quite pleasant, as long as you don't suffer from sunstroke. In the autumn, during protracted foul weather, it can give you a cold and induce melancholia. The winter is worst. There are games played in a snow storm, when you can't see more than two squares ahead and you have to be careful not to take one of your own pieces.

"At the moment it's still summer, but a rainy one. I wouldn't complain," ended my friend, "if it were not for the clouds and my tonsils. If I don't go to work to-day, they can give me notice. I'm playing a Bishop. I reached that position with a great deal of effort and to the envy of my colleagues. Will you take over for one day only? Please! Perhaps to-morrow the weather will improve. You'll get full day's pay. It's not too bad; Bishops get more because there is so much running to do. Anyway all the pieces get more. One day I might become King."

"I can't," I replied. "I can't stand people looking at me. Don't you remember how this caused difficulties at the theatre? A staring crowd embarrasses me and this leads to a counter-reaction, forcing me into excessively open and frank behaviour. It seems to me that since they come to look at me, it would be less than honest not to show them everything. I was thrown out of the theatre because during a first night, under the influence of so many pairs of eyes, I showed the spectators my boil. And you have said yourself that living chess is a spectacle."

"You needn't worry about that," my friend reassured me. "On this occasion there is no question of a spectacle. I'm working for two old men who have been advised by their doctor to seek outdoor exercise. That's why they gave up ordinary chess and took up living chess. It's a private game. Apart from the participants you won't see a soul, there won't be a single spectator."

I reflected that I had nothing else to do that day. There was no reason to refuse a favour to a friend, while earning some money at the same time.

"All right," I said, "but will I know how to do it?"

"It is quite simple and the Knight will give you the few essential bits of advice. I'm in the white team and we stand next to each other on the left. At the beginning of each game, before developments separate us, we always manage to exchange a few words."

"Fine. I'll go."

"Go. I'll retire to bed."

We parted.

The game took place in the courtyard of an old palace, enclosed on four sides by two-storied cloisters. I entered through a tunnel-like gateway. A grey square of sky covered the enormous box of the courtyard, so vast that the huge chessboard marked out on its floor did not look large at all. Here and there on the walls vertical pools of Russian vine screened the cloisters. Perhaps because of them the whole courtyard was swathed in an emerald gloom, the intensity of which varied with the passage of mists and clouds high above. A few human figures moving about looked strangely small because we are accustomed to seeing people indoors in restricted spaces, which make them appear large. Here however I found myself under an open sky and yet indoors, as if clever architecture had joined space to enclosure.

As I approached some of the figures acquired a super-natural size. It was because of their costumes. While the pawns were not much larger than normal human beings, the Bishops, Rooks and Knights looked enormous. Only their feet, protruding from under the fantastic dress, remained normal, shod in a variety of old shoes. Above them necks and heads of horses, their teeth bared, each tooth the size of a tile, the severe-looking, geometric and crenellated Rooks, the saucer-like ruffs of the Bishops.

Daunted by all this I involuntarily stopped on the edge of the courtyard. The cavernous gateway, unpleasantly ready to reflect and magnify the slightest noise, suddenly seemed friendly and snug. I did not notice that a black Rook had appeared behind me.

"You are not allowed in here," said a voice from within the castle. I looked at the Rook and noticed painted horizontal and vertical white lines imitating the point between bricks. Automatically, I looked up to the battlements, though I knew that the head of the speaker must be level with mine.

I explained politely that I was not a casual gaper, but had come to stand in for a sick colleague. The Rook towered over me silently for a while and then from within came the sound as of spitting and he moved away, his heavy shoes creaking on the stones. I entered the courtyard.

On the left wing of the whites I noticed the Knight to whose care my friend had recommended me. I spoke to him and he turned his massive *papier-mâché* chest and his mane frozen in a picturesque disarray, until his nostrils were right above his head.

"All right," he said. "I'll help you to change. Got a cigarette? We are not allowed to smoke during work, but we could have one now. Mind you, one has to make sure that the smoke doesn't go up, because this can be seen and a supervisor might pick on you. But if you blow the smoke into your trousers, it comes out at the bottom and all's well. You must learn these little tricks."

Under the Knight's guidance I put on the Bishop's involucre. It was dark and stuffy inside it. Through the eye-holes I could see the edge of my frill and a part of the courtyard plunged in a green dusk.

"Yes, my friend," said the Knight, "you've got to know the ins and outs here. Now, for instance, we can have a smoke, but we've got to be careful. We can also eat our sandwiches, but you must remember not to drop the wrapping paper on the ground. Later it is more difficult."

The Queen took her place on my right. Instinctively I looked at her feet and saw frayed trouser turn-ups and shoes with cracked uppers. A bit farther along towered the majestic silhouette of the King with tennis shoes sticking out from under it.

"The King gets the highest salary," explained the Knight, "because he is the heaviest of the lot. In spite of it he is played by an elderly man; though the piece is heavy there's not much walking to be done, and that's important when you are past sixty. Also in old age the few extra pennies come very handy indeed. Should you notice that it is his turn and he's not moving, you'll do him a service if you knock on his side, that's if you are near enough. Sometimes he falls asleep inside still standing on his feet."

The ranks of the white and black pieces were filling in. Beyond them I could see the cloisters. The air, saturated with damp, was far from clear, the clouds in the sky cast their shadows over everything, and the overhanging roof made the walls darker still. Because of all this the columns, arches and balustrades, here and there obliterated by patches of vine, looked like a flat and misty drawing.

"Oho," said the pawn in front of me, "the black Bishop has again been at the bottle."

"He really shouldn't drink," commented the Knight. "Bishops have to run in straight lines. It's different when you're a Knight. Nobody notices if you stray from your course a little bit because as it is you've got to move sideways. . . ."

"Attention," warned the pawn. "It's beginning."

I used to play chess in my time, not badly either, but one did not have to be a master to notice the low level of the game in which I had to take part. First of all the pauses between moves were of such duration that one could not help wondering if the players had fallen asleep or, perhaps, gone away altogether, forgetting to tell us that they had given up. Hidden in the cloisters they kept on falling into endless contemplation, while our legs were getting numb. Eventually their mental efforts led to hopeless and chaotic moves, which betrayed a complete lack of skill on both sides.

Like all the pieces I was moved about a few times without rhyme or reason and this began to worry me.

"What's the matter?" I whispered to the Knight when at last I found myself again at his side.

"Sclerosis," he whispered back. "A short while ago they could still get through a game in five or six hours, but it seems they've got worse."

"Which of the two plays a better game?"

"Neither. That's why it's such hard work. Sometimes they can't finish before it gets too dark and then they leave us where we stand overnight and finish the game the following day. I'm afraid this is going to happen to-night. The game is going badly and the weather is uncertain."

We walked about the chessboard hither and thither, from one square to another. A few pawns got captured. We looked at them with envy as they walked away.

It started raining. A fine rain, the sort that lasts a long time; it starts with deliberation, knowing that it has a few days in hand and need not hurry, and then gradually gathers momentum. My cardboard costume protected me at first, but I was worried about my feet shod only in light shoes.

"See that Rook in boots?" The Knight pointed at a black figure. "Watch out. He likes to give your ankle a kick when capturing you. He'll also tell on you if you squat for a moment to give your tired feet a rest. A proper patriot he is, too. God forbid that black should start losing. He's at his worst then. Sometimes he gets so excited that he starts crying."

"Is it his game, or what?"

"He's just passionate."

Something started dripping under my collar. The dome-like cardboard structure over my head had parted in one place and was letting through the rain, its drops unpleasantly cold.

The intervals between moves became incredibly long as the players seemed to have increasing difficulty in taking in the state of the game. As the rain thickened, the gargoyles, through which the rain gutters were discharging, began to sing, shyly at first, but with increasing confidence. From all sides came the individual whisper of drops falling against the general background of a noisy downpour. The black Bishop, his alcoholic euphoria gone, had obviously lost heart and swayed sadly two squares away from me. My friend, the Knight, had been shifted to the other end of the board.

Anger swelled inside me. It was all very well for all those old professionals, used to this kind of discomfort. But my feet were getting wet and I could not reconcile myself to it. And there was no prospect whatsoever of the game ever coming to an end.

"Perhaps someone will capture me," I thought hopefully for a moment. "Then I shall be able to go home. But one cannot rely on a happy accident. What else? Wait. And if they leave us overnight? The Knight said that this could happen."

I could see so many openings, which if exploited could help to bring about a decision. . . . But the most obvious, the most glittering chances were being systematically wasted by both sides. The thought that because of this incompetence I might get pneumonia gave another spur to my anger. Not able to bear it any longer I decided off my own bat to bring the game to a conclusion.

I was sure that I could get away with a little cheating, with moving one or two squares without any orders. Around me I could see only general apathy. The sclerotic players immersed in their thoughts would not notice anything. Slowly, unobtrusively, I started to shift my position and move into the next square. One had to be careful not to overdo it and brazenly move from a black into a white square, because everyone knows that a Bishop has to stick to one colour throughout the game. But if I avoided such glaring mistakes I was bound to succeed.

Now I had to make my decisive move. Having found myself on the same diagonal as the black Bishop, dare I take my courage in both hands and capture him? But there was a chance that the player directing the black side, seeing his Bishop opposite me, might decide to have me captured. I had to wait. Anyhow I did not want to move about too much. Minutes passed and nothing happened. I counted up to a hundred and decided to take the risk. Moving with purpose I walked up to the black Bishop.

"You're captured, my friend," I said. "You can go home."

In choosing him as my first victim I counted on the fact that in his drunken stupor he was paying even less attention to the game than the others. When I spoke to him he swayed, cleared his throat and did not disguise his joy.

"Splendid. I'm on my way," he cried. "What? Can't a man have a drink?" He spoke with such belligerence and fled without waiting for an answer; I occupied his square as if it was mine of right.

My calculations proved right. The general boredom and indifference were such that nobody knew or cared if it was white's move or black's. The players themselves must have had one of their mental blackouts and I was also helped by the rain and the gathering dusk.

Just in case, however, I waited a few moments before polishing off two black pawns. Neither of them uttered a word, and with obvious relief they left the chessboard. In this way acting in my own interest I was helping my colleagues.

I could not have cared less about white's victory for which I was working. All I wanted was to bring the game to a conclusion. I expected that once I had captured all the black pieces, even the dimmest idiot would be able to checkmate the lonely King. Gradually I grew insolent and captured any handy piece without stopping in between. I was, however, on guard as far as the black Rook in heavy boots was concerned. Not only did I leave him alone, but I also tried to operate as far from him as possible, so that he should not notice what I was doing.

I was just preparing to have a go at one of the black Knights when I noticed that something was wrong.

In spite of all my efforts, the numerical balance of the opposing forces remained unchanged. True that there were fewer pieces on the board, but both sides had been equally depleted. Could it be that the man playing black had suddenly woken up and shown unexpected enterprise? I started to observe closely what was happening around me and discovered that the black Rook in heavy boots was cheating.

Now I understood why, even if he suspected something, he did not expose me. His own hands were far from clean. He was doing the same as I, but from quite different motives—he was the only jingoist in the game. All my efforts were being wasted. The balance between the sides remained unchanged and the chances of the game coming to an end had not increased.

The black Rook was becoming insolent. I saw him jump at our poor Queen, kicking brutally with his heavy boots at the miserable old shoes of my colleague. The enemy had given up all pretence and

Check!

◆

I could not remain idle. Without wasting a moment I removed the black Queen. It was clear that the black Rook knew what I was doing, but he also knew that I was aware of his activities. He was avoiding me and I could see that he hated me.

On my side, apart from the King of course, only my friend the Knight and a few pawns were left in the game. On the other side the position was similar.

"I don't want to interfere," said the Knight, "but do be careful. I would like to help you, but I'm regular here. If they notice, they'll throw me out, and I want to keep the job. With you it's different. There's nothing they can do to you, because you are here only for the day. Ow! . . ." He cried out with pain as the black Rook who had approached stealthily, gave him the usual vicious kick. "Farewell," he called to me walking off the field. He was the only one who understood what was happening. But I could not stop to say good-bye, because I had to run and polish off the black Knight. Then came the turn of the remaining pawns. We finished with them in no time, without even trying to keep up appearances. Only the two Kings, the black Rook and myself were left on the board. No further cheating was possible in the now wide-open space.

It was now raining cats and dogs. My cardboard costume was sodden and heavy, my shoes full of water. The rain had softened the battlements of the Rook and paint was running off the Kings. The ingenious orchestration of drops and rivulets disappeared under the steady noise now filling the courtyard.

The players made a few primitive moves, putting each other's Kings in check, but it was all pointless and could bring no solution. Then came an endless pause and one really did not know if the players were still there or had gone home. The four of us were standing there, soaking in the rain, and with despair I could see no end to it. Worse still was the possibility, mentioned by the Knight, that we should be left there till the morning, the players hoping in vain to finish the game the following day. The light was failing and the rain splashed with increasing force.

I watched the black Rook, determined to be the first to kick should he approach me. He must have guessed and kept his distance. For a while we stood still, watching each other. At last he gave up and, turning to the white King, said: "Check!"

I decided to put an end to it.

127

"Listen," I said to the Rook, "let's not delude ourselves. It's dark and pouring with rain. I know you are a patriot and want your side to win, but you can see that the game is inconclusive. It's a draw. Let's go home."

"If I say check," he declared gloomily, "it is check!"

I could see that there was no point in arguing with him. My King had not budged, he must have fallen asleep in spite of the rain. I could not be sure that enraged by this the black Rook would not cause him some bodily harm. I knocked at the King's side.

"Eh? What is it?" The old man woke up.

"You are in check, granpa. Didn't you hear?"

"All right, all right." He shuffled to the adjoining square. The Rook immediately checked him again. Making sure that I was exposing myself to the Rook, I gently propelled the King to the edge of the board. The stillness of the courtyard, woven out of the murmur and gurgling of the rain, was interrupted by a succession of hoarse cries of "check!"

"We are going home," I managed to whisper to the black King as we passed him. He yawned, said "Good-night" and walked off. It was already so dark that the enraged black Rook didn't even notice.

When we reached the edge of the chessboard I made a dash for the cloisters, pulling the King with me. Panting we hid behind a column. I ordered the King to keep quiet and started listening.

It was now coming down in buckets and the invisible courtyard was splashing and drumming. I expected to hear the heavy boots on the pavement. We waited for a time but the sound did not come.

"Finished," I said. "We are going."

"Check!" roared a voice right behind us.

We fled across the courtyard in the direction of the gate. While running as fast as I could I figured out how he managed to surprise us. He must have taken off his boots and in stockinged feet walked stealthily along the cloisters.

I was already under the archway leading to freedom when I noticed that the old man, burdened with age and the costume made doubly heavy by the rain, had fallen behind. His heavy breathing and the squelching of his tennis shoes echoed under the vaulted ceiling. I realized that we could not escape. It was probably fear that suggested a way out. I peeled off my costume, turned back and feverishly started to remove the King's superstructure. Then I threw it as far as

Check!

◆

I could. The huge, stiff scarecrow settled on the floor with a dull thud. We jumped behind the pillars.

The black Rook was right behind us. He found what he wanted and stopped. Then in the echoing darkness we heard repeated dull blows of a knife piercing a dummy—the empty royal shell of wet cardboard and *papier-mâché*.

We walked away slowly. There was no longer any need to hurry.

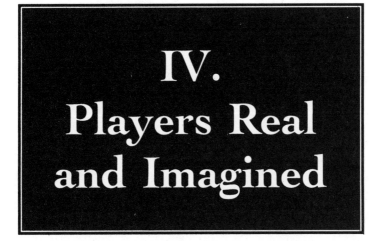

IV.
Players Real
and Imagined

Few players have had as great an impact on chess—and on the public's perception of chessplayers—as Bobby Fischer, who in 1972, in a titanic match telecast throughout the world, won the world championship from Boris Spassky and brought to an end (only temporarily, as it turned out) a Soviet chess dynasty that seemed destined to dominate the sport forever.

Fischer's stunning victory, his fame, the riches that could have been his—all had been predicted by him a decade earlier. In an interview in *Harper's Magazine*, in January 1962, Ralph Ginzburg asked the eighteen-year-old grandmaster (Fischer was born in March 1943), "Would you consider yourself the greatest player that ever lived, even better, say, than Capablanca, Steinitz, or Morphy?" Fischer's reply: "Well, I don't like to put things like that in print, it sounds so egotistical. But to answer your question, Yes."

At another point Ginzburg asked him what he planned to do when he became world champion. Fischer's reply: "I'll make a tour of the whole world, giving exhibitions. . . . I'll make them pay thousands. . . . Then I'll build me a house. . . . I want to live the rest of my life in a house built exactly like a rook."

Incredibly, all this had been said before, in strikingly similar terms, in a novel published eight years before Fischer was born, by a chessplaying character named Fischer! The novel, *Auto-da-Fé,* by Elias Canetti (born 1905), the 1981 Nobel Prize winner for Literature, was first published in German, as *Die Blendung,* in 1935. The character, a grotesque hunchbacked dwarf who dreams of defeating Capablanca, is named Fischerle, but he tells reporters after his imagined victory: "I'm surprised to find myself called Fischerle everywhere. My name is Fischer." This astounding coincidence must be unique in literature.

The novel's main character, a book-collecting scholar named Peter Kien, marries his housekeeper, who, bitterly disappointed that he has far less money than she had thought, bit by bit appropriates his library and finally drives him from his apartment. In a nightclub called the Stars of Heaven, Kien meets Fischerle and his wife, a prostitute for whom Fischerle procures clients. With his eye on the cash Kien is carrying, Fischerle takes him to a hotel, where while Kien sleeps Fischerle dreams of becoming world chess champion.

133

Elias Canetti

Fischerle might well argue with himself. Stealing had become a habit with him. For a little while he hadn't been stealing because where he lived there was nothing to steal. He didn't take part in expeditions far afield as the police had their eye on him. He could be too easily identified. Policemen's zeal for their duty knew no limits. Half the night he lay awake, his eyes forcibly held open, his hands clenched in the most complicated fashion. He expelled the heaps of money from his mind. Instead he went through all the rough passages and hard words he had ever experienced in police stations. Were such things necessary? And on top of it all they took away everything you possessed. You never saw a penny of it again. *That* wasn't stealing! When their insults ceased to be effective and he was fed to the back teeth with the police and already had one arm hanging out of bed, he fell back on some games of chess. They were interesting enough to keep him firmly fixed in bed; but his arm remained outside, ready to pounce. He played more cautiously than usual, pausing before some moves to think for a ridiculously long time. His opponent was a world champion. He dictated the moves to him proudly. Slightly bewildered by the obedience of the champion he exchanged him for another one: this one too put up with a great deal. Fischerle was playing, in fact, for both of them. The opponent could think of no better moves than those dictated to him by Fischerle, nodded his

head gratefully and was beaten hollow in spite of it. The scene repeated itself several times until Fischerle said: "I won't play with such
half-wits," and stretched his legs out of bed. Then he exclaimed: "A
world champion? Where is there a world champion? There isn't any
world champion here!"

To make sure, he got up and looked around the room. As soon
as they won the world's title people simply went and hid themselves.
He could find no one. All the same he could have sworn the world
champion was sitting on the bed playing chess with him. Surely he
couldn't be hiding in the next room? Now don't you worry, Fischerle
would soon find him. Calm as calm, he looked through the next room;
the room was empty. He opened the door of the wardrobe and made
a pounce with his hand, no chess player would escape him. He moved
very softly, who wouldn't? Why should that long creature with the
books be disturbed in his sleep only because Fischerle had to track
down his enemy? Quite possibly the champion wasn't there at all, and
for a mere whim he was throwing his beautiful job away. Under the
bed he grazed over every inch with the tip of his nose. It was a long
time since he'd been back under any bed and it reminded him of the old
days at home. As he crawled out his eyes rested on a coat folded up
over a chair. Then it occurred to him how greedy world champions
always were for money, they could never get enough; to win the title
from them one had to put down heaps of money in cash, just like that,
on the table; there was no doubt the fellow was after the money, and
was lurking about somewhere near the wallet. He might not have
found it yet, it ought to be saved from him; a creature like that could
manage anything. Tomorrow the money'd be gone and the flagpole
would think Fischerle took it. But you couldn't deceive him. With his
long arms he stretched for the wallet from below, pulled it out and
withdrew himself under the bed. He might have crawled right out, but
why should he? The world champion was larger and stronger than he,
sure as fate he was standing behind that chair, lurking for the money,
and would knock Fischerle out because he'd got in first. By this skilful
maneuver no one noticed anything. Let the dirty swindler stay where
he was. Nobody asked him to come. He could scram. That would be
best. Who wanted him?

Soon Fischerle had forgotten him. In his hiding place right at the
back under the bed he counted over the beautiful new notes, just for
the pleasure of it. He remembered exactly how many there were. As
soon as he had done he started again at the beginning. Fischerle is off

now to a far country, to America. There he goes up to the world
champion Capablanca, and says: "I've been looking for you!" puts
down his caution money and plays until the fellow is beaten hollow.
On the next day Fischerle's picture is in all the papers. He does pretty
well out of it all. At home, under the Stars of Heaven, that lot
wouldn't believe their eyes, his wife, the whore, begins to howl and
yell if she'd only know it she would have let him play all he wanted;
the others shut her up with a couple of smacks—serve her right—
that's what happens when a woman won't bother to learn about the
game. Women'll be the end of men. If he'd stayed at home, he'd
never have made good. A man must cut loose, that's the whole secret.
None but the brave deserve to be world champion. And people have
the nerve to say Jews aren't brave. The reporters ask him who he is.
Not a soul knows him. He doesn't look like an American. There are
Jews everywhere. But where does this Jew come from, who's rolled
in triumph over Capablanca? For the first day he'll let people guess.
The papers would like to tell their readers, but they don't know.
Everywhere the headlines read: "Mystery of the new World Champion." The police become interested, naturally. They want to lock
him up again. No, no, gentlemen, not so fast this time; now he
throws the money about and the police are honored to release him at
once. On the second day, a round hundred reporters turn up. Each
one promises him, shall we say, a thousand dollars cash down if he'll
say something. Fischerle says not a word. The papers begin to lie.
What else are they to do? The readers won't wait any longer. Fischerle sits in a mammoth hotel with one of those luxury cocktail
bars, like on a giant liner. The head waiter brings the loveliest ladies
to his table, not tarts mind you, millionairesses with a personal interest in him. He thanks them politely, but hasn't time, later perhaps
. . . And why hasn't he time? Because he's reading all the lies about
him in all the papers. It takes all day. How's he to get through it?
Every minute he's interrupted. Press photographers ask for a moment of his time. "But gentlemen, a hump . . . !" he protests. "A
world champion is a world champion, honored Mr. Fischerle. The
hump is quite immaterial." They photograph him right and left,
before and behind. "Why don't you retouch it," he suggests, "take
the hump out. Then you'll have a nice picture for your paper." "Just
as you please, most honored world champion!" But really, where's
he had his eyes? His picture is everywhere, without a hump. It's
gone. He hasn't one. But he worries a bit about his size. He calls the

head waiter and points to a paper. "A bad picture, what?" he asks. The head water says: "*Well.*" In America people speak English. He finds the picture excellent. "But it's only the head," he says. That's right too. "You can go now," says Fischerle and tips him a hundred dollars. In this picture he might be a fully grown man. No one would notice he was undersized. He loses his interest in the articles. He can't be bothered to read all this in English. He only understands "Well!" Later on he has all the latest editions of the papers brought to him and looks hard at all his pictures. His head is everywhere. His nose is a bit long, that's true; can't help his nose. From a child up he's been all for chess. He might have taken some other idea into his head, football or swimming or boxing. But not he. It's a bit of luck really. If he were a boxing champion, now, he'd have to be photographed half naked. Everyone would laugh at him and he'd get nothing out of it. On the next day at least a thousand reporters turn up. "Gentlemen," he says, "I'm surprised to find myself called Fischerle everywhere. My name is Fischer. I trust that you will have this error rectified." They promise they will. Then they all kneel down in front of him—how small men are—and implore him to say something at last. They'll be thrown out, they'll lose their jobs, they cry, if they get nothing out of him today. My sorrow, he thinks, nothing for nothing, he gave the head waiter a hundred dollars, but he won't give the reporters anything. "What's your bid, gentlemen?" he cries boldly. A thousand dollars shouts one. Cheek, screams another, ten thousand! A third takes him by the hand and whispers: a hundred thousand, Mr. Fischer. People throw money about like nothing. He stops his ears. Until they get into millions he won't even listen to them. The reporters go mad and begin tearing each other's hair, each one wants to give more than the other; all this fuss; auctioneering his private life! One goes up to five millions, and all at once there is absolute quiet. Not one dares offer more. World Champion Fischer takes his fingers out of his ears and declares: "I will now say something, gentlemen. What good will it do me to ruin you? None. How many of you are there? A thousand. Let each one of you give me ten thousand and I'll tell you all. Then I shall have ten millions and not one of you will be ruined. Agreed?" They fall on his neck and he's a made man. Then he clambers up on a chair, he doesn't really need to any more but he does it all the same, and tells them the simple truth. As a world champion, he fell from Heaven. It takes a good hour to convince them. He was unhappily married. His wife, a Capitalist, fell into evil ways, she was—as they used to call it in his home, the Stars of Heaven—a "whore." She wanted him to take money from her. He didn't know any way out. If he wouldn't take any, she used to say, she'd murder him. He was forced to do it. He had yielded to her blackmail and kept the money for her. Twenty long years he had to endure this. In the end he was fed up. One day he demanded categorically that she should stop or he'd become chess champion of the world. She cried, but she wouldn't stop. She was too much accustomed to doing nothing, to having fine clothes and lovely clean-shaven gentlemen. He was sorry for her but a man must keep his word. He goes straight from the Stars of Heaven to the United States, finishes off Capablanca, and here he is! The reporters rave about him. So does he. He founds a charity. He will pay a stipendium to every café in the world. In return the proprietors must undertake to put up on their walls every game played by the world champion. Any person defacing the notices will be prosecuted. Every individual person can thus convince himself that the world champion is a better player than he is. Otherwise some swindler may suddenly pop up, a dwarf or even a cripple, and brag he plays better. People may not think of checking up the cripple's moves. They are capable of believing him simply because he's a good liar. Things like that must stop. On each wall is a placard. The cheat makes one wrong move, everyone looks at the placard and who then will blush to the very hump on his miserable back. The crook! Moreover the proprietor must undertake to fetch him a sock on the jaw for saying things about the world champion. Let him challenge him openly if he's got the money. Fischerle will put down a million for this foundation. He's not mean. He'll send a million to his wife so she needn't go on the streets any more. In return she'll give it him in writing that she won't come to America and will keep mum about his former dealings with the police. Fischer's going to marry a millionairess. This will reimburse him for his losses. He'll have new suits made at the best possible tailor so that his wife'll notice nothing. A gigantic palace will be built with real castles, knights, pawns, just as it ought to be. The servants are in livery; in thirty vast halls Fischer plays night and day thirty simultaneous games of chess with living pieces which he has only to command. All he has to do is to speak and his slaves move wherever he tells them. Challengers come from all the chief countries of the world, poor devils who want to learn something from him. Many sell their coats and shoes to pay for the long journey. He receives them with hospitality, gives them a good meal, with soup, a sweet and two veg, and pretty often a nice grilled steak instead of a cut from the joint. Anyone can be beaten by him once. He asks nothing in return for his kindness. Only that each one should write his name in the visitors' book on leaving and categorically assert that he, Fischer, is the world champion. He defends his title. While he does so his new wife goes out riding in her car. Once a week he goes with her. In the castle all the chandeliers are put out, lighting alone costs him a fortune. On the door he pins up a notice: "Back soon. Fischer: World Champion." He does not stay out two hours, but visitors are queuing up like in the war when he gets back. "What are you queuing for?" asks a passer-by. "What, don't you know? You must be a stranger here." Out of pity the others tell him who it is that lives here. So that he shall understand each one tells him singly, then they all shout in a chorus: "Chess Champion of the World, Fischer, is giving alms today." The stranger is struck dumb. After an hour he finds his voice again. "Then this is his reception day?" That is just what the natives have been waiting for. "Today is not a reception day or there would be far more people." Now all of them begin talking at once. "Where is he? The castle is dark!" "With his wife in the car. This is his second wife. The first was only a simple Capitalist. The second is a millionairess. The car belongs to him. It isn't just a taxi. He had it built specially." What they are saying is the simple truth. He sits in his car, it suits him very well. It is a little too small for his wife, who has to crouch all the time. But in return she's allowed to ride with him. At other times she has her own. He doesn't go out in hers. It's much too big for him. But his was the more expensive. The factory made his car specially. He feels inside it just as if he were under the bed. Looking out of the windows is too boring. He shuts his eyes tight. Not a thing moves. Under the bed he is perfectly at home. He hears his wife's voice from above. He's fed up with her, what does she mean to him? She doesn't understand a thing about chess. The man is saying something too. Is he a player? He's obviously intelligent. Wait, now, wait; why should he wait? What's waiting to him? That man up there is talking good German. He's a professional man, sure to be a secret champion. These people are afraid of being recognized. It's with them like it is with crowned heads. They have to come to women incognito. That man's a world champion for sure, not just an ordinary champion! He must challenge him. He can't wait longer. His head bursts with good moves. He'll beat him into a cocked hat!

Brad Leithauser

In his autobiography Karpov on Karpov (*Atheneum, 1991*), *the former world champion describes Fischer's impact in the years 1970–72:*

> When Fischer began his triumphant march to the chess summit, there was a sporting—and political—fascination to it: Who would come out on top—the lone Brooklynite or the united phalanx of the strong Soviet grandmasters? It was the favorite topic of the man in the street: one against all. This heated up interest to such a degree that for a time chess became the number one sport in the world.

The fascination with Fischer—which continues today unabated—has resulted in the publication of a number of novels that feature Fischer-like characters. In a class by itself is Brad Leithauser's Hence, *the story of a chess match between Timothy Briggs, in whose speech and mannerisms Fischer is clearly recognizable (especially during the hotel-room scene in which he is visited by his chess trainer, Imre), and an obnoxious chessplaying computer named ANNDY.*

We move to the sixth game of the match, and Timothy has a decisive edge over the machine. Victory in this game is inevitable. Within the regulations governing the match, provision has been made that in such circumstances ANNDY's operators can resign on behalf of their machine. This is a provision inserted purely for Timothy's benefit; to spare him from needless exhaustion, he will not be required to pursue a foregone victory. Of course it is a provision of no possible use to ANNDY, or its makers, since the machine is indefatigable.

But Timothy—ashen-faced, and desperation blazing in his eyes, as though he stood on the threshold of another defeat rather than victory—refuses to let the machine resign. He would play on, and ANNDY must play with him. Now why would Timothy jeopardize the needed victory? It makes no sense . . . But after some shrugging of shoulders, some brief whispered consultations, it is agreed that the game will continue.

Timothy is driving his pawn to the queening square. His face has a peculiarly severe look: he is punishing the machine. He is pursuing Law. He is claiming Justice. And he is the Judge, he is the Lawman. The pawn would advance and there is no stopping it. In all the world, there can be no stopping it. Deeper, deeper must go that advance, until ANNDY is beaten, absolutely subjugated—the pawn queened, the king toppled. But when the game is concluded at last, and ANNDY's resignation accepted, Timothy rises with an uncertain look. Isn't it apparent that he wants to shake hands with the machine and not with its human operators? Triumph is on Timothy's pallid face, and a kind of stunned disbelief, but also isn't there a tinge of white-faced shame? One might suppose that having for a time ignored all the injunctions to halt, and having continued his forceful violation of this other mind, he has only now perceived, as he rises from his chair, that the victim of his advances is not living and has never been alive. . . .

That pounding, which is so insistent, and so stupidly repetitive, turns out to be a knock at the door. From great depths of sleep, where the source of a colossal humming resides, and from a dream retrievable only in jagged-edged fragments, in which his assailants have been holding his legs, to stop him from kicking out against them, Timothy is summoned—up to a view, as his eyes snap open at last, of his room at the Totaplex Hotel. His legs have been held by the tight sheets of the bed. There is another knock at the door. Because he has been sleeping in his flannel shirt and his socks, he has only to slide into his dungarees to be fully dressed.

Timothy opens the door and finds Imre standing in the corridor. Joy, surprise, relief spring upwards inside him to thicken all words of greeting in his throat. "Uh," he says as the two shake hands. "Yuhh."

Imre bustles into the room in his clipped, rapid way—those movements that are so much Imre's and no one else's—swings his big suitcase in a happy arc and lets it drop to the floor. It makes quite a thump, despite the room's carpeting.

"Books!" Timothy says.

"The best portable chess library in America. Puh," Imre adds—a familiar little snort that serves him as the equivalent of a wink or grin. He looks pleased with himself. He, too, is cheered by this reunion.

"So how dya like the room?" Timothy asks him—but Imre doesn't answer. His attention has already gone elsewhere. He hunches over the chessboard on the desk, utterly silent for almost a minute, then wheels around to make a stabbing accusation: "Sacrifices! Always those sacrifices."

Timothy has little to say to this. He can only drop his eyes, shrug, and feebly mumble, "Just investigating . . ."

"What is it with you, you always need to be giving something away, give it away just to see if you can get it back? You don't believe me, believe I'm right when I tell you how much better it is not to give anything away in the first place? Fireworks." Slowly, despairingly, Imre shakes his huge, bespectacled head. "Always the fireworks . . ."

So disproportionately large is Imre's head, and his hands as well, that in photographs he often looks achondroplastic—dwarfish. The impression is quite misleading. In fact, he is a man of about average height; he is as tall, for instance, as Timothy's brother Garner. Yet even in person, a sense of something compressed, or stunted, remains. When he goes out on the street, in his ragged clothes and his thick, powerful eyeglasses, which bulge his eyes to enormous proportions, he is apt to draw stares—especially from children, who perceive him as something of a freak. His speech, too, fosters misconceptions. The thickness of his accent, and the lumbering idiosyncrasies of his delivery, suggest an incomplete hold on the English tongue. And yet his grammar is often a good deal sounder than Timothy's own. "Fireworks," Imre says. "You saw what happened to Jeong in Amsterdam? Against Broner?"

"Oh well hey Jeong's crazy," Timothy says.

"Who do I hear saying that? When he plays so much like you? He'd sacrifice his king if only they'd permit such a thing."

Imre's huge hands scramble over the chessboard. He rearranges the pieces with brisk violence, setting them down with little knocking noises. Timothy goes over to investigate. "Thirty-two minutes Jeong looks at this position," Imre says, "and then what does he do? Doesn't he bring the bishop all the way out here?" Knock. "But let's just say he pulls the bishop back." And this time, instead of rapping the piece upon its proposed spot, Imre slides it soundlessly backwards, one diagonal space. "Wait," he barks, an order seemingly addressed not so much at Timothy as at Timothy's hand, which has sprung eagerly toward the board. Imre glares at it until it makes a full retreat into Timothy's lap. "Broner's going to bring the pawn up then? So, you think so? But maybe, then, just maybe the knight comes over . . ." Knock, knock. Pieces dance. Timothy's hand reaches out again and this time is permitted to shift a piece.

It is like a conversation between the deaf, this flood of hand signals, with its overlapping stops and starts, this onrush of motions that simply cannot keep pace with the thoughts that fly before it. Imre proposes a plausible line of discourse, Timothy counters with an objection, and Imre—proudly, having foreseen this very objection—immediately thrusts forward a pawn. Timothy's hand goes to his chin, to stroke the sandy stubble thoughtfully. "Muh," he agrees at last. "Neat. Yeah. Yeah."

Imre modestly shakes off the compliment. "Puh," he says.

"Oh yeah, neat. That's neat." . . .

He senses out there, beyond the edges of his vision, as he takes the pawn—not with the bishop, which everyone, including ANNDY, would have expected, but with the knight—Imre. He is offering ANNDY a free pawn, and he knows ANNDY's going to take it. He senses Imre's forward-lunging shock, elbows on knees and head pitched into those huge-knuckled hands, all of that massing nervous censure and all the frantic scrambling attempts to trace the strategic lines. And the possibility of Imre's anger, that stern lecture even now preparing itself for delivery, this raises the stakes and increases the sweet, dangerous racket in his veins. He is off alone, in a high, deserted angular terrain and braver than anyone knows, for they can't understand it or envision the least bit of it, bravery like this. ANNDY takes the pawn.

And when, soon, he offers ANNDY another pawn, this one on the king's side, he feels this time Imre's mind dogging along close behind his. Imre sees, it doesn't take him long at all to see how this pawn will be retrieved. Yes, Imre is right there with him. Inside the head there's a loud but muffled whirring, like the sound of a gas stove in the next room when the flame's turned up all the way, only louder, but still he can feel Imre so close beside him. ANNDY thinks for eighteen minutes when forced to trade its bishop for a knight. Trouble, it smells trouble, and knows enough to push its analysis another half-move deeper than usual. But the answer's not to be found there, not a half-move deeper, or two, or three, or even five: it's all too deep, too high, for ANNDY.

A profound reevaluation is going on. ANNDY, too, has begun to grasp the shifting current of the game, deep, right down deep in the cold pooling microlabyrinths of its circuitry, but all the machinery in the world at this point can do precisely nothing. *Yes.* ANNDY has taken a blow and all the computations in the world cannot undo the damage.

There's a kind of leakage, like a crowbar to the abdomen of a robot, the oiled wafers mangled and an ooze like blood around the edges of a wound, a sweet needed easing and a deeper wounding driving, and none of it can be halted. "ANNDY doesn't like this," Oliver Conant says, though he himself can't see why it is that ANNDY, still technically up a pawn, is hurting. But ANNDY is hurting . . .

And ANNDY's going to be liking the game less and less, five moves down the line, ten moves down; ANNDY has begun to grasp it all now, has felt the first precision-tooled advances of a raiding party that cannot be stopped. They have connected at last, come together, he and ANNDY have, and ANNDY sees just exactly what he sees: a white rook perched firmly on the seventh rank.

ANNDY is going so deep, and so far, three hundred and sixty-five thousand nodes a second, twenty million positions a minute, roads and roads almost without number and all of them leading to that towering rook on the seventh rank. Like the spokes of a wheel, the infinity of lines slicing through any particular point, but this particular point is the human rook erected at the hub of the world. Millions and millions of positions glimpsed and evaluated, and all so fast they go beyond a blur, they race on into invisibility . . . And not one of them skipped or slighted, not one dismissed at the outset, but everything tagged and stored, tagged and stored . . . Yes, yes, ANNDY is vast, ANNDY is the biggest mind in the world really, there's no use denying that, and all so clean, so beautifully pristine, with none of the world's stink and sewage getting in: just that endless hunger, that ravenous insweeping call for more positions, more positions, more positions, and yet ANNDY is missing some something . . . Something's been left out, or a pettiness has crept in, and ANNDY's greedy, for pawns, for the small stuff, too greedy and small ever to dare to lift its gaze down and out to the real beyond, where, already, the farthest future shapes are assembling themselves.

It is odd to feel this so acutely now, as the machine slowly is being cornered, all of its calculations coming together to produce nothing but a defeat, but he has never so clearly discerned those billions of numbers ANNDY's forever sifting, that generous-lapped mountain, the Everest of calculations upon which it perches. ANNDY is vast, but he knows, as the flame whirs with a loud steady slap-slapping inside his head, that Timothy Briggs is vaster. He is being drawn upward, and upward with a refining flame, when he sets the rook down, thump, in all its ponderous masonry, on the seventh rank, thump, himself inside it, high in the tower, as he knew he would be, his face inside it, thump, and all of the walls of ANNDY's defenses fixed to crumble. "ANNDY doesn't like this *at all*," Oliver says.

At this utterly safe height, high in the laddered tower, he can feel his own knowledge branching magnanimously outward, descending in sweetened sunny rays to touch the separate intellects in the audience. What Imre has seen for some time, and ANNDY for not quite so long, grows more and more apparent, until Garner can see it, and the little kids from the Boston Chess Club, and squirming bony-hipped Oliver Conant, who can't manage to keep his fly up, so that a bit of pink shirt tail pokes through today, and the television crew, and the journalists, and even Vicky, too, who hardly knows how to move the pieces—Vicky, who sits as such a potent dark configuration of entanglements there just beyond the board of his vision. He perches at such an elevation that Oliver's voice reaches him thinned by distance: "ANNDY's willing to concede this one."

Soon, or a little later, "ANNDY's had enough . . . Good game," Oliver says, and this time extends his hand. The shaking of hands awakens a bank of applause in the audience and Oliver turns toward it and gives a kind of wave and backs away into a defeated dark. And with Oliver gone, everyone is looking only at what is visible of Timothy Briggs now, and his eyes are burning in the bright flaming light as he, too, waves and nods at them. Forces are regrouping themselves. There has been a release and another sort of leakage, a puncture through which are somersaulting voices, lights, eyes, and the bigger, hungry eyes of the television cameras. Meshed microphones are held before him, with those cameras hungrily running, and he feels the whole of this as a sort of spilling in reverse, a huge and unregulated outward upflow, holes through which everything in the auditorium is cascading. He is being asked questions, one stacked upon another, but the words are not there by which they might be answered. The words will not group, they scatter in a wandering spotlit babble beneath that massed permanent tower on the seventh rank, whose stringent lessons about life's perfectability are every moment being retreated from. And then comes a question, *What does your victory today show?*, to which it turns out he has the one significant, the perfect reply: "I think this should give everybody hope . . ." He addresses these words to all of them, the microphones and the papers, the blank newspapers with boxes reserved for his photograph, the faces waiting on the other side of the camera's eye. Everything is spilling outward into place. "That's what I'm trying to do here. I'm trying to give people hope." They ask him to step over to the edge of the stage, closer to ANNDY's screen, and that's all right. They want to take photographs that will have ANNDY's screen in the background. They can't see much of anything, of course, nothing of what really happened today, nothing of what ANNDY's really like, the mountains of numbers below which they live their whole lives, but that's all right. They're blind as bats but it's all right so long as you explain things very clearly to them, because they would like to understand, truly, but they just don't have the minds for it. They want to be told what all of this means. "ANNDY's a fabulous piece of machinery," he explains. "There's no doubt about that. But it can't compare with the human mind. People need to understand how special they are."

And ANNDY, it turns out, has been elaborately prepared for a loss like this. They knew it all along, Conant and the rest of them, that the loss was inevitable, otherwise why should they have gone to the trouble of preparing all of these messages? OUCH! YOU'VE GOT THE SMARTS THAT SMART and YOU REALLY KNOW HOW TO HURT A GUY and OOH, I THINK I MUST HAVE DRUNK TOO MUCH LAST NIGHT.

The messages are flashing, nearby, behind him, as he explains it carefully to all of them out there. "This isn't John Henry all over again. This isn't a battle of muscle but of mind and that's a whole new something else. People need to see that they can do anything, once they put their minds to it." He feels his words going out, across his waiting country, and feels the need people have, from one wired, plugged-in coast to the other, for these very words. A regrouping, a disciplined reorganization from above is required in this country, and soon, by which what is at present random and all but powerless will be made efficient and powerful. The pieces, the material, are out there—have been there all along. "What I'm going to show people, in this match, is that the machine can never replace the human being. That we're special. We need to go right back to that idea. This match stands for something. It stands for something big."

They are laughing, and that's all right, for it scares them a little, and therefore they're looking for laughter, and that's what ANNDY serves up to them: JUST LET ME SULK FOR A WHILE and YOU'RE A BIG BAD BRUTE YOU ARE. They are laughing, but that's just nervousness: they *want* these words that make them jittery, they know they need to feel his voice expanding still further before them: "You know people have been calling me John Henry, but I'm not John Henry. I'm Timothy Briggs. This is a different kind of a story. He didn't use his *mind*. We're at the dawn of a new millennium and these are new issues and people need to see with their minds what this means. They don't think hard enough." He doesn't want to hurt them, but this is something they will have to face dead on. There are things they will have to face, and with this cool, crystallizing realization he feels also a kind of anger, or impatience—something smoldering hot—shrugging upward through his human insides, up to his throat. "Sometimes, ladies and gentlemen, you honestly don't think hard enough."

Laughter, like monkeys at the zoo they are always wanting to retreat behind laughter. ANYONE FOR TENNIS? asks ANNDY, and adds, after a moment's thought, IT ONLY HURTS WHEN I LAUGH.

Robert Lowell

Fischer is present also in Robert Lowell's poem "The Winner," which is, as Andrew Waterman points out in his essay earlier in this volume, an "amalgam of Fischerisms."

I had the talent before I played the game;
I made the black moves, then the white moves,
I just muled through whole matches with myself—
it wasn't too social only mating myself. . . .
But this guy in West Berlin whispers a move in my ear,
or there's a guy with his head right over my board—
they weren't too communicative with high chess.
Are most of your friends from the chess world?
I have a few peripheral friends here and there
who are non-chess players, but it's strange,
if you start partying around, it doesn't go.
I try to broaden myself, I read the racetrack,
but it's a problem if you lose touch with life . . .
because they want two world leaders to fight it out hand to hand.

Julian Barnes

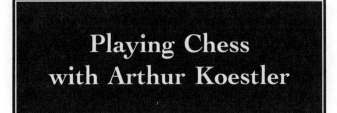

Playing Chess
with Arthur Koestler

*In the summer of 1982, Julian Barnes paid a week-long visit
to Arthur Koestler, during which the two writers—separated
in age by more than forty years—played a mini-match of
five chess games and talked of this and that. The great
Hungarian-born author of* Darkness at Noon *was then
seventy-seven years old, suffering from both leukemia and
Parkinson's disease, and already planning the double suicide
that he and his wife would carry out less than a year later—
all of which lends special poignancy to this encounter.*

GAME 1

We play not on a board but on a curious rubber traveling mat.
Perhaps it was originally magnetized to make the pieces hold firmly
to their squares, but if so, the magnetism has long worn off. The mat
has been rolled up for many years and does not flatten out properly,
despite Arthur's smoothings. The surface dips and sways like undu-
lating meadowland: bishops look even more threatening as they cant
toward you at twenty degrees to the perpendicular. Those who play
chess know how in the course of a game that bland grid of sixty-four
squares becomes charged with lines of energy, pockets of power,

backwoods domains of stagnancy and despair. As the isobars of control and vulnerability develop, this ruckled mat throws in some extra uncertainties, some distracting bits of dream and surrealism.

We begin cautiously: neither of us has played for some time. Every so often I am interrupted by the thought, *I'm playing chess with Arthur Koestler!* While it's normal to imagine how your opponent is assessing your game (will he buy that bluff? does he know I prefer bishops to knights?), it's less helpful to start worrying about what your opponent will think of you off the board because of what you do on it. But these considerations are hard to put aside when playing someone you have long admired, whose work spoke with a personal clarity during your intellectually formative years—and someone, after all, who reported the Fischer-Spassky match in Reykjavík for the London *Observer*. What does such a man think as I swap knights to double a pawn on his KB file? Is he judging this a crude maneuver that achieves a petty, vulgar advantage when one ought to be aiming for elegance, beauty, and finesse? Or is he saying to himself—like any other normal chess-playing human—"Oh damn, why did I let this whippersnapper double my pawns like that?"

Our rustiness, the joke "board," and the normal half-ludic, half-social uncertainties of playing an unfamiliar opponent are compounded by Arthur's physical condition. He is now seventy-seven, and known to be suffering from Parkinson's disease. When I arrive he remarks, in front of his wife, Cynthia, how much he has deteriorated in the last twelve months. "Zis Parkinson's—it knocks me sidevays," he says in that almost parodic Middle European accent which still comes as a surprise because you somehow expect mastery of written and spoken English to go together. (But of course they don't. See Nabokov: "I think like a genius, I write like a distinguished author, and I speak like a child.") Arthur's hand movements have lost their precision, and perhaps his eyesight is not so good anymore, because occasionally during our five games he starts to put a piece down on an impossible square, awarding himself, for example, two bishops on the same diagonal. Usually he notices; once or twice I have to point it out (and do not like to ask whether the fault is one of hand or eye). Each time, he apologizes courteously: "Zis Parkinson's, it knocks me sidevays."

The game is tedious and barely competent until I get a useful pawn pin. He struggles to shift it and loses another pawn, then I rack up the pin, he semi-blunders, and I win rook for bishop. This, I know, is the key breakthrough: queens are already off, and my two rooks look unstoppable. Then it's my turn to blunder. Like many average players, I have a visceral fear of the opponent's knight. Bishops, queens, and rooks move in that straightforward, undeceitful way of theirs; the knight—well, the opponent's knight—is sneaky and treacherous. Predicting the piece's behavior more than two moves ahead is almost impossible. So suddenly, without any decent notice at all, Arthur's whinnying horse is right in where it shouldn't be, forking my rook and king. All that hard work wasted, I think. "Analyzing the position" (as we describe sitting there and worrying a lot), I see that when he takes my rook, I recapture the knight, and we're level on material again. A long, grim struggle to come. So I move my king and *bang*, his next move is not, as I expect, to take off my rook, but to contrive a very neat mate with two bishops and knight. Ouch. You do like to be allowed at least to foresee the manner of your impending defeat. Oh well. 1–0.

GAME 2

It's the summer of 1982, and I am down at the Koestlers' farmhouse in Denston, Suffolk, for a week. I seem to be writing two novels at the same time, one of which is about Flaubert. Writers divide into those who happily talk about their work in progress and those who squirm in embarrassment at the prospect. I am a squirmer (of course, it's not just embarrassment; it's also caution that someone might steal the idea for your book, plus sheer vanity—however good you make it sound you probably won't be able to convey the full originality, daring, and brilliance of the project). Three or four times over the last year or so Arthur has asked me what I am working on, and each time I answer, with tight-lipped paranoia, "A book about Flaubert." Each time—preferring, as is his style, the challenging question to the mollifying expression of interest—he responds, "Why not Maupassant?" I never really find an answer. I suppose I should just say "Flaubert's better."

I stay in the visitor's flat at the end of the farmhouse. I write in the morning, have lunch, read, play chess with Arthur, and go for a run in the early evening (I am in what I hopefully refer to as "training" for the London Marathon, which is a safe nine months away). The weather stays fair, and a satisfying balance is held between work, exercise, and pleasure. The only bogus thing about my day is the "training." I have decided to avoid an over-hasty buildup to the twenty-six miles, and so jog around the unfrequented Suffolk lanes for twenty minutes or so, each day making it to a slightly more distant tree, a different patch of cow parsley. All kinds of mental stratagems have to be employed (dreaming up dinners, playing through sexual fantasies) to keep my legs moving, to rebuff the tempting voice which says, "What are you doing this for, you don't need this running shit, nobody can see you, come on, give up. . . ." But I just about don't give up in my low-level quest for a certain healthiness.

Arthur, as it later turns out, is worse than he lets on: he has leukemia as well as Parkinson's. Both diseases are to some extent controllable, though one or the other will get him in the end. One example of his "deterioration," he says, is that his voice is no longer reliable. It tires quickly and he can't always control the register; recently he's been turning down requests for radio and television interviews, and won't do any more. I fail to notice any fluctuations in his voice over two and a half hours the first evening, so am only half-convinced of his supposed decline, but he knows better. As it transpires, he is already planning his suicide. He has always been a firm and public believer in what is—either euphemistically or accurately, I can never quite decide—referred to as "self-deliverance." EXIT, the British organization founded to promote the cause of euthanasia, has produced a booklet offering practical advice. Arthur, in his methodical way, has already annotated his copy with a précis of what to do: "1. An hour and a half before your meal. . . ." He summarizes the amounts to drink and drugs specified, and notes for future use the shelf life of barbiturates ("eight years").

The second game lasts longer than the first, about an hour and three-quarters. Playing white, I opened with a fianchettoed bishop. There is occasionally some mild surprise value in this beginning, though I use it mainly because it tends to lead to open, attacking chess. I hate and fear those clogged games with a great ball of pawn tension in the middle of the board; one minor miscalculation and the whole thing will suddenly unravel in your face. I remind myself that Bent Larsen, the Danish grand master famous for his attacking style, frequently opens with a fianchettoed bishop. As I play p-QN3 followed by B-N2, I dream of a pair of bishops on neighboring diagonals aiming their crossbows into the heart of black's defensive nest.

But it seems I am not as good a chess player as Bent Larsen. A lot of pins and semi-pins hinder the bold maneuvers I have imagined. My diagonal threats peter out. Another loss. 2–0.

GAME 3

After the second game, I mention to Arthur that I've never played the King's Gambit. Whenever I try it out by myself, it always seems to lead to a lost position for white: it is suicidal. I only know one person—a reckless, pressing daredevil on the board—who ever plays this sharp, aggressive, old-fashioned gambit. So I ought to be less surprised when Arthur, as white, opens p-K4, p-KB4. I think, *Oh shit, the King's Gambit! I should never have told him how unfamiliar I am with it.* I picture him sneaking off the previous evening to his chess manuals and running through all the subtleties of this violent opening. Such thoughts don't help black's defenses; also, the suicidal tendencies implicit for white whenever I rehearse the King's Gambit seem mystifyingly absent for my opponent.

Now, toward the very end of his life, Arthur is mellowed by weakness. In the three or four years I have known him, he has become much less combative. I met him first at his house in Montpelier Square, at one of those London dinners at which most of those present have two houses and yet (and therefore) spend a lot of time complaining about the trade unions. It seems *de rigueur* on these occasions to have in your wallet a cutting from the *Daily Telegraph* about some obscure restrictive practice whereby workers with metal-boring drills are bringing the country to its knees by refusing to use their drills for boring wood. I was working for the *New Statesman* at the time (and living in a bed-sitter), so was unsusceptible to the inference that if only these recalcitrant workers would allow themselves to be pushed around a bit more, then people with two houses could afford a third house (which conclusion has been well borne out as Mrs. Thatcher's Britain continues). There was much disgust and dismay expressed that evening about the behavior of the National Graphical Association—the printers then being the particular object of fashionable odium among right-thinking people. (Quite by chance, I had spent that day at a small printing works in Southend, supervising the going-to-press of the *Statesman*'s back half. Everyone there had been hardworking, cooperative, and entirely lacking in a forked tail.) Not long after Mrs. Thatcher became leader of the Conservative Party, she paid a visit to Arthur. A previous prime minister, Harold Wilson, had recruited two famous Hungarian economists, Balogh and Kaldor, to his staff of special advisors. Arthur recalled that he was flattered by Mrs. Thatcher's attention but declined her casting: "I will not be your Hungarian guru."

Now he sits in the sunshine, with Mozart on the radio and a bottle of Moselle in a wine cooler before him, looking rather like a wise squaw. He walks with a stick and seems weary of his reputation for belligerence. I have recently read a new biography of Camus, and mention—thinking it might amuse him—that the historical record is confused. Some authorities maintain that he gave Camus a black eye only once; others assert that it was twice. But he is not particularly amused. "Only once," he says wearily. "It was a drunken brawl."

Despite my trepidation when faced with the King's Gambit, I seem to have chances at first; then Arthur establishes a strong center. A potential weakness is that he leaves his queen and knight on the same diagonal. But how to exploit this without being obvious? Gratifyingly, the weakness exploits itself: a forced defensive pawn-push on my part sets up a square for my bishop, which leaps out from the back rank into a killer pin on knight and queen. The queen falls. Some peril remains, as Arthur has two attacking rooks, two bishops, and a knight, plus a pawn on the sixth rank, but once all chances of a breakthrough are headed off he gently topples his king. 2–1.

Afterwards, I go for a run, light-headed and light-hearted. *Hey, I've beaten Arthur Koestler at chess!* There is nobody, alas, to tell; but I run for twenty-eight minutes nonstop, the longest for ages, without feeling too bad. When my calves begin to ache, I imagine lush country wives with throbbing décolletages who drive up alongside and implore me to take a lift; then I don't think of my calves for a while. But reality being what it is, there are no beckoning *chauffeuses;* I seem to have chosen a road driven only by careless and surly males.

GAME 4

While we are on the subject of literary brawls, there's something else to clear up. That famous occasion Arthur threw a bottle at Sartre, was it the same brawl as when he gave Camus a black eye, or a separate one? "I *never* threw a bottle at Sartre," he replies. The record on that, he insists, is false. He adds that his friendship with Sartre was "poisoned" by "Simone."

I open p-QB4, which Arthur says he has never played against (can this be true? well, it will be in this sense, that my first few moves are always divertingly ungrounded in opening theory). After a tense beginning, Arthur gradually puts on the K-side pressure and establishes—revenge for the last game—an unbreakable pin on knight and queen. For a while, I am forced into a mixture of last-ditch defense and a series of waiting moves (never good for morale). Then I see the chance of a possible breakthrough: I give up the pinned knight for two central pawns, which opens routes to his isolated king which he has overconfidently neglected to castle. Gradually, I increase the pressure and cram him into back-row submission. After an hour and a half of unremitting tension, I pummel my way to victory. 2–2.

With the game over, Arthur puts the pieces back on the board and dismisses one of his moves as a blunder—or rather, given his joke-shop pronunciation, "a blonder." If I hadn't mated him, he points out, he would have mated me. So far we have played four times, he has won twice and "blondered" twice. Tomorrow will be the decider.

Afterwards, another record-breaking run: a whole thirty minutes nonstop. Arthur's postmatch exercise is of a different nature. If he sits down for too long he gets dizzy; so while I glide puffingly past the cow parsley dreaming of delinquent wives he walks slowly twice round the house to clear his head. "Zis Parkinson's, it knocks me sideways." His attitude to his illness seems mainly one of interest. He mentions other famous people who have suffered from Parkinson's. It is a distinguished disease (a disease for people with two houses, perhaps). His response to old age is also scientific and practical. The brain needs exercise like any other muscle. He writes five hundred words a day. He does the *Times* crossword. No doubt his chess games with me are designed not just for pleasure.

Domestically, he is a frail dictator. The telephone rings while he is in the house and Cynthia is gardening. Arthur gets up and walks slowly to the front door. "Ooo-oo," he goes, an Indian brave's call not reduced, in old age, to a squaw's call. "Telephone, angel." And Cynthia comes running from the garden. Neither seems to find this system unusual. One year, my wife and I are staying at Denston on Arthur's birthday. The telephone rings several times; Cynthia screens the callers. Perhaps he takes one birthday greeting out of six. Nor is there, for the rest of that day, any acknowledgment of the date. He is devoid of sentimentality or nostalgia. In the same way, he is interested only in what he is working on now, not what he wrote thirty years ago. In another writer this might spring from irritation at being praised for your backlist while doubts are raised about your current preoccupations; with him it seems quite genuine. He once showed me a garage at Denston which he mockingly referred to as his "archive": I remember rows of steel shelving and large numbers of foreign editions. "Do you have a copy of your first book?" (I remembered it as an encyclopedia of sex written under a rather transparent pseudonym.) "Of course not," he replied. "That would be an enormous vanity."

He is a very courteous man. I quiz him about his name being on a board outside the local church: there is "Arthur Koestler" amidst a lineup of English officers, gentry, and clergymen appealing for funds. "It is expected," he replies defensively and a little stiffly, as if I should not be so openly surprised at an agnostic Hungarian Jew taking up his squirearchical responsibilities. At dinnertime he always rises to pour the first glass of wine for everyone—with however trembling a hand. His courtesy, however, should not be mistaken for indulgence. "You won't mind if I slip away after dinner?" he inquires most evenings, almost as if it were your house and his tiredness were making him a bad guest. But when, after dinner, you attempt to bid him good-night as it is only a quarter past nine and your glass has just been refilled, he responds with a slightly firmer emphasis, "I think we all go to bed now, yes?" Yes, Arthur. He needs Cynthia to help him: he has a contact lens, for instance, which he is no longer able to handle himself; she puts it in and takes it out for him. No doubt he also doesn't want you sitting up and discussing him with his wife.

GAME 5

Six in the morning. High cloud and light summer air. Moorhens are processing from the pond to the cornfield; two young rabbits are rolling on their backs in a dustheap where an elm has been removed; tits and sparrows are already in overdrive, all motion and babble. Nature is parodying itself for a city dweller charmed by the simplest country sights; and the sound of Arthur's voice is in my head as I watch the exuberant, carefree, normal scenes. "Zis Parkinson's, it knocks me sidevays."

It is our final game of the series, the decider. I am thirty-six and in full health; he is seventy-seven and very ill; the score is 2–2. Perhaps he will never play chess again. Perhaps I should lose, perhaps I should make a deliberate blonder. Like every chess player, Arthur delights in victory and loathes defeat: surely, out of gratitude for his writing, and out of affection, I should throw this last game?

Such reflections seem patronizing and irrelevant after only a couple of moves. Has any chess player *ever* thrown a match? Chess is a game of courteous aggression—and therefore very suitable for Arthur—but the courtesy and formality only serve to sharpen and focus the aggression. As Arthur's first attack develops, he immediately stops being a seventy-seven-year-old invalid who may never move p-K4 again; he becomes a ferocious assailant trying personally to damage me, to overthrow and humiliate me. How dare he! Gradually, I neutralize his first thrust, then begin a dogged pawn-march of my own. At first the maneuver is purely defensive—I push a pawn, he obliged to retreat a piece—but its nature slowly changes. I realize that a huge advancing arrowhead of pawns with one's pieces undeveloped behind them is hardly recommended by any reputable chess strategist, but in this particular game the ploy seems unfaultable: with every pawn-move he is getting more and more cramped. His pieces are pushed back until they have barely a single square left to go to: in one corner, for instance, he has a rook's pawn, doubled pawns on the knight file, plus a knight in the corner square, all of which are locked up by a mere two pawns of mine. His queen darts out, but I lay a trap and play my final push. I move a knight, which discovers a double attack on his queen. He must resign—yes, he must lose his queen, and then he must resign! I've got him beaten!

At this point an alarm clock goes off somewhere in the house. It is set for regular intervals throughout the day and designed to remind Arthur to take his medicines. Cynthia has gone out, so we set off around the house looking for the alarm, which is still buzzing. For some reason this proves difficult; eventually we track it down in Arthur's study and turn it off. He dutifully swallows a pill and we return to the board.

My inevitable feelings of pity and tenderness during this interruption do not affect my planned ruthlessness on the board. The game, after all, is serious (on move 7 Arthur attempts to vault one of his bishops over the top of a pawn; he doesn't spot the illegality, I point it out, he apologizes—"It's my eyes, you know"). Now we settle back into our chairs again. Yes, that's right, his queen is attacked by two of my pieces. There is no free square for it to run to. I must win! But then, quite unexpectedly, Arthur finds a place for his queen: on a square currently occupied by one of my pawns. Fuck! Damn! A blonder! Worse, I'm clearly due to lose another pawn (in fact, the two pawns cementing down his K-side corner). Ah well, nothing to do but push on. Arthur, having prized away one little finger of my stranglehold, is able to begin an attack; I counter by grubbing out some of his seventh-rank pawns with my rook. Queens are now off, we have one rook each, I have bishop for knight (good), but am two pawns down. Even so, I have chances, incredibly strong chances: a pawn on the seventh rank, defended by a rook, and with its queening square covering my bishop. Yes, I must surely queen, and then win his rook. How can this not happen? Victory soon! And yet, somehow, I don't manage to queen (I can't quite work out why not—his king just lolloped over and messed me up, I should never have allowed it). I lose rook and pawn for rook, and though I still have bishop for knight I'm three pawns down. Nothing for it. *Resigns. 3–2.*

Afterwards, despite the result, I don't feel as depressed as I normally would: it has been a fluctuating, violent, eccentric game in which we both had chances, and I played as well as I could. That Arthur won makes me feel, in the circumstances, a more or less grudgeless admiration. An hour and a half, a titanic struggle, and I feel shattered: what a testament to the old fighter that he overcame the young (well, youngish) whippersnapper. . . . But this magnanimity in defeat is not allowed to lie undisturbed. Arthur has the true chess victor's talent for rubbing things in: over dinner, an hour or so later, he changes the conversation to remark wistfully, "Of course, I am only fifty percent vot I vos at chess." I'm not exactly cheered by this not exactly tactful remark. But a little later I am partially restored. Cynthia says she can't remember when Arthur last had a series of daily games like this—surely not since he played George Steiner at Alpbach. That must have been interesting; what, I ask, was Steiner's game like? Arthur, a small man, has a way of puffing up his chest like a pouter pigeon at moments of pride. "He played like a *schoolboy.*" Well, that's some consolation. Oh, and did you tend to beat him, Arthur? More puffed chest: "Alvays."

ANALYSIS

We oscillate, Koestler recognized, between *la vie triviale* and *la vie tragique*. I was preparing to run the marathon; he was preparing to die. I failed (well, the winter snow interfered with my training schedule—and besides, in the end my application was rejected, probably because I put "journalist" on the form and they decided they had far too many journalists running already and didn't need any more coverage); he succeeded. We met over chess, that trivial pursuit which refers to nothing else in life, to nothing significant, and yet which engages our full seriousness. George Steiner, who like Koestler covered the Fischer-Spassky match, strove in his report to convey the powerful emotions involved in a chess match. What he wrote is certainly unforgettable:

> The poets lie about orgasm. It is a small, chancy business, its particularities immediately effaced even from the most roseate memories, compared to the crescendo of triumph in chess, to the tide of light and release that races over mind and knotted body as the opponent's king, inert in the fatal web one has spun, falls on the board.

Steiner had the grace (and humor) to add: "More often than not, of course, it is one's own king." Without this rider, sated Casanovas would probably have been rushing to the local chess club to try out a more passionate sport.

Later that year my wife and I went down to Denston. Arthur said to us quietly, "Here is a conundrum which I cannot express to Cynthia. Is it better for a writer to be forgotten before he is dead, or dead before he is forgotten?" We nodded, and I remember thinking, *Well, that's hardly a conundrum for you, Arthur, obviously your work is going to survive your death.* . . . Except, of course, that this was not his question. He was asking which was *better*.

In late February of the following year Cynthia telephoned. We had a long-standing arrangement to take them to a Hungarian restaurant; she was canceling for the second time in a fortnight. She said Arthur had the flu, and whenever he got mild secondary illnesses it made his Parkinson's worse. She sounded nervous and apologetic, but no more so than usual; we agreed to fix a new date when Arthur was feeling stronger. "We're not going to let you get out of this, Cynthia," I said.

They did get out of it. Four days later Arthur and Cynthia killed—or delivered—themselves. I was standing in the newsroom of the *Observer,* one Thursday after lunch, and saw it on a television routinely emitting Ceefax news. A journalist standing nearby glanced at the screen and commented with casual knowledgeability, "He killed her and then did himself in." I wanted to knock the journalist down, or at least insult him violently, but said nothing. There wasn't any point in being angry with the fellow himself (saying the first thing that comes into our heads on such occasions wards off the reality, denies that death will call for us too in due course); what made me angry was the realization that Arthur was finally passing into untender hands (FAMOUS AUTHOR IN SUICIDE PACT, etc.), that he would no longer be there to correct things, get annoyed, or even just laugh. He had moved from "Arthur" to "Koestler," from present to past tense. He had been handed irretrievably into the care of others: how well would they treat him? (No more accurately than he would have predicted. All his life Arthur had been sternly opposed to having children: the *Times* obituary, in its final paragraph, invented a daughter for him and Cynthia.)

The note Arthur left was dated the previous June—before I played chess with him. In it he spoke of his clear and firm intention to commit suicide before he became too enfeebled to make the necessary arrangements. He reassured his friends that he was leaving them in a peaceful frame of mind, and "with some timid hopes for a depersonalised after-life beyond due confines of space, time and matter and beyond the limits of our comprehension."

His death was exemplary, well managed, and, from the evidence, easy. Cynthia's death was, from the evidence, difficult, and causes problems. That she lived entirely for him nobody doubted; that he could be tyrannical was equally clear. Did he bully her into killing herself? This was the unmentionable, half-spoken question their friends came up against. I did not know him very well, but I seldom met anyone with less obvious romanticism or sentimentality; I would judge that a suicide pact would strike him as foolish, vulgar, and anachronistic. Indeed, I can imagine him getting irritated with Cynthia for wanting to join him: if his death, like his life, was to be part of a campaign, if it was intended to change people's minds about self-deliverance, what could be more counterproductive as propaganda than for his healthy fifty-five-year-old wife to kill herself as well? Which provokes the slimy follow-up question: if he didn't bully her into it, why didn't he bully her out of it? It seems to me that at this point speculation becomes impertinent, unless you can imagine yourself as a seventy-seven-year-old suffering from Parkinson's and leukemia and no longer able to rely on prolonged spells of lucidity. If you can do that, then I'll listen to you.

Cynthia, in the note she left, said that she didn't think much of double suicides as a rule. She wasn't a dramatic woman; she was shy, nervous, bird-like, capable of seeming in the same day both twenty-five and fifty-five. She moved awkwardly, like an adolescent unhappy with her body, who expects at any moment to knock over a coffee table and be sent to her room for doing so. I liked her, but her character evaded me: it was as if she would not show you what she was like for fear that something (what?) might happen to make her realize she'd been a fool for showing herself to you. On warm summer afternoons at Denston she used to clear the pond of weed, with a dog occasionally and unhelpfully at her heels. She had a long garden rake with a piece of rope attached to the end of the handle. She would throw the rake into the pond, haul it out with the rope, scrape the weeds off the teeth of the rake, pile them on the bank, and throw the rake back in. It looked a slow and awkward business. She herself looked awkward, liable to overbalance into the pond at any moment; but she kept at it with what looked a childlike doggedness. Splash, pull, scrape, pile; splash, pull, scrape, pile; splash, pull, scrape, pile. That last summer I played chess with Arthur she didn't clean the pond.

John Griffiths

The Memory Man

Arden Wylie, the title character in John Griffiths's espionage novel The Memory Man, *is a professional chessplayer in decline. Well past his prime and "terrified of blunders," he faces an uncertain future. When he is approached during a tournament in Moscow by a young journalist who says she wants to interview him (in reality she has been recruited by the CIA to involve him in a scheme to test the credibility of a Soviet scientist who says he wants to defect), he gives her a short course on the life-style of an itinerant American chess-master.*

Grand Master Wylie surveyed his position. He was a pawn down already; the pawn at Q4 was isolated, probably indefensible. To make matters worse, his remaining knight was badly placed and his entire position was cramped. His opponent would have no difficulty forcing an exchange of rooks, and he would be left with a lost endgame. The defeat would take his score in the tournament below fifty percent. His worst result in years. His share of the prize money would barely cover expenses.

With the air of one suddenly resolving a difficult problem, he got up and extended a hand to his opponent.

"I accept a draw," he announced.

The Australian, Greene, pulled back as though stung. "A draw? You've got to be kidding. You're lost. You ought to resign. You bloody Yanks are all alike. No fucking sportsmanship . . ."

His nasal snarl could be heard all over the hall, disturbing its cathedral-like hush. A sudden clatter of conversation from the spectators was peremptorily stilled by a glare from the tournament director. From the tables adjacent to Wylie's there came a series of urgent and irritated hisses. The tournament director left his seat and made his way toward them.

Wylie shrugged. "The position is obviously drawn. However, if you need the practice . . ." He bent down, gave his king's rook's pawn a contemptuous nudge with his middle finger, advancing it one square, and stopped his clock. Then he strolled away from the table, pausing en route to light a cigarette, and drifted toward the window, where he stood, a study of indifference, gazing out upon the scene below.

Behind him he could hear the remonstrance of the tournament director.

"Perhaps you were provoked, Greene. But I must ask you to control your temper. There are other players here. You are disturbing their concentration. Please continue your game in silence."

More hisses from the nearby tables. Wylie continued his gazing. He allowed fifteen minutes to elapse before he returned to the board.

Greene's move, the product not of thought but of overwhelming anger, had been a blunder. He had realized this even as he was making it; but his hand had touched the piece, and his instincts as a player, not to mention the inhibiting presence of the tournament director, precluded second thoughts. He could only sit, poker-faced, and pray that Wylie would overlook the fact that the rook at B5 could now be taken with impunity.

Wylie did not. He glanced briefly at the pieces, took the rook, and sauntered back to the window, neglecting to stop his clock.

Wylie crossed the hotel lobby, brooding. He had been enormously lucky. Six and a half points, out of a possible twelve so far, instead of five and a half; there was a world of difference. He might possibly make some money. There was Petrosian to come, of course—a draw there would be something. And Stein, another draw, perhaps. And Karpov? Doubtful. He had chances, certainly. But . . .

He was desperately tired. The doubts which, since Amsterdam, had gathered, like rain clouds on a clear day, slowly but perceptibly around him, could not be ignored. Draws. He was hoping for draws. His win over Greene had been a plain swindle. . . . Greene—a player whom in five previous meetings he had crushed offhandedly—had almost defeated him.

He could write it down to fatigue, of course, to that idiotic, fifteen-hour simultaneous he had given too close to the tournament. But at heart he knew better. It was always an effort now. Each time he sat down at the board it took more courage, a greater summoning of will, to peer into the swirling vortex of possibilities the black and white squares and thirty-two pieces could produce. The game, a playground he had lightheartedly inhabited for as long as he could remember, had become strange country, full of pitfalls and dark places. He played safe now, terrified of blunders. He had lost his nerve, and he was losing his talent.

It would take time. He could hang on for a few more years, his results getting worse, his rating slowly dropping. Then the tournament invitations would stop coming. He would be reduced to occasional journalism—at fifteen dollars a hundred—and teaching openings to patzers.

He was, in some ways, a proud man, conscious of belonging to a tiny, specialized aristocracy of the intellect. He had seen some of his peers deteriorate that way, painfully and in public, and he did not wish to follow their example. He did not want to be forced into more swindles, to betray, in insolence or timidity, the game that had dignified his life.

He should face facts. It was over. If he had courage he should play out this tournament and retire, resign honorably. But to what? With what?

That was the big problem. He had some money, but not enough to live on. He was virtually unemployable in any capacity he cared to contemplate. Welfare was unimaginable. So to what? With what?

On reaching his room he took his shoes off and lay down on the bed, hands behind his head, staring up at the ceiling. In this space, roughly square, its paint a drab gray, cracked and peeling in places, he now imagined a chessboard and began to reconstruct the game he had just played, trying to discover just where its pattern had begun to elude him. Perhaps it had been at move thirteen, where his pawn push, an effort to force simplifying exchanges, had ceded to his opponent the long white diagonal to his KR1. Perhaps . . . His mind, happy to abandon its contemplation to such gloomy imponderables as his future, began to sift the possibilities, sorting them into concrete variations, each to be analyzed separately.

He got up and fetched his board. Ceilings were unsuitable for serious analysis. He had begun to arrange the pieces into the position at Greene's move twelve when he heard footsteps coming to his door and then a knock, barely perceptible, and another, louder.

"Who is it?"

"Is this room forty-two? Is that Mr. Wylie?" The voice was clear and feminine. American.

"Yes to both questions. Come in, please."

He was irritated at the distraction. But when he saw her, the irritation evaporated. She was young, about thirty, he estimated, and quite pretty.

"Mr. Wylie. I hope I'm not disturbing you. I should have called first, I know. But I tried at the desk and they told me the telephones were out of order. They always are here apparently. So I decided to try your room. I hope you don't mind."

"No, I don't mind at all. But what can I do for you, Miss . . . ?"

"Mrs." She was recovering her composure. "Mrs. Anne Crossland. I'm a journalist. Free-lance. I've been commissioned by one of the women's weeklies to do an article on the status of women in Russia. But while I was here I discovered that there was this big chess tournament going on and that Americans were playing. I thought perhaps you might agree to an interview. Chess is very topical now, and I know several papers that might take it.

"By the way," she added, "I should congratulate you. I understand you had a notable victory today."

He smiled wryly. "I had a victory. But it was hardly notable."

"Why?"

"My opponent blundered in a winning position. I was lucky. Very lucky . . . What sort of interview did you have in mind?"

"Oh! 'The Life-style of a Chess Player'—that sort of thing. Nothing very technical, or very personal for that matter."

Wylie looked at her. The session of analysis was shot, obviously, and the last thing he really wanted to do was talk about himself. But he needed diversion and she really was, when you studied her closely, remarkably attractive. He decided to amuse himself.

"What do you know about chess?"

"Nothing, really. I know the moves, but that's all. I'm not really interested in you as a chess player, but more in your life away from the game. How being a professional chess player affects it."

"But I am a chess player," he objected. "It's my defining characteristic. Chess players don't have life-styles." He motioned her into one of the chairs. "They leave that to TV stars, advertising executives, or even journalists. Chess players play chess. Period. Everything else is a detail. So unless you know something about chess, how can you write intelligently about our lives? There's nothing else to write about.

"Did you know, for example, that the average professional chess player in the U.S. earns less than ten thousand dollars? Did you know that he spends probably seventy-five percent of his time in hotels—mostly cheap hotels? That ninety percent of his meals are eaten in restaurants, also cheap? Or that chess players enjoy, if that is really the word, the lowest marriage rate and the highest divorce rate of any recognized occupation?"

He had begun to enjoy himself. It was amazing, he reflected, how much conviction, a number—any number—could carry. When they came to label the twentieth century they should call it "The Age of Statistics."

"You see," he continued, "it's impossible to understand how we put up with such a life; how grown, intelligent men, who could certainly make more money in other professions, can tolerate this poverty, this lack of recognition, roots, and security, unless you can appreciate something of what the game means to us. And that, too, is probably impossible unless you yourself, however obscurely, have felt its pull."

"You're saying, in effect, that one has to be a junkie to understand junkies?"

"That's not a bad analogy."

"I see. Then I guess I'll have to approach the problem the other way round."

"How do you mean?"

"Approach an understanding of what chess means to you by discovering what you give up for it—the way we do with junkies. As a matter of fact, you told me a good deal about your life-style even while you were claiming to have none."

He smiled. "I see you're not to be discouraged."

She smiled back. "Were you really trying?"

"I guess not. I suppose everyone would like to imagine his life is interesting. I'm no exception. . . . What did you want to know?"

"Well, I suppose I could just ask you my list of twenty invariable questions, call it a day, and depart. But that sort of approach always comes out rather lifeless, I feel. I'd rather—" She hesitated. "If you have the time, and if it wouldn't be too much of a drag, I'd rather spend a couple of hours with you, walking round the city, sightseeing or sitting in the park, and see what comes out of it. I find people are always more interesting when they're just talking. Not answering direct questions."

"Ah, the New Journalism." He smiled. "Of course, you understand what a terrible burden that places on me. I have to just talk and yet I have to be interesting. I could get terribly self-conscious."

"Oh, I imagine you'll manage." Her mouth twitched ironically.

"Well, in that case, I suppose, it wouldn't be *too* much of a drag."

They smiled at one another. Two contestants in a match that had come out even.

Sholem Aleichem

From Passover to Succos, or The Chess Player's Story

Quite another sort of life-style is portrayed by the great Yiddish writer Sholem Aleichem (Solomon J. Rabinowitz) in "From Passover to Succos, or The Chess Player's Story." Ostensibly a simple tale of a poor Jewish watchmaker who is such a fine chessplayer that he attracts the attention of the Czar himself, it is in fact a grim depiction of Jewish life in Czarist Russia.

The period from Passover to Succos is roughly six months (April–October).

It was late one winter's night—long past midnight. The guests had finished a late supper and the remains on the table bore witness to the fact that they had done well by themselves. The green card tables were covered with chalk marks and scattered piles of cards from which aces and kings peeped out in profusion as though to say, "Now we are here." The guests would have loved nothing better than to sit down to a game of preference or whist, but somehow it didn't seem proper. It was much too late. So they just sat around, smoked, drank black coffee, and gossiped. The conversation was dying out when someone threw in a word about chess. Another picked it up, then another, and another. It was plain that they were trying to draw out a certain ardent chess player by the name of Rubinstein.

Rubinstein was a rabid chess fiend. He was willing to travel ten miles on foot, to go without food or drink or sleep for a game of chess. It was a passion with him. Many stories made the rounds about his chess playing. It was said: 1. That he played chess with himself all night long. 2. That he had divorced his wife three times already because of chess. 3. That he had once disappeared for three years because of a chess game. In a word, wherever you found Rubinstein, there you found chess. And wherever there was chess, there was Rubinstein. And Rubinstein loved to talk about chess as a confirmed drunkard loves to talk about liquor.

When you looked at Rubinstein, you were struck first of all by his enormous forehead—it was high and broad, and rounded like a bay window. His eyes also were enormous. They were round and black, but without expression, like two lumps of coal. He was thin and bony in build, but he had a voice like a bell, deep and sonorous. When Rubinstein was among a group of people you heard only Rubinstein and no one else.

When he heard the guests mention chess, Rubinstein wrinkled his already deeply wrinkled forehead, squinted with one eye at the coffee he was drinking as though to determine whether it smelled of soap or of dishwater, and spoke to everyone in general and to no one in particular. His voice rang out like a cathedral bell. "Ladies and gentlemen! If you want to hear a story about a chessplayer, sit down, all of you, right here near me, and I will tell you a story that happened long ago."

"A story about a chess player? A story of long ago?" The hostess who had been afraid that the gathering was about to break up caught up his words eagerly. "Wonderful! Excellent! Tell Felitchka to shut the piano, and will you please lock the doors and bring in two–three more chairs? Sit down, everybody, please sit down. Mr. Rubinstein is going to tell us a story about a chess player, a story of long ago."

Rubinstein examined the cigar his host had just handed him, from all sides, as though to determine how much it had cost; then he made a grimace and furrowed his enormous brow as though to say, "Maybe it looks like a cigar, but it tastes more like a broom." And he began his story:

"I don't have to explain to you that I am a devoted chessplayer, ladies and gentlemen, and that our whole family are chessplayers by nature. The name of Rubinstein is known all over the world. In fact, I would like to have you show me a Rubinstein who is *not* a chessplayer."

"Why, I know a fellow named Rubinstein who is an insurance salesman. He comes in to see me every week. Aside from life insurance, he knows absolutely nothing. A regular dolt."

This remark was thrown in by one of the guests, a young man with a narrow, pointed head and gold-rimmed glasses, who considered himself quite a wit. But Rubinstein remained calm. He looked the young man over with his coal-black frigid glance and said in his deep sonorous voice, "He can't be one of our Rubinsteins. A true Rubinstein has to be a chess player. That is as natural as it is natural for a buffoon to crack jokes. My grandfather Rubin Rubinstein was a true Rubinstein, for he was, ladies and gentlemen, a born chess player. The world could turn upside down and he wouldn't notice it when he was in the middle of a chess game. People came to play chess with him from all over the world—noblemen, counts, princes. By trade he was only a watchmaker, a poor workingman, but a real craftsman, an artist at his trade. But since the only thing that really mattered in his life was chess, he had difficulty in making a living, and earned barely enough to feed his family.

"And it came to pass, ladies and gentlemen, that one day there rode up to my grandfather's hut a splendid equipage drawn by two pairs of fiery steeds, and a nobleman leaped out of this equipage followed by two men-servants in livery. The nobleman was covered with medals and orders from head to foot, like royalty. He walked into the hut and asked, 'Where is the Jew Rubin Rubinstein?' At first my grandfather was a little frightened, but he recovered quickly and spoke up, 'I am the Jew Rubin Rubinstein. How can I be of service to you, your Highness?' The nobleman was pleased with this answer and said to my grandfather, 'If you are the Jew Rubin Rubinstein, then I am very happy to know you. Have the samovar put on to boil, and bring out your chessboard. I'll play you a game. I've heard it said that you are a very fine chess player and that so far no one has ever checkmated you.'

"Saying this the nobleman sat down (apparently he was a lover of chess) and began playing with my grandfather. They played on and on, one game after another, one game after another. Meanwhile the samovar boiled and tea was served in proper style, on a large tray with preserves and pastries of all sorts. My grandmother saw to that, though she hadn't a *groschen* in her purse. . . .

"Meanwhile a crowd had gathered around the carriage outside my grandfather's door. Everyone was curious to know who it was that had come to see Rubin the Watchmaker. All kinds of rumors flew around the village. It was rumored that the nobleman had come from the capital of the province to carry out an investigation—something about counterfeit money—that it was the work of an informer, a plot of some sort that had been cooked up against Rubinstein. No one dared to walk in and see for himself what was going on. For who would have dreamed that the nobleman and my grandfather were only playing chess?

"And what shall I tell you, ladies and gentlemen? Though the nobleman was a good chess player, a very good chess player indeed, he was checkmated by my grandfather over and over again, and the more he played the more excited he became, and the more excited he became the worse he played. As for my grandfather, do you think he as much as winked an eyelash? Not he. He might as well have been playing with—I don't know whom—for all the emotion he showed. The nobleman must have been pretty much put out by all this. No one likes to be beaten, and to be beaten by whom? By a Jew! But what could he say, when the other was obviously the better player? Ability cannot be denied. And besides, I will have you know, ladies and gentlemen, that a real chess player is more interested in playing the game than in winning or losing. To a real chess player the opponent is nothing, only the game itself counts. I don't know if you will understand this or not."

"We can't swim either, but we understand what swimming is," broke in the witty fellow with the gold-rimmed glasses. Rubinstein the chess player measured him with his chilly glance and said, "Yes, we can see that you know all about swimming." He took a puff of his cigar and went on:

"And since everything in this world must come to an end, ladies and gentlemen, their chess game came to an end too. The nobleman arose, buttoned up the gold buttons on his coat, extended two fingers to my grandfather, and said, 'Listen to me, Rubin Rubinstein, you have beaten me, and I concede that you are the finest chess player not only in my province, but in the whole country, and perhaps in the whole world. I consider myself fortunate to have had the honor and the pleasure of playing with the finest chess player in the whole world. Rest assured that your name will become even more famous than it has been. I shall convey this to the king's ministers. I shall report it in Court.'

"When he heard him mention the king's ministers and reports to the Court, my grandfather asked, 'And who are you, your Highness?'

"The nobleman burst out laughing, puffed out his beribboned and bemedaled chest and said to my grandfather, 'I am the Governor of the Province.'

"My grandfather's heart sank at this. If he had only known with whom he was playing he might have played differently. But it was too late. What was done couldn't be undone. The Governor made his farewells in the friendliest possible manner, went out to his carriage, got in, and rode off.

"It was then that the whole village came flocking around my grandfather wanting to know who the nobleman had been. When they found out that it was the Governor himself, they went on to ask, 'And what did the Governor want with you?' When my grandfather informed them that the Governor had come for a game of chess they spat three times to ward off the evil eye, and each one went on his way. They talked about the affair and talked about it among themselves, but in time it was forgotten. My grandfather forgot about it also. His head was filled with new chess problems and incidentally with the lesser problem of making a living.

"And it came to pass, ladies and gentlemen, a long time after, how long I do not know myself—I only know that it was Passover Eve and my grandfather had nothing with which to celebrate the holiday, not even a piece of *matzo*. He had a houseful of children and this one needed a shirt, that one a pair of shoes. Things were bad. My grandfather, poor soul, was sitting doubled up, a magnifying glass screwed into his eyes, tinkering with a watch that had stopped running and refused to start again, and thinking to himself, 'From whence shall come my help?'

"Suddenly the door opened and in walked two gendarmes and made straight for my grandfather. '*Pazhaluista*,' they said to him, 'If you please.' A thought flashed through my grandfather's head (my grandfather was a man given to strange thoughts), 'Perhaps they have come from the Governor.' Who could tell? Maybe the Governor wanted to reward him, make him wealthy? Hadn't it happened before that through some chance happening, through some little incident, a nobleman had taken a poor Jew and showered him with gold, and endowed his children and his children's children forever and ever?

"But it turned out, ladies and gentlemen, to be nothing of the sort. They were only asking him to be so kind as to pick himself up and set out at once, for—guess where—Petersburg! Why, they themselves didn't know. They had just received a paper from Petersburg on which was written: '*Niemedlannia dostavit yevreya Rubina Rubinsteina v Sankt Peterburg.*' This meant that they must this instant deliver the Jew Rubin Rubinstein to St. Petersburg. There must be a reason for this. 'Confess, fellow, what have you done?' My grandfather swore that he was innocent, in all his life he hadn't as much as hurt a fly on the wall. The whole town could vouch for him. They paid no attention to him, but ordered him to come along with them and join the convoy. The order had said to *deliver* the Jew Rubinstein, and what else could that mean except to bring him by convoy and in chains? And *this instant.* Which meant the quicker the better.

"Without wasting any more time, ladies and gentlemen, on unnecessary ceremonies, they took my grandfather, bound chains around his hands and feet, and led him away in a convoy with all the thieves and criminals. And what it meant in those days to 'go by convoy,' I don't have to explain to you. You know yourselves that an ordinary person who was led by convoy seldom reached his destination. There were no trains, no highways. People fell like flies by the roadside. More than half of them died on the way and the rest arrived worn out, sick, and crippled for life.

"But as luck would have it, my grandfather was of the same physical makeup as I am, thin and bony, but with a strong constitution. Besides he was a thinking man, a man with a philosophy of his own. 'A man,' he said, 'dies once, not twice, and if it is fated that he should continue to live, no one can take his life away.' Why did he speak thus of life and death? For it was apparent that this smacked of exile, of Siberia, or maybe even worse. He not only bade his wife and children and the whole village good-bye, he asked for the book of the dying and the dead, and wanted to make his last confession. The whole town turned out to see him off, as though it were his funeral. They mourned for him already as though he were dead, and tears poured like a deluge. . . .

"To describe to you, ladies and gentlemen, what my grandfather went through on his journey, I would have to spend not one night with you, but three nights in a row. And that would be a pity. The time could be much better spent in playing chess. Briefly I can tell you that the journey lasted the whole summer, from Passover to *Succos*. The convoy, ladies and gentlemen, was divided into stations, and at each station the prisoners had to wait a week, or two weeks, or sometimes longer, until new groups of thieves and brigands were assembled. Then they were driven farther.

"And when finally after many trials and tribulations they arrived in the great and glorious city of St. Petersburg, do you think that they were through with him? If you think so, you are greatly mistaken. For here at the end of the journey they took my grandfather and locked him up in a stone cell, a tiny dark room in which he could neither sit nor lie, nor move nor even stand upright. . . ."

"Just the place for a game of chess!" broke in the witty young man with the gold-rimmed glasses.

"Or for telling rotten jokes," added Rubinstein the chess player, and went on with his story.

"Here in this stone cell my grandfather prepared himself in earnest for death. He recited the last prayer, beheld the Angel of Death in front of his eyes, and felt his soul leaving his body before sentence could even be passed on him. And to tell the truth, he now wished for death to come. He had only one flicker of hope left. . . . He was certain that his townspeople would intercede for him. There would be mediators, people of good will who would use their influence to set him free. They would go to the various officials, offer bribes if necessary, do everything in order to deliver an innocent man who had been the victim of an ugly frame-up.

"And my grandfather was not wrong, ladies and gentlemen. From the day he had been led away, the town had busied itself about his case. The townspeople consulted lawyers, sought influence in high places, gave money wherever they could. But nothing helped.

"Their money was accepted, but no promises were made. It was impossible, said the officials, to do anything for my grandfather, and here is how they explained it. It is easy to buy the freedom of a thief or a common criminal. Why so? For the simple reason that you knew the thief had stolen a couple of horses, or the criminal had set fire to a house. But a fellow like this Rubinstein who had neither stolen horses nor set anything on fire—who could tell what sort of offender he was? Maybe he was even a 'political'? In those days a 'political' was worse than a murderer who had slaughtered a whole province. To intercede for a 'political' was very dangerous. The very word 'politichesky' couldn't be spoken out loud, only whispered in the dark. But what did Rubin Rubinstein the Watchmaker have to do with politics? Still, who could tell? Wasn't he a brainy man, a chess player, a philosopher?

"But, ladies and gentlemen, as I have said before, all things come to an end. The day arrived when the doors of the prison opened, and two gendarmes, armed from head to foot, came in, dragged my grandfather out, more dead than alive, put him into a carriage and drove off. Where to? He didn't ask. To the judgment? Let it be to the judgment. To the scaffold? Let it be to the scaffold. Anything to put an end to this. He saw himself standing in front of the Court. 'Rubin Rubinstein,' they said to him. 'Confess your guilt.' And he answered, 'I confess that I am a Jew and a poor watchmaker, and I live by the work of my hands. I have never stolen anything, never swindled anyone, nor insulted anyone. God is my witness. If you want to torture me, do so, but first take away my immortal soul. It is in your hands.'

"As my grandfather argued with the Court in this vein, the carriage drove up to a large building and my grandfather was told to get out. He obeyed. They took him into a room, then into a corridor, then into another room, and told him to take off all his clothes down to his undershirt. He couldn't figure out what this meant, but when an armed gendarme tells you to take off your clothes, you can't very well be impolite and disobey. Then they told him—and I wish to beg your pardon a thousand times for mentioning such a thing, ladies and gentlemen—to take off his undershirt, too. He took off his undershirt, too. Then they took him stark naked into a bathroom and proceeded to give him a bath. And what a bath. They scrubbed him and rubbed him, they scoured him and polished him, rinsed him and dried him. Then they let him get dressed, took him out once more, and drove off. They drove and they drove and they drove. And my grandfather thought to himself, 'Dear Lord, what will become of me now?' He tried to recall all the stories he had ever read of the Spanish Inquisition and he couldn't recall ever having read of a single instance where a condemned man was given a bath before being led to the gallows.

"As he was musing thus, ladies and gentlemen, the carriage drove up to a courtyard surrounded by an iron picket fence; each picket was tipped with gold and on each tip was an eagle. He was led through rows of generals decorated with golden epaulettes and with medals on their chests. He was told that he must not be frightened, he was going to be presented to the King. He was instructed to look straight in front of him, not to say anything unnecessary, not to complain about anything, and only answer the questions put to him with 'yes' or 'no.'

"Before my grandfather could get his bearings he found himself in a magnificent hall hung with paintings and filled with golden furniture. Opposite him stood a tall man with sideburns. The man with the sideburns (it was Czar Nicholas I) looked my grandfather over and the following conversation took place between them:

The King: 'What is your name?'

Grandfather Rubinstein: 'Rubin Sholemov Rubinstein.'

The King: 'How old are you?'

Grandfather Rubinstein: 'Fifty-seven.'

The King: 'Where did you learn to play chess?'

Grandfather Rubinstein: 'The knowledge is passed on in my family from father to son.'

The King: 'They tell me that you are the foremost chess player in my kingdom.'

"To this my grandfather wanted to say, 'Would that I were not the foremost chess player in your kingdom.' Then the King would surely have asked, 'Why do you say this?' Then my grandfather would have let him know that this was no way to treat an eminent chess player with whom the King wanted to have an audience. Grandfather Rubinstein would have known what to tell the Czar, you may be sure of that!

"But at this moment the King waved his hand, the generals leaped forward, and the same gendarmes who had brought him in led my grandfather out into the courtyard. There they set him free and ordered him to leave the city instantly, for a Jew had no right to be there. Don't ask how he finally got home. It's enough that he got there alive. He had left home before Passover and he arrived just in time to celebrate *Succos*. Ladies and gentlemen, I have finished. . . ."

Alfred Kreymborg

Chess Reclaims a Devotee

*Halfway across the world and half a century after Aleichem,
another sort of Jewish life—one that exists eternally in the
world's great metropolitan chess centers—is exuberantly
painted by Alfred Kreymborg (1883–1966), an influential
editor and poet, the author of forty books, and in his youth
a professional chessplayer until he made one of the game's
legendary blunders, following which he "gave up chess for
poetry" and twenty years later went "home again" to the
Manhattan Chess Club.*

*Here are the moves of the fateful game he describes
(slightly inaccurately) in his memoir. It was played against
Oscar Chajes in the New York National Masters' Tournament in 1911: 1 e4 c5 2 Nf3 Nc6 3 d4 exd4 4 Nxd4 Nf6 5 Nc3
d6 6 Be2 g6 7 Be3 Bg7 8 0-0 0-0 9 h3 Bd7 10 Qd2 a6 11 Nb3
b5 12 a3 Rc8 13 f4 Qc7 14 Rad1 Be6 15 Rfe1 Bxb3 16 cxb3
Na5 17 b4 Nc4 18 Bxc4 Qxc4 19 e5 dxe5 20 fxe5 Ne4 21
Nxe4 Qxe4 22 Bc5 Qb7 23 e6 f5 24 Qd7 Rc7 25 Bxe7 Ra8
26 Qd8+ Bf8 27 Bxf8 Rxd8 28 Rxd8 Rc8*

See diagram.

*29 e7?? (he should have played 29 Rxc8 first; now he
has a lost position) 29 . . . Qb6+ 30 Kh1 Rxd8 31 exd8Q
Qxd8 32 Bc5 g5 33 Rf1 f4 34 b3 Qd3 35 Rf3 Qb1+ 36 Kh2*

178

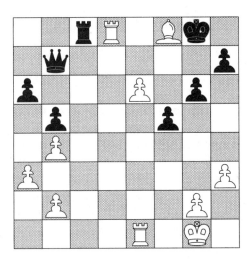

Qc2 37 Be7 h6 38 Bc5 Kh7 39 Kg1 Kg6 40 a4 bxa4 41 bxa4 Qxa4 42 g3 Qd1+ 43 Rf1 Qd3 44 gxf4 Qg3+ 45 Kh1 Qxh3+ 46 Kg1 gxf4 47 Kf2 Kf5 48 Rg1 Qc3 49 Rh1 Qd2+ 50 Kg1 Qe1+ 51 Kg2 f3+, White resigned.

Recently, after an absence of nearly twenty years from the chess world, I returned to the game of my first love, and may now be seen at the Manhattan Chess Club, along with many another ex-expert, college champion or duffer, puffing away at a pipe, stogie or cigarette, and shoving or banging white or black figures through a dreamy atmosphere, the while onlookers or kibitzers indulge in gratuitous comments at the expense of the losing players.

No game of chess in the old days had the least zest unless it was encircled by spectators infinitely wiser than the unhappy combatants; and for some time after my retirement from action I sat with the kibitzers and vied with the ancient fraternity in showing a defeated player, much against his will, how he could have won a lost game. The fraternity is open to any tyro with the requisite impudence for loosing his tongue in the face of the masters themselves; and the post-mortem is usually opened with some expletive such as *Potzer!* *Pfuscher! Nebich!* Ultimately, I drifted away from the game altogether. It had savagely reduced my energies, lost its nocturnal fascination and never earned for me more than a few dollars a week—my sole livelihood for a number of years. All in all, the mad, intricate, logical, ferociously difficult combat had subjected me to too many heartbreaks.

I played my game as most other men played theirs: with passionate intensity. To the ignorant outside world, two men over a chessboard look like a pair of dummies. And yet, inside the pale automata, dynamos pound incessantly. Here is nothing less than a silent duel between two human engines using and abusing all the faculties of the mind—the will, the imagination, logic, memory, caution, cunning, daring, foresight, hindsight, perspective, detail, unity and courage—in an effort to outwit, corner and demolish the not-less-than-hateful opponent. It is warfare in the most mysterious jungles of the human character. Chess has also its lighter, jocular, outrageously funny aspects; but first I wish to revert to its tragedies; and anyone who has ever participated in tournaments will know at once what I mean.

Those in which I took part from boyhood on—I made my début at eleven—were absolute nightmares. In my last tournament—a national contest won by Frank Marshall, with José Capablanca half a game behind—I lost nine pounds over a simple oversight I committed in a game against Chajes—then the Western champion and an East Side idol. I broke down near the close of a combination some seventeen or eighteen moves deep with all the pieces on the board, excepting a pawn or two on each side. To my king's pawn opening—a pawn which has given way to the queen's in present-day chess—Chajes retorted with the Sicilian defense: a delightfully risky game involving both players in counter-attacks from the outset. Counter-attack, the basis of chess of the classical or romantic era, gave way, about twenty years ago, to the growing inroads of safety first, conservatism and science—a movement ushered in by queen's pawn openings, a movement we'll come to later. At the moment, I must once more relieve myself of that everlasting bugaboo: the game with Chajes. Before I plunged into the mazes of the combination, I spent about fifty minutes working out in advance all the possible ramifications involving both sides of the board.

I have to explain to the layman that tournament games must be conducted with time-clocks in order to force the combatants to move at reasonable intervals. Time-clocks had to be invented against old-time players who won their games through a preponderance of

Sitzfleisch—or as my old friend, Dr. Siff, used to say: "What you need for chess isn't brains, but buttocks." During the classical era, a man with a lost position could wear down his opponent by sitting like Buddha and refusing to move—except once every hour or two. Staunton, the old British champion, won many a lost game in that fashion.

Time-clocks were the only means of keeping such devils within gentlemanly bounds, and, in the course of events, all tournaments, international, national or local, were conducted with the little double clocks ticking in accordance with which player's turn it was to move. World championships and international contests are run at the rate of fifteen moves an hour; contests of lesser importance at the rate of twenty: a fairly fast rate for players congenitally slow. I was one of these, and the tournament in question was run at the twenty-move rate. I now look upon that oversight of mine as the luckiest break in my whole existence. But at the time it was an overpowering tragedy.

Having spent fifty minutes on the first move of the combination, I would have only ten minutes to make my next nineteen moves. This, however, was a safe matter: I knew the combination by heart and, one by one, Chajes was making the anticipated moves. But I was deeply excited. Each time he made his next move and I made mine, I got up from the table and flitted about the room. My state was intensified by the interest in our game shown by the other contestants. Whenever they were free to leave their tables, they came over and followed the course of the combination—Capa and Marshall no less than the others. No one spoke to anybody else, but I could see experts nudge each other and eye me amazedly.

The whole thing went to my head. For years and years, I'd had a consuming chess ambition to rise by degrees to the New York State championship, the American and finally, nothing less than the world crown—then held by Emanuel Lasker. A year or two before, I had tied with Capa for the State championship and only lost the play-off after a long, heartrending end-game in which a mere tempo defeated me. Had it been his move, we would have drawn, but since it was mine I lost: the result, I swore, of defending the damned queen's pawn opening. Here was young Capa again; "fools" were already predicting he was destined to defeat Dr. Lasker. And here was Marshall, the American champion—and here was I, after having drawn an uphill battle, with two pawns down, against Hodges, a former American champion—and having won a game against the tantalizing Rice Club champion, Tenenwurzel. En route to victory over Chajes—the dark horse of the tournament—I would close the third round in the lead—providing I made my moves by heart. Veteran that I was at twenty-five, how could I possibly go wrong?

But I did. The general excitement was too much for my nerves. My hand began shaking with each successive move. The silence, above all, was unendurable. If I could have spoken to someone or someone could have spoken to me—but no. Chess contestants are pledged to non-communication as if they were prisoners under sentence for committing egregious crimes.

I shoved my pieces mechanically. The time-clock dangers were reduced. My opponent, beginning to detect the outcome of the combination, moved with increasing deliberation. But no matter how he pondered, he still had to make the moves I had figured on, once he'd entered the trap. They were the best at his disposal. By the time we neared the close of the combination, all the unengaged players were seated about the table, surrounded by practically all the spectators in the long, gray room. Capa and Marshall had been forgotten. I was the centre of the chess world and I paced up and down outside the dark ring, a prey to frenzied emotions. After Chajes made his sixteenth move, I would only have to make my seventeenth and he his seventeenth. Then my eighteenth, the *coup de grâce*, would force him to resign.

I kept looking at the ring for a sign that the East Side veteran had made his sixteenth move. The sign came. A number of men looked my way and respectfully opened a path. Capa was one of the men who stepped aside. I could see him smile a little. I don't quite recall what followed. I was in a tingling haze and through the haze I saw that Chajes had made the necessary move. He shook his stoical head as he made it. I haven't the slightest idea why I didn't sit down and deliberate before making my penultimate move. I remember looking at my clock: I had ample time. But I didn't take it. Nor did I sit down. Exultantly, I made the move leaning over the table and then sat down. And then—to my frozen horror—I saw I had made, not my seventeenth, but my eighteenth move! I had transposed the moves and blundered outright!

A few moves later I resigned. Instead of an immortal game, a game for chess history—as Marshall assured me later—I had blundered like a tyro. An infinitesimal aberration cost me the game, my chances in the tournament and my whole chess career. Throughout the remaining rounds, people reverted to that strange oversight. They buttonholed me in off hours and again and again I had to explain how it had happened, from the first move to the last. And abed at night, each time I lost another game—I lost game after game—I rehearsed the cause of my collapse. Instead of finishing at the head or near the head of the contestants, I finished next to last.

But I had already reached a solemn determination. While sitting petrified in a chair which should have been a throne, and accepting Chajes' cordial condolence, I resolved to have done with chess tournaments, chess clubs and chess forever after. I lost nine pounds over that oversight. And thanks to a constant devotion to poetry, side by side with chess, there wasn't another pound I could afford to lose. I was about thirty pounds underweight and poorer than a sparrow. So I gave up chess for poetry. But that, as Mr. Kipling used to say, is another story.

II

Ultimately, I caught the serene view of the Chajes tragedy. Had I won the game, I would have been lured on to further victories and defeats, only to end in a chess master's grave—a dismal profession withal. The invincible Steinitz had fallen before the invincible Lasker, and Lasker before the invincible Capablanca, and Capa before the invincible Alekhine. Chess mastery—possibly like any other mastery—is a thing to keep away from. The people who usually enjoy chess are the dubs and duffers, experts who have resigned their ambitions and now play for the pastime, and the fraternity of kibitzers.

One uncertain day, rather bored with the self-centered world of poetry and the self-centered world at large, I found myself in the neighborhood of the Manhattan Chess Club and, being able to "resist anything but temptation," I dropped in. I was greeted with a delight I could not have received anywhere else on earth. And here, scarcely a day older than when I had last beheld them, were some of the friendly enemies of my youth: Rosen, Rosenthal, Meyer, Warburg, Beihoff, Tenner—not a Gentile in sight. In chess, the Rosens bloom on and on. In the old days, over on Second Avenue, the crack players numbered Rosen, Rosenbaum, Rosenfeld, Rosenthal, Rosenzweig— the last truly a twig compared with the others.

I had done well to give up tournament chess, but nothing less than an idiotic whim had forced me to desert my old friends. I cannot attempt to describe how their welcome stirred me. The affections are outmoded these days: sentiment has been gobbled down by the sciences and by dollars mounting on dollars. One has to be hard-boiled. But hard-boiled here? Impossible. The chess world anywhere is a world unto itself, and when a gang of dark Jews welcome a goy with unrestraint, there's nothing to do but enthuse. For nowhere else is the goy held in greater contempt. The man who dubbed chess Jewish athletics, dubbed it correctly. With rare exceptions, Jews have graced Caissa's throne for a century past. And what, over on Second Avenue, did they used to call the insignificant pawn? A goy, a little goy! But even the Gentile rises to honors in time. Look at your Jewish Who's Who and you'll find me there. And why not? I bragged about that once too often and was hailed by a Jew: "Dirty climber!"

Well, I was at home again, more at home than ever before. No time-clock was in evidence; no tourney in progress. Safe from the past, was I safe from the present? What was going on here? What had happened to chess? "Pots—" Rosen ventured.

"What are pots?"

I was swiftly initiated. Pots is a game invented by a fellow named Calladay—"Cal, he's called"— by way of destroying serious chess. And who is this Cal? A third-class goy who's just as poor at this game as he was at the old game. But pots are now the rage all over the chess world.

I watched the marvelous invention. Three players take turns playing one another the while the odd or disengaged player acts as the referee calling time. He calls time, not at the rate of fifteen or twenty moves an hour, but at ten seconds a move! I never saw so many blunders in my life—it was delightful. And the best of players blundered—still more delightful. No wonder Cal had invented Pots. If a fellow didn't move on time, "Forfeit!" the referee called and took the place of the offender, who took the place of the referee. The stakes are always a quarter a game. They are called "union rates." And shades of Caissa, what a noise—noise of all things at a chess club! It was all most alluring.

We had played rapid-transit chess in the past, but never with such wholesale gusto. In the earlier days on the East Side, where chess could be seen at its best and grimmest, a man named Louis Hein invented a game called the Marathon, in which twenty, thirty or forty dynamos engaged in a round-robin the while Hein bellowed "Move!" That was also ten-second chess, but Marathons used to drag on for hours, and long sessions of any sort were precisely the torture most old-timers had begun to revolt against.

Before I knew where I was at, I was seated at one of these crazy tables— "Try it and see, you old duffer," I was challenged. Never a fast player, and long out of practice, I could barely see two moves ahead. Still worse, my lack of ambition undermined the will to win. I lost often and didn't mind losing. What had happened to me? I dropped in at the club again, merely to look on—and then to play, always to the friendly greeting, "you old duffer!" The name didn't nettle me. There were always old experts who recalled my former exploits to the youngsters who derided me. One day, I won a quick game from the Intercollegiate champion and the old-timers chortled. A large, grave gentleman, watching proceedings, remarked: *"Das war wie Eisen gespielt!"* The speaker was Alexander Alekhine. I thanked him and fled the table.

No one could rouse my ambition again, least of all the new world's champion. I'd sought the old haunt in pursuit of that momentary Nirvana which chess clubs afford to any profession: the law, medicine, music, commerce, religion or what not. I recalled a chess proverb: You can lose your wife one day and come here and forget her the next. Each of these men came here for relaxation, had always done so and always would. Best of all, these pots had buried the cut and dried queen's pawn opening. Chess was irregular again, adventurous, delirious, novel, absurd, human. The mummies who formerly shoved pieces about were flesh and blood again. And the laughter I heard had not been heard in my world for years. The rude explosion was neither ironical nor cynical. It had nothing to do with modernity, psychology, reasoning. It was forthright. And no one laughed louder than the dubs.

Men who had rarely won a game before won many a game now, and won it from many a master. The master resigned with grace and then proceeded to trounce the potzer as the potzer had never been trounced before. Nothing pleased me more than the momentary rise of the duffers. Among my chess memories—or memories in general—none cling more tenaciously, or with more enduring affection, than those which shadow underdogs I have known. Here I have to revert again to the Second Avenue of my youth and young manhood.

III

I was then the queer little shaver who earned his livelihood by playing anyone and everyone at so much a game at all hours of the day and night. One thing that attracted me to the East Side was the fact that most men earned their living in just the same way. Another thing—most of the men were older than I, much older, some of them patriarchs. Still another—they were cultivated. When we weren't playing or talking chess, we talked about music and books: I went to school over there. And I learned philosophy without calling it such. We had no abstract words for what we felt and thought. When we wearied of talk, "Let's have another game—" there was always that. And no one was so hard up that there wasn't someone worse off. I remember the proprietor of a chess café who let the addicts sleep on or under tables overnight. I remember a potzer too proud for such beds. If he lost instead of won, he'd sleep on park benches. None of us found that out till he died on one. Then we chipped in to save him from Potter's Field. A witty fellow he was; none wittier over there where wit is an essential weapon to losers.

I remember a game I played with a rabbi old enough to be my father's grandfather. He had a beard longer than the beard of Moses. He combed it with care and let it hang at ease over one corner of the board. It was too long to hang anywhere else. We were in the midst of an exciting game in the midst of an excited band of kibitzers. I noticed nothing at the time but the game itself. The old rascal had "swindled" me out of the first game: a legitimate swindle, a coffee-house trap. I vowed vengeance and dug myself into the table. The smoke was terrific—I didn't smoke in those days. The pieces we handled were heterogeneous: queens looked like bishops, bishops like pawns, and some of the knights had no heads. I was nearsighted, but I didn't mind. I'd got the hang of the pieces. And I'd got the hang of the position. But I didn't get the hang of the beard. I paid no attention to that.

The game was going my way. The rabbi was attacking on all sides, but I revelled in such tactics. I was always at my best building up walls against attacks, and then forcing a hole with a pawn, another pawn and then the counter-attack. The counter-attack was at work; it was working beautifully. The old fellow shook his head; so did the other old fellows. They began poking fun at him, unmerciful fun. "*Warte nur*," he said, but kept on retreating. "*Warte nur* yourself," I retorted, and went on advancing.

Suddenly, I detected a mate in three and cried, "Check!" He moved his king. Then I shouted, "Check again!" and he moved his king. Then I grabbed my queen, banged her down and crowed, "Checkmate, my friend!" The rabbi shook his head calmly. "Not yet, my friend," he replied, lifting his magnificent beard off the corner of the board. Out came a rook that removed my queen!

Then there was an old fellow named Ziegenschwarz who hated to win games that didn't end in checkmates. He took a sadistic delight in encouraging his victims to struggle on to the very end. He simply wouldn't let them resign. He'd even make bad moves to keep them going awhile longer, and chattered away in an effort to keep them cheerful. His favorite opponent was a melancholy soul named Levkowitz.

Levkowitz was an ideal loser: he not only lost as a rule, but he lost with a series of groans that deepened and lengthened with each hopeless move. One evening I watched the pair: Levkowitz looked not alone forlorn, but ill, very ill. He kept complaining about his *Magen*: he'd eaten some indigestible herring.

"There's nothing the matter with herring," Ziegenschwarz argued; "it's your game disagrees with you."

"I've got a lost game!"

"No, you haven't, move, you *Pfuscher!*"

Levkowitz made a lame move—"I've got a lost game, I resign."

"No, you don't—" and Ziegenschwarz made a weak move.

Levkowitz brightened a little, but suddenly scowled and moaned:

"I feel sick."

"No, you don't—move, *Dummkopf!*"

Levkowitz made a heroic effort, moved—and was sick in earnest. He tried to get up, but Ziegenschwarz wiped off the board with his sleeve, made a move and grabbed his victim's sleeve.

"I'm nearly mate."

"No you're not. Move, move!"

Levkowitz moved and was violently sick again. His tormentor wiped and moved with mad acceleration.

"I'm lost, lost," Levkowitz moaned.

"Move once more, just once more."

Levkowitz moved and staggered from the table.

"*Schachmatt!*" howled Ziegenschwarz without wiping the table and hustled after his friend: "Come, I'd better take you home."

IV

The crown prince of East Side chess was and still is Charles Jaffe. It is impossible to convey the weird type of game he used to play and the respect it won him among the cohorts along the avenue. If ever a man held court around a table, it was this very dark, slender, cigarette-smoking gypsy. The moment he arrived and sat down with some dub, most other tables were deserted. I venture to say that if Capa and Lasker had fought out their battles on the avenue and Jaffe and his dubs sat down nearby, the world warriors would have been deserted by the kibitzers.

Jaffe kept up a running fire of caustic badinage and could give amazing odds to the potzers. I never saw any high-class player give such odds and get away with them. The reverence in which he was held was mainly due to this faculty. He was a genius against weaker players. And they measured the rest of the chess world accordingly. If a better player than Jaffe (there were, of course, none better!) failed to win games at the odds the prince gave, he was treated with comparative contempt.

The ability to play coffee-house chess was one in which Jaffe surpassed any master. Coffee-house chess depends on an alert ingenuity in waylaying the opponent through subtle little traps or swindles. Usually the trap is baited with a sacrificial pawn no potzer can resist smelling and seizing. Were the pawn a consequential piece, the fellow would hesitate and look around. But the little goys overwhelm his appetite. It is almost an axiom that most games have been lost and won through hastily grabbing those innocent pawns.

Jaffe was a veritable devil in leaving them about and in keeping up an undercurrent of teasing cajolery, mock-heroics, encouragement, quips and puns. No wonder Second Avenue held him in awe! And no wonder the avenue held the outside masters in comparative contempt! Even Lasker, king of the Jews and the whole chess world, was held in doubt where Jaffe was concerned. As for the Gentile Capa, he was a duffer by comparison. "Jaffe could beat Capa blindfolded!"

Unhappily, once the crown prince left the avenue he was not so invulnerable. Invite him to a tournament among his peers, take away his magic banter and force him to face sound, scientific chess, and his traps proved of little avail. Traps were often his own undoing. What we call playing for position—a damnable modern invention—was something his valiant combinations couldn't penetrate. The extreme caution of modern chess wore down his temperamental inspirations. He belonged to the school of Paul Morphy, giant meteor of the romantic era.

Jaffe, in truth, should have been born among the Labordonnais and MacDonnells who never defended themselves, but went on attacking till the other fellow's attacks demolished them. Even inferior players, by playing book openings and developing "according to Hoyle," could defeat him by letting him defeat himself. Jaffe seldom disgraced himself in tournaments. He had the habit of defeating superiors and losing to inferiors, which seems to be the outcome of taking chances. No matter how he fared, he was always defended by the cohorts.

I recall the international tournament in Europe he embarked on some years ago. He didn't have the fare abroad and had to raise it through subscription—so I was told at the time. Doubtless, most of it was raised east of Third Avenue and south of Fourteenth Street. Over on Second Avenue, newspapers were scanned as they had never been scanned before, and there was only one daily event the readers turned to. I'm not in the mood for rehearsing those long days of silent gloom. Jaffe went abroad to show the *Schachmeister* what duffers they were and finished, not on top, nor anywhere near the top. When he returned, did the avenue upbraid him or drape itself in mourning? I went across town with that question in mind, ready to say what I could if necessary. I didn't have to say it. Jaffe was surrounded by a ring of laughing, gossiping kibitzers. Opposite him sat a time-honored potzer.

The potzer was eyeing and trying not to eye a terribly tempting pawn. I prayed to all the gods that the fellow would nab it. He didn't nab it. He hesitated, circled the board with his eyes and looked at everything but the little goy. The suspense was growing quite awful. It silenced the kibitzers. It silenced Jaffe himself. He looked rather drawn after the foreign débâcle. I wanted to shake hands with him, wring his arm off, slap his back, hug him—but I'd have to wait.

He was smoking away as usual. His side of the board was strewn with cigarette stubs, ashes and burnt matches. The famous lurking smile was absent. Confound that *Pfuscher!* Why didn't he relieve our suspense? All he'd lose would be a dime, and that pawn was worth a fortune to us. His glance no longer circled, but concentrated on one spot. The spot, confound him, was far removed from the pawn. Then he smiled slyly and lifted his left hand. Why did he lift that hand—he always moved with the other?

Then, praise Elohim, the hand closed round his queen and quietly clipped off the pawn. Jaffe smiled, lifted a knight and put it down ever so gently—forking the duffer's king, queen and two rooks. Hysteria rent the air. Jaffe raised his hand—"Wait, let him look!"

"I have to lose the exchange," sighed the duffer.

"Look again."

"I have to lose one of my rooks or the queen—"

"Look again."

"I'm in check—wait—I'll move my king—but wait—I don't want to lose my queen—why didn't you say check?"

"I didn't have to say check, potzer! Where are your ears? Didn't you hear me say mate?"

The hysteria revived. Pandemonium smote the table. *"Rinnsvieh, Nebich, Dummkopf, Schlemiel!"* the cohorts clamored. . . .

V

Well, here I am, here I am again, a ghost unashamed of his past. The game I now play is less than the shadow of the game I used to play. Fellows I formerly gave odds to, now play me even, or have the impudence to offer me odds. Worst of all, I'm no longer a hard loser; and if I leave a rook enprise in one game, I leave my queen in the next. *Sic transit et cetera!*

Luckily, I'm in first-class company. Other old-timers who sit down with me are not much better than I. Sometimes I pay them a quarter; sometimes they pay me—and we always play Pots. We open our sessions with a few plausible alibis. One man has a headache from trying to sell life insurance policies; another looks weary from having done nothing all day, and the third—I mention actual cases—has read a rotten review of his latest poems.

Somehow, on the evening in question, the weary gentleman had won three pots in a row: an unheard-of record for him. The life-insurance salesman—who is none other than George Beihoff—let it go at that and shrugged his shoulders. Throughout chess history, vanquished players are entitled to the immortal post-mortem: "I had a won game." The third time I sang the slogan, Anonymous—I have to call him that—shot back: "You had a won game, but I won it." We started to sputter and argue. Beihoff finally cut us short and turned on Anonymous: "Why shouldn't you beat us at chess? You've retired from business, you live on your income and your sex-life is over."

Without further ado, I rejoined the Manhattan Club in earnest. I entered my name for a life-membership. But there's a special clause in my application. It provides that if I'm ever caught starting anything remotely resembling a serious game, I'm to be expelled without trial by the board of governors.

David Delman

The Last Gambit

The hero of David Delman's detective novel The Last Gambit, *a chessplaying New York police lieutenant named Jacob Horowitz, has come to Philadelphia, his original hometown, to play in an open chess tournament. The day before the first round, he visits his old chess club—which turns out to be not much different from the place Alfred Kreymborg called home fifty years earlier in another city—and encounters Grandmaster Dmitri Kaganovich, who is also scheduled to play in the tournament but is murdered before he gets the chance.*

Stripped of the social engagement that would have occupied the early part of the afternoon, Jacob found himself at loose ends. The tournament didn't get under way until tomorrow. He could do some additional studying, he supposed—review the various Sicilian defenses he'd be counting on heavily, for instance—but he knew that wouldn't be really useful. Too much like last-minute exam cramming. He sauntered along Broad Street for a while, stopping here and there to watch it being torn up. Jacob was fond of Philadelphia. Not only was it his birthplace, but it was where he had spent the early, happy years of his first marriage. As with most big cities, however, it was not at its best when viewed casually. You had to live in a city, Jacob knew, in order to hear its music. Like an experienced woman,

Philadelphia played it safe with strangers. Barebacked construction workers hovered over a hole in the ground, but their approach to widening it was too desultory to sustain interest. Jacob did not attach blame to that. It was a sweltering day in early July, temperature and humidity suddenly skyrocketing after a spell of unseasonal balminess. How hot was it? Hot enough to get the hell out of it. Screw Foxy Farrington, Jacob decided, and made for the Quaker Chess Club as if it were an oasis. If Farrington had preceded him Jacob would coolly grin and bear it, coolly the operative word.

The building was shabby enough to suggest that its history might be interesting. It wasn't. It was merely a relatively new building that had gone to seed fast. The rent was predictably cheap. An ambulance-chasing lawyer, a small-time accountant and an employment agency for domestic help were its star tenants. Quaker Chess, with its modest membership roll—80 thereabouts—felt right at home.

Jacob stepped out of the arthritic elevator on the fourth (and top) floor. He pushed open the heavy door, and in the tiny anteroom saw at once that Teddy Sherman and the ancient doctor who was his archenemy were, as ever, locked in combat. Teddy was the club caretaker, about 75, whose style of play was ferocious. The doctor, about 80, was if anything even more aggressive. In fact both old men moved pieces so quickly that sometimes—watch intently as he might—it was hard for Jacob to assess positions since they changed so rapidly.

As Jacob entered he heard Teddy's raspy voice in its habitual complaint to the chess gods. "Man's too good for me. Look at him, a friggin' machine. How about a mistake, Krueger? One lousy mistake. Is that too much to ask?"

"Come on, come on," Doc Krueger said. "You're a piece ahead. You're everything ahead. Stop complaining and move already."

Jacob grinned. It could have been yesterday, not three months ago, that he'd been here last.

"Don't know why I sit down with the *momser*," Teddy said and attacked violently with a rook that almost instantly found itself beleaguered.

"Check, if you don't mind." Doc Krueger's voice had become unctuously apologetic now that he was closing in for the kill. Two moves later an enraged Teddy knocked his king down in token of defeat and paid the quarter that made it binding.

Both oldsters had been well aware of Jacob's presence, but neither spoke until the issue between them was decided. Nor had Jacob expected them to. Chess players, a diverse enough breed, all had that much in common: the game first, civilities a distant second.

Teddy—tiny and frail with unkempt white hair and the sharp stare of a former high-roller—allowed himself to smile welcomingly now. "Jacob, where you been? I could have been dead you stayed away so long."

"Dead? You? You'll outlive me by fifty years. And Doc Krueger will outlive us both."

The doctor dissolved in laughter.

"Foxy was around this morning looking for you," Teddy said.

"He found me."

"Sure he did. Krueger here couldn't keep his mouth shut and told him try Barney's."

"He needed me to tell him that?" Doc Krueger demanded defensively. "Since when don't the whole world know when Jacob's in town, try Barney's for him. I did wrong, Jacob?"

Jacob patted the old man's shoulder.

Teddy was studying him. "You're entered in the Capa, I hear. Why?"

Jacob shrugged. "Something to tell my grandchildren."

"Wrong, bubby. I think it's because you like punishment. All right, there's a babyface in the back room waiting for you."

"What kind of a babyface?"

"With mean eyes."

"Let him wait. I didn't come to Philly to be hustled by one of your babyfaces."

"Nah! Nah! He won't hustle yet. Next year maybe. Go, Jacob. I'll yak to you later. Right now, the doctor wants another piece of me. Look, he's slobbering."

The gleeful doctor bounced a bit in demonstration.

As he moved off towards the back room, Jacob heard Teddy trying to get a knight as a handicap. Moans and groans on behalf of the effort, but Jacob knew the doc was too canny. Still, Teddy might talk a pawn out of him. If he could, he might well get his quarter back.

Quaker Chess was laid out like an archetypal railroad flat—four rooms one after the other. Nothing seedy about its interior, however. Not plush either, but the walls were freshly painted white and the photos of club members—a handful of them quite well known—were respectfully arranged and dust free. Teddy did look after things. Depending on its size, each room had six to eight chessboards set up. Players for them were still sparse, though in about half an hour they would not be. By then, around noon, as many as 20 would probably be in attendance, while by day's end an average of 60 would have passed through.

The babyface in the back room might or might not have been mean-eyed, but he was certainly tender in years. Jacob guessed about 13. He was thin and very black. Bent over the current issue of *Chess Life*, he was so deep in a problem that an army of Jacobs would not have claimed his full attention. As he lifted his head, blinking, he looked like a cranky old owl encountering sudden daylight. Jacob identified himself, held out a hand in greeting. It was shaken absently. The problem was still much more with him than Jacob was, large as Jacob was.

"Want a game?" Jacob asked politely.

The invitation was taken under advisement. "Do you have a rating?"

Jacob announced it and watched as his fate hung in the balance. Perhaps because there was no one else in the room, no witness to this stepping down in class, Babyface decided in his favor.

"Mine's 58 points higher," he said, "but all right, I'll play you. Sometimes I don't mind playing patzers. I get a chance to try things."

Instantly then he reached for the white pieces—and their inherent advantage—to set them up on his side of the board. Try things, my ass, Jacob thought. The kid's a born chess player. The only vein he knows is the jugular.

But Babyface was merely OK, not the *Wunderkind* he thought himself. Soon enough Jacob was a pawn up with potential developing for a bruising kingside attack. Babyface was not happy.

"You lied about your rating," he said. "You lowered it, so you could sandbag me."

"Nary a point," Jacob said.

It was then they heard a stirring in the front room—Teddy's distinctive rasp a decibel or so above other raised voices. It took a moment to be reassured that the clamor was essentially benign. Jacob had risen to investigate. So, too, had his opponent, who managed to knock the board over in the process. Jacob stared at him. He stared back.

"Sure am one clumsy Robert," he said blandly.

"Yeah," Jacob said. "Start over?"

"No way," clumsy Robert said. "I don't play with no sandbag-gers."

He strolled nonchalantly out of the room.

Impressed, Jacob watched after him. If he survives to fifteen, he told himself, he may make champion.

By now it was clear the raised voices signified excitement and welcome. Teddy was sounding a clarion call. "Hey, look who's here—friggin' Dimmie Kaganovich."

The room just at the head of the skinny corridor was the club's largest, and, after replacing the scattered pieces, Jacob worked his way towards it. He heard a burst of laughter and arrived as a second, larger burst detonated. Jacob had no trouble identifying Kaganovich. He was poised over a board, moving chessmen with a kind of neg-ligent grace—not really moving them, just sort of flicking at them. As a result they didn't quite fill the squares they were aimed at, but young Robert, exuding amiability now, was there to do the neatening up. Kaganovich was slim, good-looking, and expensively dressed. Jacob, no men's wear model, nevertheless knew he'd be right to put high figures on the smooth linen shirt with initials discreetly embroi-dered on the pocket, the well-cut worsted trousers, and the gorgeous tasselled loafers. He had thick, black, curly hair, and high cheek-bones, testament to the Slav in him. His skin was dark, not sun-tanned, but gypsy-dark, as were his eyes—dark and almost violently expressive. At first glance Jacob thought early thirties, revising this upward on closer inspection. There was something sad, even har-rowed, about those dark, expressive eyes. Still, it was clear that just then at least he was enjoying himself. In turn his audience—of two dozen or so—was finding him irresistible.

As Jacob entered Kaganovich was replaying his climactic game against Boris Tsarkov, the one preceding his defection. Even Jacob knew the bare bones of that story, at least the *Chess Life* version, but the version Kaganovich was in the midst of was a lot livelier. It was unorthodox, outrageous, and, Jacob felt, improvised as well. In fact Kaganovich seemed to be surprising—and delighting—not only his audience with its twists and turns but himself even more so.

Suddenly, as if it were a pinch of salt, Kaganovich dropped the black king over his shoulder. "And just like that I had him," he said in the American English so unsettling to D'Agostino. "Why? Tell me why." A variety of suggestions were put forward. "No, sir. No, no, and hell no. I had him because he's Boris and I'm Dimmie, and I know him better than anyone else in the whole world. Better than his mother. Better than any broad he ever slept with, not that there have been all that many. And I knew Capablanca was in his mind. You heard me, Capa! Remember Capa versus Menchik, what Capa said about the trap he sprung? He said my opponent should have considered that a player of my experience and strength would never have made such a move if it were really that inviting. So I *knew* I could leave that bishop hanging for at least one more shot. Anyone else, Boris would have grabbed it. Me, he didn't dare. Because every contest we'd ever had he lost to me. Chess, girls, soccer, spelling bees, for God's sake. He was spooked, is what I'm telling you. Convinced by history that he was staring into a trap, he let the bishop go, and that gave me the time I needed to set up queenside and smash him. After that he was so shaken he lost two straight to Cyril Cunningham, that in and out Brit he'd never lost to before or since, and kissed goodbye his shot at the world championship that year. Maybe forever. Because the next time he looked around there were Karpov and Kasparov."

"And he's never forgiven you," someone said.

Kaganovich grinned. "You noticed."

Other questions and comments followed, and the next ten minutes featured an animated give and take between Kaganovich and his audience. It was a representative Quaker Club turnout, Jacob thought, which meant a variety of ages, colors, and social classes. He recognized a couple of lawyers, a cop, an accountant, an advertising copywriter, and a reformed alcoholic with a penchant for becoming unreformed (and unglued) whenever he entered a tournament. There was also a sporting goods salesman, and a fat, fortyish dockworker who some said was "family-connected." And of course there were Teddy (beaming, reflecting the glow of a great occasion), Doc Krueger, and, conspicuously, young Robert. No females, however. Women were still relatively exotic in the world of chess, and the Quaker Club membership reflected this. Two belonged, Jacob knew, though he'd never seen either of them.

Demographically diverse, the Quaker Clubbers were uniformly savvy about chess, and the questions aimed at Kaganovich gave him ample opportunity to be wittily irreverent at the expense of Tsarkov and other Russians, the American chess establishment, the murky politics of international chess, and, most charmingly, at his own expense. Then someone suggested an impromptu simul—Kaganovich against six boards. He hesitated and seemed, for some reason, to send a glance Jacob's way, but after a moment agreed. The boards were set up. Jacob watched for a bit, saw without regret that Kaganovich was going to crush young Robert, whereupon, nudged by a certain gnawing in his stomach, he decided to go to lunch. He kissed the bald spot atop Teddy's head and left.

The elevator had lurched to three on its way down when the club door opened. It was Kaganovich.

"Good," he said. "I caught you. You're Jacob Horowitz, aren't you?"

Jacob acknowledged that he was.

"Barney guessed you might be here. I need to talk to you."

"Sure," Jacob said.

Kaganovich gestured towards the club. "Got myself into something I hadn't intended to." Rueful grin. "Story of my life. About half an hour, I figure."

Jacob nodded.

"Hey, have you had lunch? No? Good. We'll have it together, OK? Pick a place."

Jacob named a restaurant frequented by Quaker Club members and told Kaganovich how to get there, after it was agreed that Jacob should go on ahead and book a table. Jacob hit the elevator button once more, but Kaganovich did not immediately return to the club. Jacob looked at him. The Kaganovich smile was charmingly in place.

"The thing is," he said, "someone wants to kill me. And I'm damned if I know what to do about it."

With that as his exit line he opened and then shut the door behind him. Jacob thought of following but decided there wasn't much he could accomplish in that crowded club. The elevator finally arrived again, and he got in it. He would go to the restaurant and wait. He waited a long time. When the complaints of his stomach became clamorous he lunched—alone. Later he called the Dunsany, the hotel where the tournament was being held and where most of the out of town players usually stayed. Mr. Kaganovich was not in his room, the desk clerk told him, adding that he had not long ago crossed the lobby with a young woman. They were heading towards the coffee shop. Jacob decided it was just his day for getting stood up.

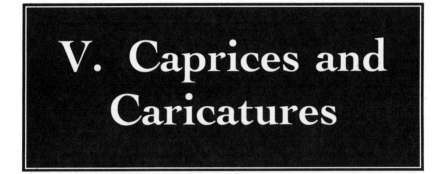

V. Caprices and Caricatures

The Twelve Chairs, a classic of popular Russian literature, was written in 1928 by two young journalists named Ilya Fainzilberg and Yevgeny Katayev, who called themselves Ilf and Petrov. The plot is set in motion when an old woman on her deathbed tells her son-in-law, Vorobyaninov, that she has hidden her diamonds in one of the family's twelve dining-room chairs, which have since been expropriated by Soviet authorities and scattered who knows where. Vorobyaninov teams up with a con man named Ostap Bender, and they set out on a quest for the chairs. One day they arrive in the small town of Vasyuki, where Ostap, who has played chess only once in his life, attempts to raise money by passing himself off as a grandmaster and persuading the gullible townspeople to buy tickets to his simultaneous exhibition.

Although *The Twelve Chairs* is a satire—very much in the tradition of Swift's *Gulliver's Travels*—that pokes fun at the absurdities of Soviet life and the pomposity of Soviet bureaucrats, the two American films that have been based on it ignore the satire and center almost entirely on the picaresque or comic aspects of the plot: *It's in the Bag* (1945) starring Fred Allen, and Mel Brooks's hilarious *Twelve Chairs* (1970).

Ilf and Petrov

The Twelve Chairs

A tall, thin, elderly man in a gold pince-nez and very dirty paint-splashed boots had been walking about the town of Vasyuki since early morning, attaching handwritten notices to walls. The notices read:

On June 22, 1927,

a lecture entitled

A FRUITFUL OPENING IDEA

will be given at the Cardboardworker Club
by *Grossmeister* (Grand Chess Master) O. Bender
after which he will play

A SIMULTANEOUS CHESS MATCH
on 160 boards

Admission ....20 kopeks
Participation ....50 kopeks
Commencement at 6 P.M. sharp
Bring your own chessboards

MANAGER: *K. Michelson*

The *Grossmeister* had not been wasting his time, either. Having rented a club for three roubles, he hurried across to the chess section, which for some reason or other was located in the corridor of the Horse-Breeding Administration.

In the chess section sat a one-eyed man reading a Panteleyev edition of one of Spielhagen's novels.

"*Grossmeister* O. Bender!" announced Bender, sitting down on the table. "I'm organizing a simultaneous chess match here."

The Vasyuki chessplayer's one eye opened as wide as its natural limits would allow.

"One moment, Comrade *Grossmeister*," he cried. "Take a seat, won't you? I'll be back in a moment."

And the one-eyed man disappeared. Ostap looked around the chess-section room. The walls were hung with photographs of race-horses; on the table lay a dusty register marked "Achievements of the Vasyuki Chess Section for 1925."

The one-eyed man returned with a dozen citizens of varying ages. They all introduced themselves in turn and respectfully shook hands with the *Grossmeister*.

"I'm on my way to Kazan," said Ostap abruptly. "Yes, yes, the match is this evening. Do come along. I'm sorry, I'm not in form at the moment. The Carlsbad tournament was tiring."

The Vasyuki chessplayers listened to him with filial love in their eyes. Ostap was inspired, felt a flood of new strength and chess ideas.

"You wouldn't believe how far chess thinking has advanced," he said. "Lasker, you know, has gone as far as trickery. It's impossible to play him any more. He blows cigar smoke over his opponents and smokes cheap cigars so that the smoke will be fouler. The chess world is greatly concerned."

The *Grossmeister* then turned to more local affairs.

"Why aren't there any new ideas about in the province? Take, for instance, your chess section. That's what it's called—the chess section. That's boring, girls! Why don't you call it something else, in true chess style? It would attract the trade-union masses into the section. For example, you could call it 'The Four Knights Chess Club,' or 'The Red Endgame,' or 'A Decline in the Standard of Play with a Gain in Pace.' That would be good. It has the right kind of sound."

The idea was successful.

"Indeed," exclaimed the citizens, "why shouldn't we rename our section 'The Four Knights Chess Club'?"

Since the chess committee was there on the spot, Ostap organized a one-minute meeting under his honorary chairmanship, and the chess section was unanimously renamed 'The Four Knights Chess Club.' Benefiting from his lessons aboard the *Scriabin*, the *Grossmeister* artistically drew four knights and the appropriate caption on a sheet of cardboard.

This important step promised the flowering of chess thought in Vasyuki.

"Chess!" said Ostap. "Do you realize what chess is? It promotes the advance of culture and also the economy. Do you realize that 'The Four Knights Chess Club,' given the right organization, could completely transform the town of Vasyuki?"

Ostap had not eaten since the day before, which accounted for his unusual eloquence.

"Yes," he cried, "chess enriches a country! If you agree to my plan, you'll soon be descending marble steps to the quay! Vasyuki will become the center of ten provinces! What did you ever hear of the town of Semmering before? Nothing! But now that miserable little town is rich and famous just because an international tournament was held there. That's why I say you should organize an international chess tournament in Vasyuki."

"How?" they all cried.

"It's a perfectly feasible plan," replied the *Grossmeister*. "My connections and your activity are all that are required for an international tournament in Vasyuki. Just think of how fine that would sound—'The 1927 International Tournament to be held in Vasyuki!' Such players as José-Raoul Capablanca, Lasker, Alekhine, Reti, Rubinstein, Tarrasch, Vidmar, and Dr. Grigoryev are bound to come. What's more, I'll take part myself!"

"But what about the money?" groaned the citizens. "They would all have to be paid. Many thousands of roubles! Where would we get it?"

"A powerful hurricane takes everything into account," said Ostap. "The money will come from collections."

"And who do you think is going to pay that kind of money? The people of Vasyuki?"

"What do you mean, the people of Vasyuki? The people of Vasyuki are not going to pay money, they're going to receive it. It's all extremely simple. After all, chess enthusiasts will come from all over the world to attend a tournament with such great champions.

Hundreds of thousands of people—well-to-do people—will head for Vasyuki. Naturally, the river transport will not be able to cope with such a large number of passengers. So the Ministry of Railroads will have to build a main line from Moscow to Vasyuki. That's one thing. Another is hotels and skyscrapers to accommodate the visitors. The third thing is improvement of the agriculture over a radius of five hundred miles; the visitors have to be provided with fruit, vegetables, caviar, and chocolate candy. The building for the actual tournament is the next thing. Then there's construction of garages to house motor transport for the visitors. An extra-high power radio station will have to be built to broadcast the sensational results of the tournament to the rest of the world. Now about the Vasyuki railroad. It most likely won't be able to carry all the passengers wanting to come to Vasyuki, so we will have to have a 'Greater Vasyuki' airport with regular flights by mail planes and airships to all parts of the globe, including Los Angeles and Melbourne."

Dazzling vistas unfolded before the Vasyuki chess enthusiasts. The walls of the room melted away. The rotting walls of the stud farm collapsed and in their place a thirty-story building towered into the sky. Every hall, every room, and even the lightning-fast elevators were full of people thoughtfully playing chess on malachite-encrusted boards.

Marble steps led down to the blue Volga. Oceangoing steamers were moored on the river. Cablecars communicating with the town center carried up heavy-faced foreigners, chess-playing ladies, Australian advocates of the Indian defense, Hindus in turbans, devotees of the Spanish gambit, Germans, Frenchmen, New Zealanders, inhabitants of the Amazon basin, and finally Muscovites, citizens of Leningrad and Kiev, Siberians and natives of Odessa, all envious of the citizens of Vasyuki.

Lines of cars moved in between the marble hotels. Then suddenly everything stopped. From out of the fashionable Pass Pawn hotel came the world champion Capablanca. He was surrounded by women. A militiaman dressed in special chess uniform (checked breeches and bishops in his lapels) saluted smartly. The one-eyed president of the "Four Knights Club" of Vasyuki approached the champion in a dignified manner.

The conversation between the two luminaries, conducted in English, was interrupted by the arrival by air of Dr. Grigoryev and the future world champion, Alekhine.

Cries of welcome shook the town. Capablanca glowered. At a wave of one-eye's hand, a set of marble steps was run up to the plane. Dr. Grigoryev came down, waving his hat and commenting, as he went, on a possible mistake by Capablanca in his forthcoming match with Alekhine.

Suddenly a black dot was noticed on the horizon. It approached rapidly growing larger and larger until it finally turned into a large emerald parachute. A man with an attaché case was hanging from the harness like a huge radish.

"Here he is!" shouted one-eye. "'Hooray, hooray, I recognize the great philosopher and chessplayer Dr. Lasker. He is the only person in the world who wears those green socks."

Capablanca glowered again.

The marble steps were quickly brought up for Lasker to alight on, and the cheerful ex-champion, blowing from his sleeve a speck of dust which had settled on him over Silesia, fell into the arms of one-eye. The latter put his arm around Lasker's waist and walked him over to the champion, saying:

"Make up your quarrel! On behalf of the popular masses of Vasyuki, I ask you to make up your quarrel."

Capablanca sighed loudly and, shaking hands with the veteran, said: "I always admired your idea of moving QK5 to QB3 in the Spanish gambit."

"Hooray!" exclaimed one-eye. "Simple and convincing in the style of a champion."

And the incredible crowd joined in with: "Hooray! Vivat! Banzai! Simple and convincing in the style of a champion!"

Express trains sped into the twelve Vasyuki stations, depositing ever greater crowds of chess enthusiasts.

Hardly had the sky begun to glow from the brightly lit advertisements when a white horse was led through the streets of the town. It was the only horse left after the mechanization of the town's transportation. By special decree it had been renamed a stallion, although it had actually been a mare the whole of its life. The lovers of chess acclaimed it with palm leaves and chessboards.

"Don't worry," continued Ostap, "my scheme will guarantee the town an unprecedented boom in your production forces. Just think what will happen when the tournament is over and the visitors have left. The citizens of Moscow, crowded together on account of the housing shortage, will come flocking to your beautiful town. The capital will be automatically transferred to Vasyuki. The government will move there. Vasyuki will be renamed New Moscow, and Moscow will become Old Vasyuki. The people of Leningrad and Kharkov will gnash their teeth in fury but won't be able to do a thing about it. New Moscow will soon become the most elegant city in Europe and, soon afterward, in the whole world."

"The whole world!!!" gasped the citizens of Vasyuki in a daze.

"Yes, and, later on, in the universe. Chess thinking—which has turned a regional center into the capital of the world—will become an applied science and will invent ways of interplanetary communication. Signals will be sent from Vasyuki to Mars, Jupiter, and Neptune. Communication with Venus will be as easy as going from Rybinsk to Yaroslavl. And then who knows what may happen? In maybe eight or so years the first interplanetary chess tournament in the history of the world will be held in Vasyuki."

Ostap wiped his noble brow. He was so hungry he could have eaten a roasted knight from the chessboard.

"Ye-es," said the one-eyed man with a sigh, looking around the dusty room with an insane light in his eye, "but how are we to put the plan into effect, to lay the basis, so to say?"

They all looked at the *Grossmeister* tensely.

"As I say, in practice the plan depends entirely on your activity. I will do all the organizing myself. There will be no actual expense, except for the cost of the telegrams."

One-eye nudged his companions. "Well?" he asked, "what do you say?"

"Let's do it, let's do it!" cried the citizens.

"How much money is needed for the . . . er . . . telegrams?"

"A mere bagatelle. A hundred roubles."

"We only have twenty-one roubles in the cash box. We realize, of course, that it is by no means enough. . . ."

But the *Grossmeister* proved to be accommodating. "All right," he said, "give me the twenty roubles."

"Will it be enough?" asked one-eye.

"It'll be enough for the initial telegrams. Later on we can start collecting contributions. Then there'll be so much money we shan't know what to do with it."

Putting the money away in his green field jacket, the *Grossmeister* reminded the gathered citizens of his lecture and simultaneous match on one hundred and sixty boards, and, taking leave of them until evening, made his way to the Cardboardworker Club to find Ippolit Matveyevich.

"I'm starving," said Vorobyaninov in a tremulous voice.

He was already sitting at the window of the box office, but had not collected one kopek; he could not even buy a hunk of bread. In front of him lay a green wire basket intended for the money. It was the kind that is used in middle-class houses to hold the cutlery.

"Listen, Vorobyaninov," said Ostap, "stop your cash transactions for an hour and come and eat at the caterers' union canteen. I'll describe the situation as we go. By the way, you need a shave and brush-up. You look like a bum. A *Grossmeister* cannot have such suspicious-looking associates."

"I haven't sold a single ticket," Ippolit Matveyevich informed him.

"Don't worry. People will come flocking in toward evening. The town has already contributed twenty roubles for the organization of an international chess tournament."

"Then why bother about the simultaneous match?" whispered his manager. "You may lose the games anyway. With twenty roubles we can now buy tickets for the ship—the *Karl Liebknecht* has just come in—travel quietly to Stalingrad and wait for the theater to arrive. We can probably open the chairs there. Then we'll be rich and the world will belong to us."

"You shouldn't say such silly things on an empty stomach. It has a bad effect on the brain. We might reach Stalingrad on twenty roubles, but what are we gong to eat with? Vitamins, my dear comrade marshal, are not given away free. On the other hand, we can get thirty roubles out of the locals for the lecture and match."

"They'll slaughter us!" said Vorobyaninov.

"It's a risk, certainly. We may be manhandled a bit. But, anyway, I have a nice little plan which will save you, at least. But we can talk about that later on. Meanwhile, let's go and try the local dishes."

Toward six o'clock the *Grossmeister*, replete, freshly shaven, and smelling of eau de cologne, went into the box office of the Cardboardworker Club.

Vorobyaninov, also freshly shaven, was busily selling tickets.

"How's it going?" asked the *Grossmeister* quietly.

"Thirty have gone in and twenty have paid to play," answered his manager.

"Sixteen roubles. That's bad, that's bad!"

"What do you mean, Bender? Just look at the number of people standing in line. They're bound to beat us up."

"Don't think about it. When they hit you, you can cry. In the meantime, don't dally. Learn to do business."

An hour later there were thirty-five roubles in the cash box. The people in the clubroom were getting restless.

"Close the window and give me the money!" said Bender. "Now listen! Here's five roubles. Go down to the quay, hire a boat for a couple of hours, and wait for me by the riverside just below the warehouse. We're going for an evening boat trip. Don't worry about me. I'm in good form today."

The *Grossmeister* entered the clubroom. He felt in good spirits and knew for certain that the first move—pawn to king four—would not cause him any complications. The remaining moves were, admittedly, rather more obscure, but that did not disturb the smooth operator in the least. He had worked out a surprise plan to extract him from the most hopeless game.

The *Grossmeister* was greeted with applause. The small clubroom was decorated with colored flags left over from an evening held a week before by the lifeguard rescue service. This was clear, furthermore, from the slogan on the wall:

ASSISTANCE TO DROWNING PERSONS IS IN
THE HANDS OF THOSE PERSONS THEMSELVES

Ostap bowed, stretched out his hands as though restraining the public from undeserved applause, and went up onto the dais.

"Comrades and brother chessplayers," he said in a fine speaking voice, "the subject of my lecture today is one on which I spoke, not without certain success, I may add, in Nizhni-Novgorod a week ago. The subject of my lecture is 'A Fruitful Opening Idea.'

"What, Comrades, is an opening? And what, Comrades, is an idea? An opening, Comrades, is *quasi una fantasia*. And what, Comrades, is an idea? An idea, Comrades, is a human thought molded in logical chess form. Even with insignificant forces you can master the whole of the chessboard. It all depends on each separate individual. Take, for example, the fair-haired young man sitting in the third row. Let's assume he plays well. . . ."

The fair-haired young man turned red.

"And let's suppose that the brown-haired fellow over there doesn't play as well."

Everyone turned around and looked at the brown-haired fellow.

"What do we see, Comrades? We see that the fair-haired fellow plays well and that the other one plays badly. And no amount of lecturing can change this correlation of forces unless each separate individual keeps practicing his check—I mean chess. And now, Comrades, I would like to tell you some instructive stories about our esteemed ultramodernists, Capablanca, Lasker, and Dr. Grigoryev."

Ostap told the audience a few antiquated anecdotes, gleaned in childhood from the *Blue Magazine*, and this completed the first half of the evening.

The brevity of the lecture caused certain surprise. The one-eyed man was keeping his single peeper firmly fixed on the *Grossmeister*.

The beginning of the simultaneous chess match, however, allayed the one-eyed chessplayer's growing suspicions. Together with the rest, he set up the tables along three sides of the room. Thirty enthusiasts in all took their places to play the *Grossmeister*. Many of them were in complete confusion and kept glancing at books on chess to refresh their knowledge of complicated variations, with the help of which they hoped not to have to resign before the twenty-second move, at least.

Ostap ran his eyes along the line of black chessmen surrounding him on three sides, looked at the door, and then began the game. He went up to the one-eyed man, who was sitting at the first board, and moved the king's pawn forward two squares.

One-eye immediately seized hold of his ears and began thinking hard.

A whisper passed along the line of players. "The *Grossmeister* has played pawn to king four."

Ostap did not pamper his opponents with a variety of openings. On the remaining twenty-nine boards he made the same move—pawn to king four. One after another the enthusiasts seized their heads and launched into feverish discussions. Those who were not playing followed the *Grossmeister* with their eyes. The only amateur photographer in the town was about to clamber onto a chair and light his magnesium flare when Ostap waved his arms angrily and, breaking off his drift along the boards, shouted loudly:

"Remove the photographer! He is disturbing my chess thought!"

"What would be the point of leaving a photograph of myself in this miserable town," thought Ostap to himself. "I don't much like having dealings with the militia."

Indignant hissing from the enthusiasts forced the photographer to abandon his attempt. In fact, their annoyance was so great that the photographer was actually put outside the door.

At the third move it became clear that in eighteen games the *Grossmeister* was playing a Spanish gambit. In the other twelve the blacks played the old-fashioned, though fairly reliable, Philidor defense. If Ostap had known he was using such cunning gambits and countering such tested defenses, he would have been most surprised. The truth of the matter was that he was playing chess for the second time in his life.

At first the enthusiasts, and first and foremost one-eye, were terrified at the *Grossmeister*'s obvious craftiness.

With singular ease, and no doubt scoffing to himself at the backwardness of the Vasyuki enthusiasts, the *Grossmeister* sacrificed pawns and other pieces left and right. He even sacrificed his queen to the brown-haired fellow whose skill had been so deprecated during the lecture. The man was horrified and about to resign; it was only with a terrific effort of will that he was able to continue.

The storm broke about five minutes later.

"Mate!" babbled the brown-haired fellow, terrified out of his wits. "You're checkmate, Comrade *Grossmeister!*"

Ostap analyzed the situation, shamefully called a rook a "castle" and pompously congratulated the fellow on his win. A hum broke out among the enthusiasts.

"Time to push off," thought Ostap, serenely wandering up and down the rows of tables and casually moving pieces about.

"You've moved the knight wrongly, Comrade *Grossmeister*," said one-eye, cringing. "The knight doesn't go like that."

"So sorry," said the *Grossmeister*, "I'm rather tired after the lecture."

During the next ten minutes the *Grossmeister* lost a further ten games.

Cries of surprise echoed through the Cardboardworker clubroom. Conflict was near. Ostap lost fifteen games in succession, and then another three.

Only one-eye was left. At the beginning of the game he had made a large number of mistakes from nervousness and was only now bringing the game to a victorious conclusion. Unnoticed by those around, Ostap removed the black rook from the board and hid it in his pocket.

A crowd of people pressed tightly around the players.

"I had a rook on this square a moment ago," cried one-eye, looking around, "and now it's gone!"

"If it's not there now, it wasn't there at all," said Ostap, rather rudely.

"Of course it was. I remember it distinctly!"

"Of course it wasn't!"

"Where's it gone, then? Did you take it?"

"Yes, I took it."

"At which move?"

"Don't try to confuse me with your rook. If you want to resign, say so!"

"Wait a moment, Comrades, I have all the moves written down."

"Written down my foot!"

"This is disgraceful!" yelled one-eye. "Give me back the rook!"

"Come on, resign, and stop this fooling about."

"Give back my rook!"

At this point the *Grossmeister*, realizing that procrastination was the thief of time, seized a handful of chessmen and threw them in his one-eyed opponent's face.

"Comrades!" shrieked one-eye. "Look, everyone, he's hitting an amateur!"

The chessplayers of Vasyuki were taken aback.

Without wasting valuable time, Ostap hurled a chessboard at the lamp and, hitting out at jaws and faces in the ensuing darkness, ran out into the street. The Vasyuki chess enthusiasts, falling over each other, tore after him.

It was a moonlit evening. Ostap bounded along the silvery street as lightly as an angel repelled from the sinful earth. On account of the interrupted transformation of Vasyuki into the center of the world, it was not between palaces that Ostap had to run, but wooden houses with outside shutters.

The chess enthusiasts raced along behind.

"Catch the *Grossmeister!*" howled one-eye.

"Twister!" added the others.

"Jerks!" snapped back the *Grossmeister*, increasing his speed.

213

"Stop him!" cried the outraged chessplayers.

Ostap began running down the steps leading down to the quay. He had four hundred steps to go. Two enthusiasts, who had taken a shortcut down the hillside were waiting for him at the bottom of the sixth flight. Ostap looked over his shoulder. The advocates of Philidor's defense were pouring down the steps like a pack of wolves. There was no way back, so Ostap kept gong.

"Just wait till I get you, you bastards!" he shouted at the two-men advance party, hurtling down from the sixth flight.

The frightened troopers gasped, fell over the balustrade, and rolled down into the darkness of mounds and slopes. The path was clear.

"Stop the *Grossmeister!*" echoed shouts from above.

The pursuers clattered down the wooden steps with a noise like falling bowling balls.

Reaching the river bank, Ostap made to the right, searching with his eyes for the boat containing his faithful manager.

Ippolit Matveyevich was sitting serenely in the boat. Ostap dropped heavily into a seat and began rowing for all he was worth. A minute later a shower of stones flew in the direction of the boat, one of them hitting Ippolit Matveyevich. A yellow bruise appeared on the side of his face just above the volcanic pimple. Ippolit Matveyevich hunched his shoulders and began whimpering.

"You are a softie! They practically lynched me, but I'm perfectly happy and cheerful. And if you take the fifty roubles net profit into account, one bump on the head isn't such an unreasonable price to pay."

In the meantime, the pursuers, who had only just realized that their plans to turn Vasyuki into New Moscow had collapsed and that the *Grossmeister* was absconding with fifty vital Vasyukian roubles, piled into a barge and, with loud shouts, rowed out into midstream. Thirty people were crammed into the boat, all of whom were anxious to take a personal part in settling the score with the *Grossmeister*. The expedition was commanded by one-eye, whose single peeper shone in the night like a lighthouse.

"Stop the *Grossmeister!*" came shouts from the overloaded barge.

"We must step on it, Kisa!" said Ostap. "If they catch up with us, I won't be responsible for the state of your pince-nez."

Both boats were moving downstream. The gap between them was narrowing. Ostap was going all out.

"You won't escape, you rats!" people were shouting from the barge.

Ostap had no time to answer. His oars flashed in and out of the water, churning it up so that it came down in floods in the boat.

"Keep going!" whispered Ostap to himself.

Ippolit Matveyevich had given up hope. The larger boat was gaining on them and its long hull was already flanking them to port in an attempt to force the *Grossmeister* over to the bank. A sorry fate awaited the concessionaires. The jubilance of the chessplayers in the barge was so great that they all moved across to the side to be in a better position to attack the villainous *Grossmeister* in superior forces as soon as they drew alongside the smaller boat.

"Watch out for your pince-nez, Kisa," shouted Ostap in despair, throwing aside the oars. "The fun is about to begin."

"Gentlemen!" cried Ippolit Matveyevich in a croaking voice, "you wouldn't hit us, would you?"

"You'll see!" roared the enthusiasts, getting ready to leap into the boat.

But at that moment something happened which will outrage all honest chessplayers throughout the world. The barge keeled over and took in water on the starboard side.

"Careful!" squealed the one-eyed captain.

But it was too late. There were too many enthusiasts on one side of the Vasyuki dreadnought. As the center of gravity shifted, the boat stopped rocking, and, in full conformity with the laws of physics, capsized.

A concerted wailing disturbed the tranquility of the river.

"Ooooooh!" groaned the chessplayers.

All thirty enthusiasts disappeared under the water. They quickly came up one by one and seized hold of the upturned boat. The last to surface was one-eye.

"You jerks!" cried Ostap in delight. "Why don't you come and get your *Grossmeister*? If I'm not mistaken, you intended to trounce me, didn't you?"

Ostap made a circle around the shipwrecked mariners.

"You realize, individuals of Vasyuki, that I could drown you all one by one, don't you? But I'm going to spare your lives. Live on, citizens! Only don't play chess any more, for God's sake. You're just no good at it, you jerks! Come on, Ippolit Matveyevich, let's go. Goodbye, you one-eyed amateurs! I'm afraid Vasyuki will never become a world center. I doubt whether the masters of chess would ever visit fools like you even if I asked them to. Goodbye, lovers of chess thrills! Long live the 'Four Knights Chess Club'!"

Samuel Beckett

In Samuel Beckett's Murphy *(1938), the title character, an Irishman living in London, finds employment as a male nurse at Magdalen Mental Mercyseat, where during his rounds one evening he plays a game of chess with a patient named Mr. Endon. The game is purest nonsense, and the annotations, presented in the style of chess tournament books of the day, are full of little jokes. For instance, the German name for a certain popular chess opening is Zweispringerspiel (Two Knights Game); in the Murphy–Endon game the opening is* Zweispringerspott *(Two Knights Joke). The comment that 1. P-K4 is "the primary cause of all of White's subsequent difficulties" is a mocking reference to the rallying cry of the "hypermodern" revolution in chess theory in the first decades of this century: "After 1. P-K4 White's game is in its last throes."*

The first cell to be revisited, that at the south-westernmost corner of the nave, contained Mr. Endon, voted by one and all the most biddable little gaga in the entire institution, his preoccupation with apnœa notwithstanding. Murphy switched on the thousand candles, shot back the judas shutter and looked in. A strange sight met his eye.

Mr. Endon, an impeccable and brilliant figurine in his scarlet gown, his crest a gush of vivid white against the black shag, squatted tailor-fashion on the head of his bed, holding his left foot in his right hand and in his left hand his right foot. The purple poulaines were on his foot and the rings were on his fingers. The light spurted off Mr. Endon north, south, east, west and in fifty-six other directions. The sheet stretched away before him, as smooth and taut as a groaning wife's belly, and on it a game of chess was set up. The little blue and olive face, wearing an expression of winsome fiat, was upturned to the judas.

Murphy resumed his round, gratified in no small measure. Mr. Endon had recognised the feel of his friend's eye upon him and made his preparations accordingly. Friend's eye? Say rather, Murphy's eye. Mr. Endon had felt Murphy's eye upon him. Mr. Endon would have been less than Mr. Endon if he had known what it was to have a friend; and Murphy more than Murphy if he had not hoped against his better judgment that his feeling for Mr. Endon was in some small degree reciprocated. Whereas the sad truth was, that while Mr. Endon for Murphy was no less than bliss, Murphy for Mr. Endon was no more than chess. Murphy's eye? Say rather, the chessy eye. Mr. Endon had vibrated to the chessy eye upon him and made his preparations accordingly.

Murphy completed his round, an Irish virgin. (Finished on time a round was called a virgin; ahead of time, an Irish virgin.) The hypomanic it is true, in pad since morning with a big attack blowing up, had tried to come at his tormentor through the judas. This distressed Murphy, though he rather disliked the hypomanic. But it did not delay him. Quite the reverse.

He hastened back westward down the nave with his master key at the ready. He stopped short of the wreck, switched on Mr. Endon's light and entered bodily into his cell. Mr. Endon was in the same position all but his head, which was now bowed, whether over the board or merely on his chest it was hard to say. Murphy sank down on his elbow on the foot of the bed and the game began.

Murphy's functions were scarcely affected by this break with the tradition of night duty. All it meant was that he took his pauses with Mr. Endon instead of in the wreck. Every ten minutes he left the cell, pressed the indicator with heartfelt conviction and did a round. Every ten minutes and sometimes even sooner, for never in the history of the M.M.M. had there been such a run of virgins and Irish virgins as on this Murphy's maiden night, he returned to the cell and resumed

the game. Sometimes an entire pause would pass without any change
having been made in the position; and at other times the board would
be in an uproar, a torrent of moves.

The game, an Endon's Affence, or *Zweispringerspott*, was as
follows:

White (MURPHY)	*Black* (MR. ENDON) (*a*)
1. P-K4 (*b*)	1. Kt-KR3
2. Kt-KR3	2. R-KKt1
3. R-KKt1	3. Kt-QB3
4. Kt-QB3	4. Kt-K4
5. Kt-Q5 (*c*)	5. R-KR1
6. R-KR1	6. Kt-QB3
7. Kt-QB3	7. Kt-KKt1
8. Kt-QKt1	8. Kt-QKt1 (*d*)
9. Kt-KKt1	9. P-K3
10. P-KKt3 (*e*)	10. Kt-K2
11. Kt-K2	11. Kt-KKt3
12. P-KKt4	12. B-K2
13. Kt-KKt3	13. P-Q3
14. B-K2	14. Q-Q2
15. P-Q3	15. K-Qt (*f*)
16. Q-Q2	16. Q-K1
17. K-Q1	17. Kt-Q2
18. Kt-QB3 (*g*)	18. R-QKt1
19. R-QKt1	19. Kt-QKt3
20. Kt-QR4	20. B-Q2
21. P-QKt3	21. R-KKt1
22. R-KKt1	22. K-QB1 (*h*)
23. B-QKt2	23. Q-KB1
24. K-QB1	24. B-K1
25. B-QB3 (*i*)	25. Kt-KR1
26. P-QKt4	26. B-Q1
27. Q-KR6 (*j*)	27. Kt-QR1 (*k*)
28. Q-KB6	28. Kt-KKt3
29. B-K5	29. B-K2
30. Kt-QB5 (*l*)	30. K-Q1 (*m*)
31. Kt-KR1 (*n*)	31. B-Q2
32. K-QKt2!!	32. R-KR1
33. K-QKt3	33. B-QB1
34. K-QR4	34. Q-K1 (*o*)

35. K-R5	35. Kt-QKt3
36. B-KB4	36. Kt-Q2
37. Q-QB3	37. R-QR1
38. Kt-QR6 (p)	38. B-KB1
39. K-QKt5	39. Kt-K2
40. K-QR5	40. Kt-QKt1
41. Q-QB6	41. Kt-KKt1
42. K-QKt5	42. K-K2 (q)
43. K-R5	43. Q-Q1 (r)

And White surrenders.

(a) Mr. Endon always played Black. If presented with White he would fade, without the least trace of annoyance, away into a light stupor.

(b) The primary cause of all White's subsequent difficulties.

(c) Apparently nothing better, bad as this is.

(d) An ingenious and beautiful début, sometimes called the Pipe-opener.

(e) Ill-judged.

(f) Never seen in the Café de la Régence, seldom in Simpson's Divan.

(g) The flag of distress.

(h) Exquisitely played.

(i) It is difficult to imagine a more deplorable situation than poor White's at this point.

(j) The ingenuity of despair.

(k) Black has now an irresistible game.

(l) High praise is due to White for the pertinacity with which he struggles to lose a piece.

(m) At this point Mr. Endon, without as much as "J'adoube," turned his King and Queen's Rook upside down, in which position they remained for the rest of the game.

(n) A *coup de repos* long overdue.

(o) Mr. Endon, not crying "Check!," nor otherwise giving the slightest indication that he was alive to having attacked the King of his opponent, or rather vis-à-vis, Murphy was absolved, in accordance with Law 18, from attending to it. But this would have been to admit that the salute was adventitious.

(p) No words can express the torment of mind that goaded White to this abject offensive.

(q) The termination of this solitaire is very beautifully played by Mr. Endon.

(r) Further solicitation would be frivolous and vexatious, and Murphy, with fool's mate in his soul, retires.

Stephen Leacock

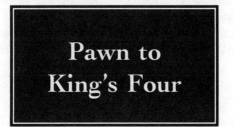

Pawn to
King's Four

The Canadian humorist Stephen Leacock takes a few wicked potshots at chessplayers in his famous story "Pawn to King's Four." Especially notable is the observation by the narrator's host and chess opponent that the head of the Criminal Lunatic Asylum goes back and forth between the chess club and the asylum "making comparative studies."

There is no readier escape from the ills of life than in a game of chess.

—Francis Bacon, and Eggs

"Pawn to King's Four," I said as I sat down to the chess table.

"Pawn to King's Four, eh?" said Letherby, squaring himself comfortably to the old oak table, his elbows on its wide margin, his attitude that of the veteran player. "Pawn to King's Four," he repeated. "Aha, let's see!"

It's the first and oldest move in chess, but from the way Letherby said it you'd think it was as new as yesterday . . . Chess players are like that . . . "Pawn to King's Four," he repeated. "You don't mind if I take a bit of a think over it?"

222

"No, no," I said, "not at all. Play as slowly as you like. I want to get a good look round this wonderful room."

It was the first time I had ever been in the Long Room of the Chess Club—and I sat entranced with the charm and silence of the long wainscotted room—its soft light, the blue tobacco smoke rising to the ceiling—the grate fires burning—the spaced-out tables, the players with bent heads, unheeding our entry and our presence . . . all silent except here and there a little murmur of conversation, that rose only to hush again.

"Pawn to King's Four," repeated Letherby, "let me see!"

It was, I say, my first visit to the Chess Club; indeed I had never known where it was except that it was somewhere down town, right in the heart of the city, among the big buildings. Nor did I know Letherby himself very well, though I had always understood he was a chessplayer. He looked like one. He had the long, still face, the unmoving eyes, the leathery, indoor complexion that marks the habitual chessplayer anywhere.

So, quite naturally, when Letherby heard that I played chess he invited me to come round some night to the Chess Club. . . . "I didn't know you played," he said. "You don't look like a chess player—I beg your pardon, I didn't mean to be rude."

So there we were at the table. The Chess Club, as I found, was right down town, right beside the New Commercial Hotel; in fact, we met by agreement in the rotunda of the hotel . . . a strange contrast—the noise, the lights, the racket of the big rotunda, the crowding people, the call of the bellboys—and this unknown haven of peace and silence, somewhere just close above and beside it.

I have little sense of location and direction so I can't say just how you get to the Club—up a few doors in the elevator and along a corridor (I think you must pass out of the building here) and then up a queer little flight of stairs, up another little stairway and with that all at once you come through a little door, a sort of end-corner door in the room and there you are in the Long Room. . . .

"Pawn to King's Four," said Letherby, decided at last, moving the piece forward. . . . "I thought for a minute of opening on the Queen's side, but I guess not."

All chess players think of opening on the Queen's side but never do. Life ends too soon.

"Knight to Bishop's Three," I said.

"Knight to Bishop's Three, aha!" exclaimed Letherby, "oho!" and went into a profound study. . . . It's the second oldest move in chess; it was old three thousand years ago in Persepolis . . . but to the real chess player it still has all the wings of the morning.

So I could look around again, still fascinated with the room.

"It's a beautiful room, Letherby," I said.

"It is," he answered, his eyes on the board, "yes . . . yes . . . It's really part of the old Roslyn House that they knocked down to make the New Commercial. . . . It was made of a corridor and a string of bedrooms turned into one big room. That's where it got the old wainscotting and those old-fashioned grate fires."

I had noticed them, of course, at once—the old-fashioned grates, built flat into the wall, the coal bulging and glowing behind bars, with black marble at the side and black marble for the mantel above. . . . There were three of them, one at the side, just near us, one down the end. . . . But from none of them came noise or crackle —just a steady warm glow. Beside the old-fashioned grate stood the long tongs, and the old-fashioned poker with the heavy square head that went with it.

"Pawn to Queen's Third," said Letherby.

Nor in all the room was there a single touch of equipment that was less than of fifty years ago, a memory of a half century. . . . Even the swinging doors, paneled with Russian leather, the main entrance on the right hand at the furthest end, swung soundlessly, on their hinges as each noiseless member entered with a murmured greeting.

"Your move," said Letherby. "Bishop to Bishop's Four? Right." . . . Most attractive of all, perhaps, was a little railed-in place at the side near the fireplace, all done in old oak . . . something between a bar and a confessional, with coffee over low blue flames, and immaculate glasses on shelves . . . lemons in a bag. . . . Round it moved a waiter, in a dinner jacket, the quietest, most unobtrusive waiter one ever saw . . . coffee to this table . . . cigars to that . . . silent work with lemons behind the rails . . . a waiter who seemed to know what the members wanted without their asking. . . . This must have been so, for he came over to our table presently and set down long glasses of Madeira—so old, so brown, so aromatic that there seemed to go up from it with the smoke clouds a vision of the sunny vineyards beside Funchal. . . . Such at least were the fancies that my mind began to weave around this enchanted place. . . . And the waiter, too, I felt there must be some strange romance about him; no one could have a face so mild, yet with the stamp of tragedy upon it. . . .

I must say—in fact, I said to Letherby—I felt I'd like to join the club, if I could. He said, oh, yes, they took in new members. One came in only three years ago.

"Queen's Knight to Bishop's Third," said Letherby with a deep sigh. I knew he had been thinking of something that he daren't risk. All chess is one long regret.

We played on like that for—it must have been half an hour—anyway we played four moves each. To me, of course, the peace and quiet of the room was treat enough . . . but to Letherby, as I could see, the thing was not a sensation of peace but a growing excitement, nothing still or quiet about it; a rush, struggle—he knew that I meant to strike in on the King's side. Fool! he was thinking, that he hadn't advanced the Queen's Pawn another square . . . he had blocked his Bishop and couldn't Castle. . . . You know, if you are a chess player, the desperate feeling that comes with a blocked Bishop. . . . Look down any chess room for a man whose hands are clenched and you'll know that he can't Castle.

So it was not still life for Letherby, and for me, perhaps after a while I began to feel that it was perhaps just a little *too* still. . . . The players moved so little . . . they spoke so seldom, and so low . . . their heads so gray under the light . . . especially, I noticed, a little group at tables in the left-hand corner.

"They don't seem to talk much there," I said.

"No," Letherby answered without even turning his head, "they're blind. Pawn to Queen's Four."

Blind! Why, of course. Why not? Blind people, I realized, play chess as easily as any other people when they use little pegged boards for it. . . . Now that I looked I could see—the aged fingers lingering and rambling on the little pegs.

"You take the Pawn?" said Letherby.

"Yes," I said and went on thinking about the blind people . . . and how quiet they all were. . . . I began to recollect a play that was once in New York—people on a steamer, wasn't it? People standing at a bar . . . and you realized presently they were all dead. . . . It was a silly idea, but somehow the Long Room began to seem like that . . . at intervals I could even hear the ticking of the clock on the mantel.

I was glad when the waiter came with a second glass of Madeira. It warmed one up. . . .

"That man seems a wonderful waiter," I said.

"Fred?" said Letherby. "Oh, yes, he certainly is. . . . He looks after everything—he's devoted to the club."

"Been here long?"

"Bishop to Bishop's Four," said Letherby. . . . He didn't speak for a little while. Then he said, "Why, practically all his life—except, poor fellow, he had a kind of tragic experience. He put in ten years in jail."

"For what?" I asked, horrified.

"For murder," said Letherby.

"For murder?"

"Yes," repeated Letherby, shaking his head, "poor fellow, murder. . . . Some sudden, strange impulse that seized him . . . I shouldn't say jail. He was in the Criminal Lunatic Asylum. Your move."

"Criminal Asylum!" I said. "What did he do?"

"Killed a man; in a sudden rage. . . . Struck him over the head with a poker."

"Good Lord!" I exclaimed. "When was that? In this city?"

"Here in the club," said Letherby, "in this room."

"What?" I gasped. "He killed one of the members?"

"Oh, no!" Letherby said reassuringly. "Not a member. The man was a guest. Fred didn't know him . . . just an insane impulse. . . . As soon as they let him out, the faithful fellow came right back here. That was last year. Your move."

We played on. I didn't feel so easy. . . . It must have been several moves after that that I saw Fred take the poker and stick its head into the coals and leave it there. I watched it gradually turning red. I must say I didn't like it.

"Did you see that?" I said. "Did you see Fred stick the poker in the coals?"

"He does it every night," said Letherby, "at ten; that means it must be ten o'clock. . . . You can't move that; you're in check."

"What's it for?" I asked.

"I take your Knight," Letherby said. Then there was a long pause—Letherby kept his head bent over the board. Presently he murmured, "Mulled beer," and then looked up and explained. "This is an old-fashioned place—some of the members like mulled beer—you dip the hot poker in the tankard. Fred gets it ready at ten—your move."

I must say it was a relief. . . . I was able to turn to the game again and enjoy the place . . . or I would have done so except for a sort of commotion that there was presently at the end of the room.

Somebody seemed to have fallen down . . . others were trying to pick him up . . . Fred had hurried to them. . . .

Letherby turned half round in his seat.

"It's all right," he said. "It's only poor Colonel McGann. He gets these fits . . . but Fred will look after him; he has a room in the building. Fred's devoted to him; he got Fred out of the Criminal Asylum. But for him Fred wouldn't be here tonight. Queen's Rook to Bishop's square."

I was not sure just how grateful I felt to Colonel McGann. . . .

A few moves after that another little incident bothered me, or perhaps it was just that my nerves were getting a little affected . . . one fancied things . . . and the infernal room, at once after the little disturbance, settled down to the same terrible quiet . . . it felt like eternity. . . .

Anyway—there came in through the swinging doors a different kind of man, brisk, alert, and with steel-blue eyes and a firm mouth. . . . He stood looking up and down the room, as if looking for someone.

"Who is he?" I asked.

"Why, that's Dr. Allard."

"What?" I said. "The alienist?"

"Yes, he's the head of the Criminal Lunatic Asylum. . . . He's a member here; comes in every night; in fact, he goes back and forward between this and the Asylum. He says he's making comparative studies. Check."

The alienist caught sight of Letherby and came to our table. Letherby introduced me. Dr. Allard looked me hard and straight in the eyes; he paused before he spoke. "Your first visit here?" he said.

"Yes . . ." I murmured, "that is, yes."

"I hope it won't be the last," he said. Now what did he mean by that?

Then he turned to Letherby.

"Fred came over to see me today," he said. "Came of his own volition. . . . I'm not quite sure. . . . We may not have been quite wise." The doctor seemed thinking. . . . "However, no doubt he's all right for a while apart from sudden shock . . . just keep an eye. . . . But what I really came to ask is, has Joel Linton been in tonight?"

"No. . . ."

"I hope he doesn't come. He'd better not. . . . If he does, get someone to telephone to me." And with that the doctor was gone.

"Joel Linton," I said. "Why, he's arrested."

"Not yet . . . they're looking for him. You're in check."

"I beg your pardon," I said. Of course I'd read—everybody had—about the embezzlement. But I'd no idea that a man like Joel Linton could be a member of the Chess Club—I always thought, I mean people said, that he was the sort of desperado type.

"He's a member?" I said, my hand on the pieces.

"You can't move that, you're still in check. Yes, he's a member, though he likes mostly to stand and watch. Comes every night. Somebody said he was coming here tonight just the same. He says he's not going to be taken alive. He comes round half past ten. It's about his time . . . that looks like mate in two moves."

My hands shook on the pieces. I felt that I was done with the Chess Club. . . . Anyway I like to get home early . . . so I was just starting to say . . . that I'd abandon the game, when what happened happened so quickly that I'd no more choice about it.

"That's Joel Linton now," said Letherby, and in he came through the swing doors, a hard-looking man, but mighty determined. . . . He hung his overcoat on a peg, and as he did so, I was sure I saw something bulging in his coat pocket—eh? He nodded casually about the room. And then started moving among the tables, edging his way toward ours.

"I guess, if you don't mind," I began. . . . But that is as far as I got. That was when the police came in, two constables and an inspector.

I saw Linton dive his hand toward his pocket.

"Stand where you are, Linton," the inspector called. . . . Then right at that moment I saw the waiter, Fred, seize the hand-grip of the poker. . . .

"Don't move, Linton," called the inspector; he never saw Fred moving toward him. . . .

Linton didn't move. But I did. I made a quick back bolt for the little door behind me . . . down the little stairway . . . and down the other little staircase, and along the corridor and back into the brightly lighted hotel rotunda, just the same as when I left it—noise and light and bellboys, and girls at the newsstand selling tobacco and evening papers . . . just the same, but oh, how different! For peace of mind, for the joy of life—give me a rotunda, and make it as noisy as ever you like.

I read all about it next morning in the newspapers. Things always sound so different in the newspaper, beside a coffee pot and a boiled egg. Tumults, murders, floods—all smoothed out. So was this, *Arrest Made Quietly at Chess Club*, it said. *Linton Offers No Resistance . . . Members Continue Game Undisturbed.* Yes, they *would*, the damned old gravestones. . . . Of Fred it said nothing. . . .

A few days later I happened to meet Letherby. "Your application is all right," he said. "They're going to hurry it through. You'll get in next year. . . ."

But I've sent a resignation in advance; I'm joining the Badminton Club and I want to see if I can't get into the Boy Scouts or be a Girl Guide.

Woody Allen

The Gossage–Vardebedian Papers

Correspondence chess offers opportunities not available to players in across-the-board contests—namely, the temptation to claim that a move made earlier was not the blunder it appeared to be but rather the result of excusable inattention in transcribing or transmitting it. But a move made is a move played, says Vardebedian in Woody Allen's "The Gossage-Vardebedian Papers," probably the funniest story ever written about chess.

My Dear Vardebedian:

I was more than a bit chagrined today, on going through the morning's mail, to find that my letter of September 16, containing my twenty-second move (knight to the king's fourth square), was returned unopened due to a small error in addressing—precisely, the omission of your name and residence (how Freudian can one get?), coupled with a failure to append postage. That I have been disconcerted of late due to equivocation in the stock market is no secret, and though on the above-mentioned September 16 the culmination of a long-standing downward spiral dropped Amalgamated Anti-Matter off the Big Board once and for all, reducing my broker suddenly to the legume family, I do not offer this as an excuse for my negligence and monumental ineptitude. I goofed. Forgive me. That you failed to notice the missing letter indicates a certain disconcertion on your part, which I put down to zeal, but heaven knows we all make mistakes. That's life—and chess.

Well, then, the error laid bare, simple rectification follows. If you would be so good as to transfer my knight to your king's fourth square I think we may proceed with our little game more accurately. The announcement of checkmate which you made in this morning's mail is, I fear, in all fairness, a false alarm, and if you will reexamine the positions in light of today's discovery, you will find that it is *your* king that lies close to mate, exposed and undefended, an immobile target for my predatory bishops. Ironic, the vicissitudes of miniature war! Fate, in the guise of the dead-letter office, waxes omnipotent and—*voilà!*—the worm turns. Once again, I beg you accept sincerest apologies for the unfortunate carelessness, and I await anxiously your next move.

Enclosed is my forty-fifth move: My knight captures your queen.

Sincerely,
Gossage

Gossage:

Received the letter this morning containing your forty-fifth move (your knight captures my queen?), and also your lengthy explanation regarding the mid-September ellipsis in our correspondence. Let me see if I understand you correctly. Your knight, which I removed from the board weeks ago, you now claim should be resting on the king's fourth square, owing to a letter lost in the mail twenty-three moves ago. I was not aware that any such mishap had occurred, and remember distinctly your making a twenty-second move, which I think was your rook to the queen's sixth square, where it was subsequently butchered in a gambit of yours that misfired tragically.

Currently, the king's fourth square is occupied by *my* rook, and as you are knightless, the dead-letter office notwithstanding, I cannot quite understand what piece you are using to capture my queen with. What I think you mean, as most of your pieces are blockaded, is that you request your king be moved to my bishop's fourth square (your only possibility)—an adjustment I have taken the liberty of making and then countering with today's move, my forty-sixth, wherein I capture your queen and put your king in check. Now your letter becomes clearer.

I think now the last remaining moves of the game can be played out with smoothness and alacrity.

Faithfully,
VARDEBEDIAN

VARDEBEDIAN:

I have just finished perusing your latest note, the one containing a bizarre forty-sixth move dealing with the removal of my queen from a square on which it has not rested for eleven days. Through patient calculation, I think I have hit upon the cause of your confusion and misunderstanding of the existing facts. That your rook rests on the king's fourth square is an impossibility commensurate with two like snowflakes; if you will refer back to the ninth move of the game, you will see clearly that your rook has long been captured. Indeed, it was that same daring sacrificial combination that ripped your center and cost you *both* your rooks. What are they doing on the board now?

I offer for your consideration that what happened is as follows: The intensity of foray and whirlwind exchanges on and about the twenty-second move left you in a state of slight dissociation, and in your anxiety to hold your own at that point you failed to notice that my usual letter was not forthcoming but instead moved your own pieces twice, giving you a somewhat unfair advantage, wouldn't you say? This is over and done with, and to retrace our steps tediously would be difficult, if not impossible. Therefore, I feel the best way to rectify this entire matter is to allow me the opportunity of two consecutive moves at this time. Fair is fair.

First, then, I take your bishop with my pawn. Then, as this leaves your queen unprotected, I capture her also. I think we can now proceed with the last stages unhampered.

Sincerely,
GOSSAGE

P.S.: I am enclosing a diagram showing exactly how the board now looks, for your edification in your closing play. As you can see, your king is trapped, unguarded and alone in the center. Best to you.

G.

GOSSAGE:

Received your latest letter today, and while it was just shy of coherence, I think I can see where your bewilderment lies. From your enclosed diagram, it has become apparent to me that for the past six weeks we have been playing two completely different chess games—myself according to our correspondence, you more in keeping with the world as you would have it, rather than with any rational system of order. The knight move which allegedly got lost in the mail would have been impossible on the twenty-second move, as the piece was then standing on the edge of the last file, and the move you describe would have brought it to rest on the coffee table, next to the board.

As for granting you two consecutive moves to make up for one allegedly lost in the mail—surely you jest, Pops. I will honor your first move (you take my bishop), but I cannot allow the second, and as it is now my turn, I retaliate by removing your queen with my rook. The fact that you tell me I have no rooks means little in actuality, as I need only glance downward at the board to see them darting about with cunning and vigor.

Finally, that diagram of what you fantasize the board to look like indicates a freewheeling, Marx Brothers approach to the game, and, while amusing, this hardly speaks well for your assimilation of *Nimzowitsch on Chess*, which you hustled from the library under your alpaca sweater last winter, because I saw you. I suggest you study the diagram I enclose and rearrange your board accordingly, that we might finish up with some degree of precision.

Hopefully,
VARDEBEDIAN

VARDEBEDIAN:

Not wanting to protract an already disoriented business (I know your recent illness has left your usually hardy constitution somewhat fragmented and disorganized, causing a mild breach with the real world as we know it), I must take this opportunity to undo our sordid tangle of circumstances before it progresses irrevocably to a Kafkaesque conclusion.

Had I realized you were not gentleman enough to allow me an equalizing second move, I would not, on my forty-sixth move, have permitted my pawn to capture your bishop. According to your own diagram, in fact, these two pieces were so placed as to render that impossible, bound as we are to rules established by the World Chess Federation and not the New York State Boxing Commission. Without doubting that your intent was constructive in removing my queen, I interject that only disaster can ensue when you arrogate to yourself this arbitrary power of decision and begin to play dictator, masking tactical blunders with duplicity and aggression—a habit you decried in our world leaders several months ago in your paper on "De Sade and Non-Violence."

Unfortunately, the game having gone on non-stop, I have not been able to calculate exactly on which square you ought to replace the purloined knight, and I suggest we leave it to the gods by having me close my eyes and toss it back on the board, agreeing to accept whatever spot it may land on. It should add an element of spice to our little encounter. My forty-seventh move: My rook captures your knight.

Sincerely,

GOSSAGE

GOSSAGE:

How curious your last letter was! Well-intended, concise, containing all the elements that would appear to make up what passes among certain reference groups as a communicative effect, yet tinged throughout by what Jean-Paul Sartre is so fond of referring to as "nothingness." One is immediately struck by a profound sense of despair, and reminded vividly of the diaries sometimes left by doomed explorers lost at the Pole, or the letters of German soldiers at Stalingrad. Fascinating how the senses disintegrate when faced with an occasional black truth, and scamper amuck, substantiating mirage and constructing a precarious buffer against the onslaught of all too terrifying existence!

Be that as it may, my friend, I have just spent the better part of a week sorting out the miasma of lunatic alibis known as your correspondence in an effort to adjust matters, that our game may be finished simply once and for all. Your queen is gone. Kiss it off. So are both your rooks. Forget about one bishop altogether, because I took it. The other is so impotently placed away from the main action of the game that don't count on it or it'll break your heart.

As regards the knight you lost squarely but refuse to give up, I have replaced it at the only conceivable position it could appear, thus granting you the most incredible brace of unorthodoxies since the

Persians whipped up this little diversion way back when. It lies at my bishop's seventh square, and if you can pull your ebbing faculties together long enough to appraise the board you will notice this same coveted piece now blocks your king's only means of escape from my suffocating pincer. How fitting that your greedy plot be turned to my advantage! The knight, grovelling its way back into play, torpedoes your end game!

My move is queen to knight five, and I predict mate in one move.

Cordially,

VARDEBEDIAN

VARDEBEDIAN:

Obviously the constant tension incurred defending a series of numbingly hopeless chess positions has rendered the delicate machinery of your psychic apparatus sluggish, leaving its grasp of external phenomena a jot flimsy. You give me no alternative but to end the contest swiftly and mercifully, removing the pressure before it leaves you permanently damaged.

Knight—yes, knight—to queen six. Check.

GOSSAGE

GOSSAGE:

Bishop to queen five. Checkmate.

Sorry the competition proved too much for you, but if it's any consolation, several local chess masters have, upon observing my technique, flipped out. Should you want a rematch, I suggest we try Scrabble, a relatively new interest of mine, and one that I might conceivably not run away with so easily.

VARDEBEDIAN

VARDEBEDIAN:

Rook to knight eight. Checkmate.

Rather than torment you with the further details of my mate, as I believe you are basically a decent man (one day, some form of therapy will bear me out), I accept your invitation to Scrabble in good spirits. Get out your set. Since you played white in chess and thereby enjoyed the advantage of the first move (had I known your limitations, I would have spotted you more), I shall make the first play. The seven letters I have just turned up are O, A, E, J, N, R, and

Caprices and Caricatures
◆

Z—an unpromising jumble that should guarantee, even to the most suspicious, the integrity of my draw. Fortunately, however, an extensive vocabulary, coupled with a penchant for esoterica, has enabled me to bring etymological order out of what, to one less literate, might seem a mishmash. My first word, is "ZANJERO." Look it up. Now lay it out, horizontally, the E resting on the center square. Count carefully, not overlooking the double word score for an opening move and the fifty-point bonus for my use of all seven letters. The score is now 116–0.

Your move.

GOSSAGE

E. M. Forster

Chess at Cracow

Not many Westerners have been privileged to witness a living chess exhibition in Poland. One of them was the English novelist and critic—and avid chessplayer—E. M. Forster, whose description of such an event has made it unnecessary for anyone else to journey to Cracow for that purpose.

WHITE	BLACK
P-K4.	P-K4.
P-KB4.	P×P.
B-B4.	Q-R5 (check).
K-B.sq.	

That is to say, White advanced his king's pawn two squares, Black did the same, White did the same with another pawn and Black took it—traditional, but risky. White's next move, bringing out the bishop, will strike the experts as odd. It is usual to bring out the knight. But why talk of oddness when the pawns were eight feet high, and the bishops ten, and the queen twelve? At Cracow, in the courtyard of the Wawel, how can anything be odd? The great renaissance arcades, the gay soldierly music, the black-and-white squares on the gravel, the soft black sky, the cathedral close by, the Vistula below, made a universe in which only human beings seemed out of place, and chessmen became real.

Chess, that inestimable possession, that precious game made and moulded by history, and by our desire for intellectual happiness, that game which the experts have not yet ruined and which has drawn together different races and classes for centuries, that man's game, if I may say so (for even the queen was a prime minister once, and even the bishop an elephant)—chess took new beauty and strength that evening in Poland, in that magic castle, the refuge of dead kings, it looked backward triumphantly, recalled the past, adorned itself with music and light. There are moments when the world is compelled to rearrange itself, and one of these occurred when the pawns came toddling in. For a long time the courtyard had been empty, while the band played and the audience sorted themselves in the four tiers of the arcades. Then, to a special little tune, great structures of red and gold entered through a dark archway—the eight pawns of the "White" side, suggesting Saracens, followed by eight others in green and blue, Mongolian. When they had taken their places on their squares and bowed to each other, the music became more grandiose, and the larger pieces began to emerge, culminating in the stupendous monarchs, who supported their frameworks with difficulty and sometimes had to be towed to their squares. It was a heartening sight, especially to anyone who had suffered under the fatuities of pageantry in England—Druids, Drake, the Lady Mary receiving the keys of the city in all her dowdiness. A pageant requires not only splendour, but a touch of the grotesque, which should lurk like onion in a salad. One ought to feel "Oh, how splendid!" then smile, and to realize the splendour better than before, and there are smiles which cannot be raised by Friar Tuck. There are smiles which never interrupt beauty. How charmingly, on this occasion, was the stupidity of the castles indicated by some low, eye-shaped windows in the neighbourhood of their knees! I had never before understood why castles are so difficult to manage. What a settled despair lurked in the beards of the kings! The knights rocked to and fro on their squares, even more indifferent than usual to their immediate neighbours, and the pawns were like overgrown children, defenceless yet dangerous.

But I must describe how the game was played.

When the thirty-two pieces were in position, a mannikin in red and gold appeared, attended by two torch bearers. He inspected the "White" pieces with all the aplomb characteristic of the human race;

he was, as a matter of fact, a man, and, immensely tiny, he ascended a little dais when he had finished and gazed over the board, simulating now intelligence and now emotion, as he touched his turbaned forehead or waved his draped arms. He was followed by a mannikin in green and blue, the player of "Black." The band played wildly and was silent. Then, to a new tune, the red and gold mannikin leapt from his dais with a Japanese lantern in his hand. What was he going to do? He seemed not to know; he had the air of never having walked on a chessboard before. But he gravitated, like many a previous player, towards his king's pawn. Finally, he approached the expectant infant and waved his lantern at its stomach. The pawn stumbled forward and, dancing before it, he caused it to advance two squares, then he went back to the dais. The second player adopted the prowling style. With the air of one who walks by night, he stole to his pawn and beckoned with his lantern stealthily. The game went on as shown at the beginning of this article, and those who do not play chess had better be told that the blue-and-green mannikin was, with his second move, faced with a crisis. Should he or should he not take the pawn offered by the other fellow? To take it would not be rank folly— generations of previous players had taken it—but experts are now in favour of resisting the temptation and doing something else instead. Long did he meditate. Then, his sombre decision taken, he summoned his two torchbearers, and they led the pawn away into outer darkness, to the sound of cymbals and drums. This interruption in the music always occurred when a capture was made. It was very effective, and I wished that there could be a special sound for "check," too—the moaning of an oboe, perhaps. Check occurred as early as the third move, and by then I was already puzzled over the quality of the game. It was either too good for me or too bad.

Cracow is a strange place. What other town has threaded a golden crown on the spire of its church, or has installed a trumpeter to play every hour and to end his tune with a gasp because, centuries ago, a trumpeter was shot through the throat by the Mongols? And the strangest thing in Cracow is the royal enclosure of the Wawel, with its conflicting hints of Russia and of Rome. Self-contained, it dominates the city and the river from its height like a Kremlin, but it is all Catholicism within, and Italian artists have worked there among builders from the East. It is being repaired, and there are no more funds; and the game of Living Chess had been organized in the hope of bringing in a little money. I had paid sixpence and watched with sympathy, and I was soon engrossed by the difficulties surrounding the black queen. She had never liked being moved out so early, she had a haggard, offended look, as a matron compelled to join in a party too soon, and was fain to rest on the hem of her mighty crinoline. By the eighth move, pawns were closing her in. I suspected collusion, and withdrew. The cathedral outside was dark and silent, and great blocks of buildings extended in various directions to the edges of the plateau, which were diversified by various towers. While I hesitated in which direction to go, there was a sound of cymbals and drums from the interior of the castle. The queen had fallen.

VI. Love New and Remembered

The erotic symbolism that can be seen in chess if one wishes to see it, combined with the game's inherent combativeness, makes it particularly useful to a writer wanting to show that courtship is, in part, a struggle for dominance. Many a fictional chess game has been contested by a man and a woman who are still working out the ground rules of their relationship.

Anne Brontë, the younger sister of Charlotte and Emily, died before reaching the age of thirty (1820–49), having written many poems and two novels. Her last novel, *The Tenant of Wildfell Hall* (1848), is the story of Helen Huntingdon and her alcoholic, philandering husband, to whom she is impossibly, maddeningly loyal. Mr. Hargrave, a family friend, believing that the long-suffering Mrs. Huntingdon has been suffering long enough, challenges her to a game of chess hoping to win more than her king.

Anne Brontë

The Tenant of Wildfell Hall

Mr. Hargrave entered the drawing-room a little before the others, and challenged me to a game of chess. He did it without any of that sad but proud humility he usually assumes in addressing me, unless he is excited with wine. I looked at his face to see if that was the case now. His eyes met mine keenly but steadily: there was something about him I did not understand, but he seemed sober enough. Not choosing to engage with him, I referred him to Milicent.

"She plays badly," said he; "I want to match my skill with yours. Come now!—you can't pretend you are reluctant to lay down your work—I know you never take it up except to pass an idle hour, when there is nothing better you can do."

"But chess-players are so unsociable," I objected; "they are no company for any but themselves."

"There is no one here but Milicent, and she—"

"Oh, I shall be delighted to watch you!" cried our mutual friend. "Two such players—it will be quite a treat! I wonder which will conquer."

I consented.

"Now, Mrs. Huntingdon," said Hargrave, as he arranged the men on the board, speaking distinctly, and with a peculiar emphasis, as if he had a double meaning to all his words, "you are a good player—but I am a better: we shall have a long game and you will give me some trouble; but I can be as patient as you, and, in the end, I shall certainly win." He fixed his eyes upon me with a glance I did not like—keen, crafty, bold, and almost impudent; already half triumphant in his anticipated success.

"I hope not, Mr. Hargrave!" returned I, with vehemence that must have startled Milicent at least; but he only smiled and murmured—

"Time will show!"

We set to work: he, sufficiently interested in the game, but calm and fearless in the consciousness of superior skill; I, intensely eager to disappoint his expectations, for I considered this the type of a more serious contest—as I imagined he did—and I felt an almost superstitious dread of being beaten: at all events, I could ill endure that present success should add one tittle to his conscious power (his insolent self-confidence, I ought to say), or encourage for a moment his dream of future conquest. His play was cautious and deep, but I struggled hard against him. For some time the combat was doubtful; at length, to my joy, the victory seemed inclining to my side: I had taken several of his best pieces, and manifestly baffled his projects. He put his hand to his brow and paused, in evident perplexity. I rejoiced in my advantage, but dared not glory in it yet. At length he lifted his head, and quietly making his move, looked at me and said, calmly—

"Now, you think you will win, don't you?"

"I hope so," replied I, taking his pawn that he had pushed into the way of my bishop with so careless an air that I thought it was an oversight, but was not generous enough, under the circumstances, to direct his attention to it, and too heedless, at the moment, to foresee the after consequences of my move.

"It is those bishops that trouble me," said he; "but the bold knight can overleap the reverend gentleman," taking my last bishop with his knight; "and now, those sacred persons once removed, I shall carry all before me."

"Oh, Walter, how you talk!" cried Milicent; "she has far more pieces than you still."

"I intend to give you some trouble yet," said I; "and perhaps, sir, you will find yourself checkmated before you are aware. Look to your queen."

The combat deepened. The game was a long one, and I did give him some trouble; but he was a better player than I.

"What keen gamesters you are!" said Mr. Hattersley, who had now entered, and been watching us for some time. "Why, Mrs. Huntingdon, your hand trembles as if you had staked your all upon it! and Walter—you dog—you look as deep and cool as if you were certain of success, and as keen and cruel as if you would drain her heart's blood! But if I were you, I wouldn't beat her for very fear: she'll hate you if you do—she will, by Heaven! I see it in her eye."

"Hold your tongue, will you?" said I—his talk distracted me, for I was driven to extremities. A few more moves, and I was inextricably entangled in the snare of my antagonist.

"Check," cried he: I sought in agony some means of escape— "mate!" he added quietly, but with evident delight. He had suspended the utterance of that last fatal syllable the better to enjoy my dismay. I was foolishly disconcerted by the event. Hattersley laughed; Milicent was troubled to see me so disturbed. Hargrave placed his hand on mine that rested on the table, and squeezing it with a firm but gentle pressure, murmured, "Beaten—beaten!" but gazed into my face with a look where exultation was blended with an expression of ardour and tenderness yet more insulting.

"No, never, Mr. Hargrave!" exclaimed I, quickly withdrawing my hand.

"Do you deny?" replied he, smilingly pointing to the board.

"No, no," I answered, recollecting how strange my conduct must appear; "you have beaten me in that game."

"Will you try another, then?"

"No."

"You acknowledge my superiority?"

"Yes—as a chess-player."

I rose to resume my work.

Thomas Hardy

A Pair of Blue Eyes

Thomas Hardy's 1878 novel, A Pair of Blue Eyes, *is a romantic tragedy that contains two parallel chess episodes. In the first, early in the story, blue-eyed Elfride Swancourt plays chess with her young suitor, Stephen Smith, and beats him easily.*

Stephen Smith revisited Endelstow Rectory, agreeably to his promise. He had a genuine artistic reason for coming, though no such reason seemed to be required. Six-and-thirty old seat-ends, of exquisite fifteenth-century workmanship, were rapidly decaying in an aisle of the church; and it became politic to make drawings of their worm-eaten contours ere they were battered past recognition in the turmoil of the so-called restoration.

He entered the house at sunset, and the world was pleasant again to the two fair-haired ones. A momentary pang of disappointment had, nevertheless, passed through Elfride when she casually discovered that he had not come that minute post-haste from London, but had reached the neighbourhood the previous evening. Surprise would have accompanied the feeling had she not remembered that several tourists were haunting the coast at this season, and that Stephen might have chosen to do likewise.

They did little besides chat that evening, Mr. Swancourt begin-

248

ning to question his visitor, closely yet paternally, and in good part, on his hopes and prospects from the profession he had embraced. Stephen gave vague answers. The next day it rained. In the evening, when twenty-four hours of Elfride had completely re-kindled her admirer's ardour, a game of chess was proposed between them.

The game had its value in helping on the developments of their future.

Elfride soon perceived that her opponent was but a learner. She next noticed that he had a very odd way of handling the pieces when castling or taking a man. Antecedently she would have supposed that the same performance must be gone through by all players in the same manner; she was taught by his differing action that all ordinary players, who learn the game by sight, unconsciously touch the men in a stereotyped way. This impression of indescribable oddness in Stephen's touch culminated in speech when she saw him, at the taking of one of her bishops, push it aside with the taking man instead of lifting it as a preliminary to the move.

"How strangely you handle the men, Mr. Smith!"

"Do I? I am sorry for that."

"O no—don't be sorry; it is not a matter great enough for sorrow. But who taught you to play?"

"Nobody, Miss Swancourt," he said. "I learnt from a book lent me by my friend Mr. Knight, the noblest man in the world."

"But you have seen people play?"

"I have never seen the playing of a single game. This is the first time I ever had the opportunity of playing with a living opponent. I have worked out many games from books, and studied the reasons of the different moves, but that is all."

This was a full explanation of his mannerism; but the fact that a man with the desire for chess should have grown up without being able to see or engage in a game astonished her not a little. She pondered on the circumstance for some time, looking into vacancy and hindering the play. . . .

The game proceeded. Elfride played by rote; Stephen by thought. It was the cruellest thing to checkmate him after so much labour, she considered. What was she dishonest enough to do in her compassion? To let him checkmate her. A second game followed; and being herself absolutely indifferent as to the result (her playing was above the average among women, and she knew it), she allowed him to give checkmate again. A final game, in which she adopted the

Muzio gambit as her opening, was terminated by Elfride's victory at the twelfth move.

Stephen looked up suspiciously. His heart was throbbing even more excitedly than was hers, which itself had quickened when she seriously set to work on this last occasion. Mr. Swancourt had left the room.

"You have been trifling with me till now!" he exclaimed, his face flushing. "You did not play your best in the first two games?"

Elfride's guilt showed in her face. Stephen became the picture of vexation and sadness, which, relishable for a moment, caused her the next instant to regret the mistake she had made.

"Mr. Smith, forgive me!" she said sweetly. "I see now, though I did not at first, that what I have done seems like contempt for your skill. But, indeed, I did not mean it in that sense. I could not, upon my conscience, win a victory in those first and second games over one who fought at such a disadvantage and so manfully."

He drew a long breath, and murmured bitterly, "Ah, you are cleverer than I. You can do everything—I can do nothing! O Miss Swancourt!" he burst out wildly, his heart swelling in his throat, "I must tell you how I love you! All these months of my absence I have worshipped you."

He leapt from his seat like the impulsive lad that he was, slid round to her side, and almost before she suspected it his arm was round her waist, and the two sets of curls intermingled. . . .

[*Stephen's ardor has the desired effect, and he and Elfride run off to be married. When she has second thoughts, Stephen goes to India to find his fortune, which he hopes will make him more suitable. While he is gone, Elfride accepts the attentions of Henry Knight, with whom she plays chess as she did with Stephen.*]

In the drawing-room, after having been exclusively engaged with Mr. and Mrs. Swancourt through the intervening hour, Knight again found himself thrown with Elfride. She had been looking over a chess problem in one of the illustrated periodicals.

"You like chess, Miss Swancourt?"

"Yes. It is my favourite scientific game; indeed, excludes every other. Do you play?"

"I have played; though not lately."

"Challenge him, Elfride," said the rector heartily. "She plays very well for a lady, Mr. Knight."

"Shall we play?" asked Elfride tentatively.

"Oh, certainly. I shall be delighted."

The game began. Mr. Swancourt had forgotten a similar performance with Stephen Smith the year before. Elfride had not; but she had begun to take for her maxim the undoubted truth that the necessity of continuing faithful to Stephen, without suspicion, dictated a fickle behaviour almost as imperatively as fickleness itself; a fact, however, which would give a startling advantage to the latter quality should it ever appear.

Knight, by one of those inexcusable oversights which will sometimes afflict the best of players, placed his rook in the arms of one of her pawns. It was her first advantage. She looked triumphant—even ruthless.

"By George! what was I thinking of?" said Knight quietly; and then dismissed all concern at his accident.

"Club laws we'll have, won't we, Mr. Knight?" said Elfride suasively.

"O yes, certainly," said Mr. Knight, a thought, however, just occurring to his mind, that he had two or three times allowed her to replace a man on her religiously assuring him that such a move was an absolute blunder.

She immediately took up the unfortunate rook and the contest proceeded, Elfride having now rather the better of the game. Then he won the exchange, regained his position, and began to press her hard. Elfride grew flurried, and placed her queen on his remaining rook's file.

"There—how stupid! Upon my word, I did not see your rook. Of course nobody but a fool would have put a queen there knowingly!"

She spoke excitedly, half expecting her antagonist to give her back the move.

"Nobody, of course," said Knight serenely, and stretched out his hand towards his royal victim.

"It is not very pleasant to have it taken advantage of, then," she said with some vexation.

"Club laws, I think you said?" returned Knight blandly, and mercilessly appropriating the queen.

She was on the brink of pouting, but was ashamed to show it; tears almost stood in her eyes. She had been trying so hard—so very hard—thinking and thinking till her brain was in a whirl; and it seemed so heartless of him to treat her so, after all.

"I think it is—" she began.

"What?"

"—Unkind to take advantage of a pure mistake I make in that way."

"I lost my rook by even a purer mistake," said the enemy in an inexorable tone, without lifting his eyes.

"Yes, but—" However, as his logic was absolutely unanswerable, she merely registered a protest. "I cannot endure those cold-blooded ways of clubs and professional players, like Staunton and Morphy. Just as if it really mattered whether you have raised your fingers from a man or no!"

Knight smiled as pitilessly as before, and they went on in silence.

"Check-mate," said Knight.

"Another game," said Elfride peremptorily, and looking very warm.

"With all my heart," said Knight.

"Check-mate," said Knight again at the end of forty minutes.

"Another game," she returned resolutely.

"I'll give you the odds of a bishop," Knight said to her kindly.

"No, thank you," Elfride replied in a tone intended for courteous indifference; but, as a fact, very cavalier indeed.

"Check-mate," said her opponent without the least emotion.

O, the difference between Elfride's condition of mind now, and when she purposely made blunders that Stephen Smith might win!

It was bed-time. Her mind as distracted as if it would throb itself out of her head, she went off to her chamber, full of mortification at being beaten time after time when she herself was the aggressor. Having for two or three years enjoyed the reputation throughout the globe of her father's brain—which almost constituted her entire world—of being an excellent player, this fiasco was intolerable; for unfortunately the person most dogged in the belief in a false reputation is always that one, the possessor, who has the best means of knowing that it is not true.

In bed no sleep came to soothe her; that gentle thing being the very middle-of-summer friend in this respect of flying away at the merest troublous cloud. After lying awake till two o'clock an idea seemed to strike her. She softly arose, got a light, and fetched a Chess Praxis from the library. Returning and sitting up in bed she diligently studied the volume till the clock struck five, and her eyelids felt thick and heavy. She then extinguished the light and lay down again.

"You look pale, Elfride," said Mrs. Swancourt the next morning at breakfast. "Isn't she, cousin Harry?"

A young girl who is scarcely ill at all can hardly help becoming so when regarded as such by all eyes turning upon her at the table in obedience to some remark. Everybody looked at Elfride. She certainly was pale.

"Am I pale?" she said with a faint smile. "I did not sleep much. I could not get rid of armies of bishops and knights, try how I would."

"Chess is a bad thing just before bed-time; especially for excitable people like yourself, dear. Don't ever play late again."

"I'll play early instead. Cousin Knight," she said in imitation of Mrs. Swancourt, "will you oblige me in something?"

"Even to half my kingdom."

"Well, it is to play one game more."

"When?"

"Now, instantly; the moment we have breakfasted."

"Nonsense, Elfride," said her father. "Making yourself a slave to the game like that."

"But I want to, papa! Honestly, I am restless at having been so ignominiously overcome. And Mr. Knight doesn't mind. So what harm can there be?"

"Let us play, by all means, if you wish it," said Knight.

So, when breakfast was over, the combatants withdrew to the quiet of the library, and the door was closed. Elfride seemed to have an idea that her conduct was rather ill-regulated and startlingly free from conventional restraint. And worse, she fancied upon Knight's face a slightly amused look at her proceedings.

"You think me foolish, I suppose," she said recklessly; "but I want to do my very best just once, and see whether I can overcome you."

"Certainly: nothing more natural. Though I am afraid it is not the plan adopted by women of the world after a defeat."

"Why, pray?"

"Because they know that as good as overcoming is skill in effacing recollection of being overcome, and turn their attention to that entirely."

"I am wrong again, of course."

"Perhaps your wrong is more pleasing than their right."

"I don't quite know whether you meant that, or whether you are laughing at me," she said, looking doubtingly at him, yet inclining to accept the more flattering interpretation. "I am almost sure you think it vanity in me to think I am a match for you. Well, if you do, I say that vanity is no crime in such a case."

"Well, perhaps not. Though it is hardly a virtue."

"O yes, in battle! Nelson's bravery lay in his vanity."

"Indeed! Then so did his death."

"O no, no! For it is written in the book of the prophet Shakespeare—

> *'Fear and be slain? no worse can come to fight;*
> *And fight and die, is death destroying death.'* "

And down they sat, and the contest began, Elfride having the first move. The game progressed. Elfride's heart beat so violently that she could not sit still. Her dread was lest he should hear it. And he did discover it at last—some flowers upon the table being set throbbing by its pulsations.

"I think we had better give over," said Knight, looking at her gently. "It is too much for you, I know. Let us write down the position, and finish another time."

"No, please not," she implored. "I should not rest if I did not know the result at once. It is your move."

Ten minutes passed.

She started up suddenly. "I know what you are doing!" she cried, an angry colour upon her cheeks, and her eyes indignant. "You were thinking of letting me win to please me!"

"I don't mind owning that I was," Knight responded phlegmatically, and appearing all the more so by contrast with her own turmoil.

"But you must not—I won't have it!"

"Very well."

"No, that will not do; I insist that you promise not to do any such absurd thing. It is insulting me!"

"Very well, madam. I won't do any such absurd thing. You shall not win."

"That is to be proved!" she returned proudly; and the play went on.

Nothing is now heard but the ticking of a quaint old timepiece on the summit of a bookcase. Ten minutes pass; he captures her knight; she takes his knight, and looks a very Rhadamanthus.

More minutes tick away; she takes his pawn and has the advantage, showing her sense of it rather prominently.

Five minutes more: he takes her bishop: she brings things even by taking his knight.

Three minutes: she looks bold, and takes his queen: he looks placid, and takes hers.

Eight or ten minutes pass: he takes a pawn; she utters a little "pooh!" but not the ghost of a pawn can she take in retaliation.

Ten minutes pass: he takes another pawn and says, "Check." She flushes, extricates herself by capturing his bishop, and looks triumphant. He immediately takes her bishop: she looks surprised.

Five minutes longer: she makes a dash and takes his only remaining bishop; he replies by taking her only remaining knight.

Two minutes: he gives check; her mind is now in a painful state of tension, and she shades her face with her hand.

Yet a few minutes more: he takes her rook and checks again. She literally trembles now lest an artful surprise she has in store for him shall be anticipated by the artful surprise he evidently has in store for her.

Five minutes: "Check-mate in two moves!" exclaims Elfride.

"If you can," says Knight.

"O, I have miscalculated; that is cruel!"

"Check-mate," says Knight; and the victory is won.

Elfride arose and turned away without letting him see her face. Once in the hall she ran upstairs and into her room, and flung herself down upon her bed, weeping bitterly.

"Where is Elfride?" said her father at luncheon.

Knight listened anxiously for the answer. He had been hoping to see her again before this time.

"She isn't well, Sir," was the reply.

Mrs. Swancourt rose and left the room, going upstairs to Elfride's apartment.

At the door was Unity, who occupied in the new establishment a position between young lady's maid and middle-housemaid.

"She's sound asleep, ma'am," Unity whispered.

Mrs. Swancourt opened the door. Elfride was lying full-dressed on the bed, her face hot and red, her arms thrown abroad. At intervals of a minute she tossed restlessly from side to side, and indistinctly moaned words used in the game of chess.

Mrs. Swancourt had a turn for doctoring, and felt her pulse. It was twanging like a harp-string, at the rate of nearly a hundred and fifty a minute. Softly moving the sleeping girl to a little less cramped position she went downstairs again.

"She is asleep now," said Mrs. Swancourt. "She does not seem very well. Cousin Knight, what were you thinking of? her tender brain won't bear cudgelling like your great head. You should have strictly forbidden her to play again."

In truth, the essayist's experience of the nature of young women was far less extensive than his abstract knowledge of them led himself and others to believe. He could pack them into sentences like a workman, but practically was nowhere.

"I am indeed sorry," said Knight, feeling even more than he expressed. "But surely, the young lady knows best what is good for her!"

"Bless you, that's just what she doesn't know. She never thinks of such things, does she, Christopher? Her father and I have to command her and keep her in order, as you would a child. She will say things worthy of a French epigrammatist, and act like a robin in a greenhouse. But I think we will send for Doctor Granson—there can be no harm."

A man was straightway dispatched on horseback to Castle Boterel, and the gentleman known as Doctor Granson came in the course of the afternoon. He pronounced her nervous system to be in a decided state of disorder; forwarded some soothing draught, and gave orders that on no account whatever was she to play chess again.

Sinclair Lewis

Cass Timberlane

"I'm mildly insane about it," Sinclair Lewis wrote to a friend of his passion for chess. In the early 1940s, writes Mark Schorer in his biography of Lewis, "chess . . . became a compulsion. He would insist that his friends play with him. . . . Thomas Costain . . . like others, remembers how much Lewis hated to lose."

Despite his consuming passion for the game, there appears to be only one fully developed chess scene in all of Lewis's many works. It occurs in the middle of Cass Timberlane, *when Judge Timberlane tries to explain the game to his recalcitrant young bride.*

He had at last the chance to complete her instruction in chess.

It was an edifying and domestic sight: the large man in a doubtful brown-flannel dressing-gown and red slippers; the girl in quilted pink silk, with her small white woolly slippers; the board and the old ivory pieces which Cass's father had bought in San Francisco; all before the fire in the library, where now a clearer light displayed the blue buckram set of "The World's Most Distinguished Legal Orations, with Sketches of Leaders of the Bench and Bar, Profusely Illustrated."

Jinny took to chess with zeal and lawlessness. She began with an eloquent prejudice against the rooks.

She was a true animist; she believed that all inanimate objects—gloves, flatirons, automobiles, stars, lilies, pork chops—had souls and that all animals had human intelligence; and furthermore she almost one-quarter believed in her own belief.

Brooding over the chessmen, she said that the rooks were smug-looking and flat-headed, with stubbly cropped hair, and she scolded them for loafing in the home rank all through the hottest of the game, and then sneaking out to kidnap some bishop who had been working hard and taking risks, and who looked so slim and neat and friendly.

She developed a surrealist criticism of the chess-rules. Why shouldn't a king be able to castle under check?

"Because it's the rule," said Judge Timberlane.

"Why is it the rule?"

"Because it is!"

"Look, silly," she explained. "The king, bless his poor scared heart—the way he has to skip around, with even these G.I. pawns threatening to bump him off all the time—and so when he's in check, when he's in danger and really *needs* to castle, then you won't let him! Why not?"

"Because it's the—"

"Who ever made the rule?"

"Heavens, I don't know. I suppose some old Persian."

"Persians make rugs. They don't make rules."

"Well, this one did."

"How do you know he was a Persian? How do you know he was old?"

"I don't." She was so spirited a debater, so much more belligerent an advocate than any Hervey Plint or Vincent Osprey, that by now he was half-serious.

"You don't know? Then maybe there isn't any such a rule! Maybe you just dreamed it."

"Well, good Lord, all players keep it—"

"How do you know they do? Did you ever see Capablanca or Reuben Fine refuse to castle just because a king was being bullied by some mean bishop? (And I used to *like* the bishops, silly girl that I was, but now I'm on to them.) Did you?"

"Of course I didn't. I've never seen any master play."

"There! Maybe there isn't any such a rule. Maybe they only have it in Minnesota. We're wonderful in Minnesota about wheat and iron and removing gall-stones, but what right have we got to dictate to the rest of the world about castling?"

"Dear idiot child, you'll be asking next how I know you and I are really married, and who made up the marriage code."

"I do ask it! How do you know we aren't living in sin, according to the Mohammedans?"

"I—"

"Maybe I ought to walk right out of here, and go to living with Abby Tubbs or Jay Laverick or Senator Hudbury, or my sweet Bertie. What's to prevent it?"

"Only me and a shotgun."

"You see? You only believe in violence; you don't believe in the rules of marriage—or of my not castling, either!"

"Just the same, you can't castle."

"Bully!"

"Get on with the game, and don't be so reasonable. A girl that would criticize the corpus of chess-laws would criticize chastity."

"I'm not sure that's so hot, either."

"Get on with the game!"

But the real debate—and he was never quite sure that there was not some reality at the core of her pretended rebellions against Authority—came when he first revealed to her, from among the more appalling secret human motives, that by creeping up to the eighth rank, his pawn had suddenly become a queen, and that she was thus about to be checkmated.

"That's the most ridiculous claim I ever heard in my life! Why? Now don't tell me it's the rule. It can't be. I know that pawn. It's got a tiny nick in its head." (This was true, though Cass had never noticed it.) "It's an unusually stupid, uncooperative pawn. It *never* could be a queen. Impossible! I won't recognize the government!"

"Don't you like rules, Jinny?"

"Well, I like you."

"Let me be didactic, Jin."

"Okay."

"Don't say 'Okay'!"

"Why not?"

"It sounds like a gum-chewer."

"But I am a gum-chewer."

"You are not, and you're not going to be. Look. I don't bully you about many things—I'd like to, but I'm too scared of you. But I want each of us to teach the other something of his attitude: me teach you that there's satisfaction in being a sober grind and mastering even a game, like chess; and you teach me that there's nothing legally wrong about letting go and just having a good time. Can't we?"

They gravely shook hands on it, seeing before them the white highway of pious self-instruction whereon every day in every way they would get not only better but more blithe; assured that he would become a first-class grasshopper and she one of the most social-minded ants in the whole three-foot mountain.

She said, with a slight shade of reverence, "When you lecture me, you sound like a real judge on the bench."

"Does it annoy you?"

"I love it. You know, pal, I'm not too sure I'm going to win this battle of marriage. I get around you by being the gay 'ittle girl—the blasted little gold-digger!—but you're too accurate and dependable for me."

"And sometimes I'm fun, ain't I?"

"Ye-es, sometimes—oh, quite often."

"But you won't lose the battle, Jin. The worthy blacksmith hasn't much chance against Ariel."

"You're balled up in your mythology, Judge. Ariel was not a girl."

"Which you distinctly are, my dear."

There was something in the smile with which she acknowledged this alluring fact which made him blush. Then, like a cat, her head low and a little sidewise, she cautiously stalked a pawn with her queen's bishop, and pounced.

E. R. Bulwer Lytton

The Chess-Board

The rueful poem "The Chess-Board" was composed not by Edward George Lytton Bulwer-Lytton, first Baron Lytton (1803–73), the author of The Last Days of Pompeii *and* Rienzi *(on which Wagner based his early opera of that name), but by his son, Edward Robert Bulwer, first Earl of Lytton (1831–91), a recognized poet who sometimes used the pseudonym Owen Meredith.*

Irene, do you yet remember
Ere we were grown so sadly wise,
Those evenings in the bleak December,
Curtain'd warm from the snowy weather,
When you and I play'd chess together,
  Checkmated by each other's eyes?
  Ah, still I see your soft white hand
Hovering warm o'er Queen and Knight,
  Brave Pawns in valiant battle stand:
The double Castles guard the wings:
The Bishop, bent on distant things,
Moves, sidling, through the fight,
  Our fingers touch; our glances meet,
  And falter; falls your golden hair

Love New and Remembered

◆

Against my cheek; your bosom sweet
Is heaving. Down the field, your Queen
Rides slow her soldiery all between,
   And checks me unaware.
   Ah me! the little battle's done,
Disperst is all its chivalry;
Full many a move, since then, have we
'Mid Life's perplexing chequers made,
And many a game with Fortune play'd,—
   What is it we have won?
   This, this at least—if this alone;—
That never, never, never more,
As in those old still nights of yore,
   (Ere we were grown so sadly wise)
   Can you and I shut out the skies,
Shut out the world, and wintry weather,
And, eyes exchanging warmth with eyes,
Play chess, as then we play'd, together!

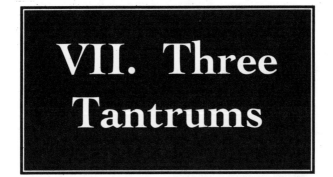

VII. Three Tantrums

Chess is a game of pure skill: There are no dice, no cards, no random events to blame when you lose. But to be forced to acknowledge the superiority of your opponent is, as anyone who has ever had to do it will agree, a mortifying experience, and not everyone can endure it with equanimity.

Tennyson's verse play *Becket* (1884) opens with a chess game between King Henry II and Becket accompanied by some not very subtle double-meaning dialogue. The king will soon make Becket archbishop of Canterbury and later have him executed in the cathedral. The deed will be carried out—the perfect chessplayer's revenge—by four knights.

Alfred, Lord Tennyson

Becket

A Castle in Normandy. Interior of the Hall. Roofs of a City seen thro' Windows.

HENRY and BECKET at chess.

HENRY So then our good Archbishop Theobald
    Lies dying.
BECKET   I am grieved to know as much.
HENRY But we have a mightier man than he
    For his successor.
BECKET   Have you thought of one?
HENRY A cleric lately poisoned his own mother,
    And being brought before the courts of the Church,
    They but degraded him. I hope they whipped him.
    I would have hanged him.
BECKET   It is your move.
HENRY Well—there.   [*Moves.*
    The Church in the pell-mell of Stephen's time
    Hath climbed the throne and almost clutched the crown;
    But by the royal customs of our realm

The Church should hold her baronies of me,
Like other lords amenable to law.
I'll have them written down and made the law.
BECKET My liege, I move my Bishop.
HENRY   And if I live,
No man without my leave shall excommunicate
My tenants or my household.
BECKET   Look to your King.
HENRY No man without my leave shall cross the seas
To set the Pope against me—I pray your pardon.
BECKET Well—will you move?
HENRY   There then!   [*Moves.*
BECKET Why—there then, for you see my Bishop
Hath brought your King to a standstill. You are beaten.
HENRY   [*Kicks over the board.*
Why, there then—down go Bishop and King together.
I loathe being beaten; had I fixed my fancy
Upon the game I would have beaten thee.

Claud Cockburn

Beat the Devil

Claud Cockburn's 1951 novel Beat the Devil *(published under the pseudonym James Helvick) concerns a group of Englishmen and their wives who, early in the story, are stranded in southern France while they wait for repairs to be made on the ship that will take them to the Congo, where they have various licit and illicit designs on certain uranium mines. One afternoon in the Universe and Madagascar Café, an idle game of chess between Harry Chelm and his wife, Gwendolen, ends abruptly in her noisy display of temper, which brings Gwendolen to the attention of Billy Dannreuther, a fellow traveler with whom she will soon begin an affair.*

In John Huston's 1954 film based on the novel, Gwendolen was played by Jennifer Jones and Billy by Humphrey Bogart.

Incidentally, Alexander Cockburn, the author of Idle Passion: Chess and the Dance of Death, *the "hilariously reductionist interpretation of chess" so neatly skewered by Charles Krauthammer in "The Romance of Chess" earlier in this volume, is Claud Cockburn's son.*

"Chess, eh?" said Mr. Wagwood. He looked them up and down as though considering whether this did or did not constitute a valid ground for an application for leave.

"Chess," he repeated, and Gwendolen said, "Yes, chess, Mr. Wagwood," and Conquest said, "Bit highbrow of you, isn't it, Mrs. Chelm?"

But she waved them good-bye, and a step or two ahead of Harry walked through the windy sunshine towards the glitter of glasses and colored drinks under the tossing awning of the big café, whose interior opened out into a large, shadowy room, baroque in decoration, criss-crossed with shafts of dusty sunlight and noisy with the click of snooker balls.

"Do you," Chelm said, "really want to play chess, or were you just escaping from that fellow?"

"I really want to play. It's a long time since we did."

They sat down at one of several similar tables consisting of a single three-footed leg of wrought iron, supporting a heavy marble slab inlaid with the colored squares of a chessboard.

Chelm still wore a gloomy look, possibly a hangover from the spitting business, or caused by annoyance at the contact with Mr. Wagwood. Mrs. Chelm was again helpful. She said, "Don't look now, but that tigress woman is simply lusting after you."

"No need to shout."

"As we came in, I heard her say, 'That really is the best-looking man I've seen in years.' "

Chelm looked down the room out of the corner of his eye. There was Mrs. Dannreuther, looking magnificent.

He said, "But who was she talking to? She's alone as far as I can see."

"He's there too, somewhere. Her husband. With that secretary man."

Chelm held out his closed hands to her, with a white pawn in one and a black pawn in the other.

"Which hand?"

"Right."

"You're white, then."

"Good. I bet she'd exhaust you. She'd seize you and knock you about. It would be like having a thing with a mettlesome horse."

"I suppose you know you're talking practically at the top of your voice?"

"They can't hear. There. Your move."

"Sorry. Didn't notice you'd played."

His attention came back from a further squint in the direction of Mrs. Dannreuther and he looked at the board complacently.

"She," said Gwendolen, "will be in her element in Africa. She'll drive chains of slaves about with whips."

"Slavery has been abolished."

"Well anyway. And please don't interrupt me when I'm thinking."

"If you want to develop that King's Knight's opening properly, there's only one right move you can make at this point."

"We shall see about that."

She bent over the board, her eyes glowing. She made a move, by no means out of the book.

"There," she said.

"Well. If you think so. I shall get that pawn."

"Just you wait. That may be part of my plan. I suppose you think I don't have a plan."

In the distant background Mrs. Dannreuther uncrossed her legs and stood up.

"I'm tired," she said. "I'm going over to the hotel. Don't drink too much coffee, Billy. Jack, watch Billy doesn't drink too much coffee. It's bad for his blood pressure."

Major Jack Ross achieved a tiny movement of his malarial face, giving the effect of this being the maximum that could be expected of a man sunk to the ears in a quagmire of tedium and indifference.

Mrs. Dannreuther stretched slightly, looked down the room towards the Chelms' table, and went out. Dannreuther made a perfunctory gesture of farewell with one powerful hand, which he then dropped again upon the table and left lying there, as motionless as the Major, the two of them sitting in fossilized silence amid the noise of Brahms' Hungarian dances which the orchestra of the Universe and Madagascar had now got around to.

Mr. Dannreuther's enormous head of sun-bleached hair stood out in the half dark of the café's interior as though it had been floodlit.

A waiter came near them with a pot of coffee and got ready to refill their glasses. Before anything more could happen, the Major moved to the extent of waggling one finger forbiddingly to and fro, and the waiter went away again without offering anything to Dannreuther, who might really have been asleep and awakened only by the crash when Mrs. Chelm, her design for victory on the chessboard thwarted at every point, convulsively gripped the edge of the table top, tipped it on its iron pedestal, and let it go crack on the tessellated floor, where the pieces rolled rattling.

On Dannreuther's florid, heavy Hanoverian face was an expression so intense that it seemed actually felt by Major Ross, apparently causing him to switch his attention over from the Chelm situation to Dannreuther, whom he fixed with a look as malignant as an oath. Insensitive to this, Dannreuther, with a blue blaze in his eyes, watched Mrs. Chelm. Oddly illuminated by a sunbeam, she was leaning forward past the now naked table leg, denouncing Mr. Chelm, her curved body quivering with passion, her throat panting, her face abandoned.

Major Ross gave a sharp preliminary snarl, which failed, however, to engage Dannreuther's notice.

"Be your age, Billy," said the Major, in his cracked, burned-out voice.

Dannreuther simply licked his lips.

"Seen a woman before, haven't you?" said the Major.

Mrs. Chelm seemed to reach a peak point in her furious transport, stopped speaking, shivered slightly and relaxed. Dannreuther relaxed too. Mr. Chelm was making deprecatory gestures and mouthing.

"Leave it alone," advised Major Ross.

"My God," said Dannreuther, looking at him for the first time, "did you see that?"

"Just because," said the Major, in his tone of bitter exhaustion, "some bitch . . . wrought up . . . chess game . . . no reason you to behave . . . dog. Rut."

"Wonderful," said Dannreuther. "She was absolutely shaking."

"Forget it," said the Major.

"What's her name?" said Dannreuther. "I never noticed her before. Only noticed that damn great Greek god she goes about with."

"Husband. Name of Chelm. Snap out of it."

"Absolutely blazing," said Dannreuther.

"Watch yourself," said the Major, speaking now in the tone of an order, and menacing at that.

This time Dannreuther condescended to take notice of the Major's remarks.

"Look here," he said violently, "don't you try any schoolmaster tricks on me. I know what I'm up to."

"Trouble is," the Major said, "you don't. You get struck. You're not normal. First few days you get after a new woman you're no good for anything."

"I'll do what I damn well choose, *Major*," said Dannreuther, with a heavy sneer.

"This is no time for it," said Major Ross. "Big job on hand."

"Thanks for the kind advice." Dannreuther resumed contemplation of Mrs. Chelm, who was watching Chelm apologize angrily to the waiter about the table.

Spencer Holst

Spencer Holst is a modern-day fabulist who writes tiny tales for adults in the guise of children's stories. "Chess" is from his collection The Language of Cats and Other Stories.

Once upon a time there was a demonstration of Russian courtesy.

There is a fair-sized city in Russia, the center of a great gray barren region.

In this town there is a chess club and anyone in the whole area at all seriously interested in chess belongs to this club.

For a number of years there had been two old men who were head and shoulders above all the rest of the club members. They weren't masters, but in this area they were the chief players, and for years the club members had been attempting to decide which of them was the better; each year there was a contest, and each year these two tied: First one would win, then the other, and then they would draw, or stalemate; the club was divided, half the members thought one was superior, half the other.

The club members wanted to have one champion.

So they decided this year to hold a different sort of contest: They decided to bring in an inferior player, an utterly unknown person from outside the area, and each of the candidates would play him a game, and they simply assumed each of the candidates would win against the mediocre player so there was no question of winning or losing; but rather they decided to vote afterward, after studying and discussing each of the candidates' games, and award the championship to him who played with better style.

The tournament evening arrived, and the first candidate played with the inferior player—until the inferior player finally shrugged his shoulders and said, "I concede. You obviously win." Whereupon the first candidate leaned over and turned the chessboard around, himself taking the position the inferior player had given up, and said, "Continue." They played longer until finally the inferior player was checkmated.

Then the second candidate played the inferior player until finally the outsider threw up his hands and said, "I concede." And the second candidate, exactly as the first candidate had done, turned the board around, and said, "Continue."

They played for a while until the harassed inferior player, looking blank, leaned back and shrugged his shoulders and said, "I don't know what to do. I don't know where to move. What should I do?"

The second candidate twisted his head around to get more of his opponent's view of the board, and then said tentatively, "Well, why don't you move *that* piece *there*." The outsider stared at the board uncomprehendingly, and finally shrugged his shoulders as if to say, "Well, it can't do any harm, and after all, what does it matter, as I know I'm going to lose anyway." With that gesture he moved the piece *there*.

The master frowned and pondered the board for several minutes before moving.

His frown deepened.

The corners of his mouth turned down.

His eyes hardened, he turned a sullen, stony, defiant stare at his audience for a moment before whispering in a choked voice all could hear, "I concede!"

He leaped up from his chair, raised his gold-headed cane quickly into the air, smashed it down onto the ebony and ivory chessboard, and split it in half.

He rushed from the room muttering loudly a long, strong string of profanities that were marvelous to hear.

He was, of course, awarded the club championship, and had, I think, incidentally demonstrated the proper way to lose a game.

VIII. Moved to Murder

His tantrum spent, the defeated player now coolly plots a more realistic revenge. What form will it take? Study a new opening, perhaps, practice the endgame, somehow win the next game. . . . But murder? Only in fiction.

In Theodore Mathieson's story "The Chess Partner," Martin Chronister, unable to bear the humiliation of losing continually to a rival who also seems about to win the heart of the woman Chronister loves, plans his lethal strategy. But he overlooks one or two unexpected moves.

Theodore Mathieson

The Chess Partner

Sweating with apprehension, for he was gun-shy, Martin Chronister cocked the trigger of the Colt .38 and sighted down the barrel for the last time.

The gun, held between the jaws of a vise clamped to the top of a bookcase in his bedroom, was aimed—through a small hole he had cut through the plywood wall—at a chair drawn up to a chess table in the adjacent living room.

After examining, without touching, the dark twine that was tied to the trigger and which passed through a staple to the floor, Chronister followed the line through the door and into the living room, making sure it lay free along the wainscoting, to where it ended at his own chair at the chess table, opposite the first chair.

For a moment he thought he heard Banning's car, but decided that it was the evening wind beginning to sough among the pines. He added a log to the fire, then turned to look at the painting of his deceased father in the heavy, gilt frame, beneath which the lethal hole in the wall was concealed in shadow.

"I'm using your old Army gun, too." Chronister smiled up at the portrait which he'd lugged down from the attic that afternoon. In the gloomy oils, the medals on the uniform of the disabled old soldier shone dully, like golden poppies through the smoke of battle, and the grim lips seemed to be forming a question.

Why pull a string to do it?

Sure, the Old Man knew what it was to kill an enemy, and might even understand doing it across a chessboard instead of on a battle-field, but he'd always had contempt for his son's fear of guns.

"It isn't just gun-shyness, Martin," he'd said once. "You shrink from every bit of reality and involvement in life!"

No matter. Chronister knew that if he faced Banning with a live gun, he'd botch the job. Doing it his way made the act less personal and more—mechanical.

A crunch of footsteps on the path outside the cabin alerted Chronister to the fact that, having missed the sound of Banning's motor, the zero hour was almost upon him. Flinging open the front door, he greeted his enemy with a false smile of friendship . . .

If Banning were actually to die that night, it was because he'd made three mistakes, one of which he couldn't help.

First, he'd barged into Chronister's relationship with Mary Rob-bins. Not that the relationship was much to speak of at the beginning. For two years Chronister had met Mary at the store in town every week when he went to buy his groceries, but the contact had become a cherished event. Always a loner—he had worked for years as a bookkeeper in small-town businesses before he'd retired, unmarried, at forty-nine—Chronister had always been afraid of women. But Mary was different.

She, too, lived in the woods, tending an invalid father, in a house at the foot of Chronister's hill, but he'd always been too shy to pay them a visit. Although she might be, as the storekeeper said, rather long in the tooth, she had a gentle voice and nice hands and eyes, and above all she seemed maternal, which perhaps was her greatest at-traction for him.

Then came the Saturday when he'd met Mary in the canned goods section, and they'd struck up a conversation that seemed even livelier than usual, over the quality of different brands of tuna fish. Suddenly Banning happened along, looking remarkably distinguished in his tan raincoat, with his prematurely graying hair.

"I couldn't help overhearing," he'd said in his knowing way. "Fresh *anything* is better than canned, unless you're afraid that build-ing up your red corpuscles will make you wayward."

Mary had looked uncomfortable, and murmuring something about finding it difficult to buy fresh fish in a mountain community, moved away. Chronister was outraged, but he waited until they were outside the store and he had put his groceries in his pickup before he spoke.

"When I'm talking with my friends, I'd appreciate your waiting until you're introduced before you volunteer your opinions."

"I hate to hear phony talk, that's all," Banning said. "She isn't really interested in tuna fish, Martin. What she really wants is a man in bed with her. You'll never make the grade with that kind of talk!"

Chronister felt a sudden rush of blood to his head. "What gives you the right to interfere in my business?" he shouted. "Just because you come out once a week and play chess with me doesn't make you my adviser. And your winning lately doesn't make you my mental superior!"

"You must feel it does, or you wouldn't mention it," Banning said.

Chronister nearly struck out at him then. Until a few months ago, Banning and he had been pretty evenly matched upon the board. Then his chess partner had started winning relentlessly, which seemed to Chronister to give his partner a psychological ascendency over him. No matter how hard Chronister worked to improve his game, he had continued to lose, and Banning seemed to grow more sure of his domination.

After what had happened in the store, Chronister was beside himself. "Well, Miss Robbins and I are not chessmen," he said, "so keep your damned fingers off us!"

"Sure," Banning said.

He walked away abruptly, crossing the highway to the hotel where he lived alone on a modest disability pension.

"I always wanted to be an intellectual bum," he'd told Chronister once, "and the Army helped me do it."

Banning had lost his left arm in Korea . . .

For the next two weeks Chronister lived without having a single visitor at his cabin. Twice he saw Mary at the store and the last time she asked him to come to visit her and her father.

Chronister kept putting off the visit, largely out of a lifetime habit of avoiding entanglements, but Mary was often in his thoughts.

Meanwhile he worked hard at his chess books, playing games

against the masters. He had a hunch that Banning would be back, and sure enough, one Friday around the end of April his chess partner appeared, full of conciliatory smiles.

"No use holding a grudge, I figure," Banning said. "Besides, I miss our games."

"So do I," Chronister agreed. "I've been boning up on the books, and I think I can take you now."

"Let's find out."

The struggle this time was more even, and up to the end game Chronister felt he had a fair chance of winning. But in the final moves, Banning brought his hopes down crashing, and then checkmated him.

Once again came Banning's smile of superiority, his almost physical levitation—which was Banning's second mistake.

"By the way," he said from his height, "I paid a couple of visits to Mary and the old man. You're quite right in giving her the eye. In a housecoat she's not bad at all. Although her pa is a dreary lump. Every time he looks at my arm, he fights the Battle of the Marne all over again!"

If Chronister had had his gun handy, he might have used it personally then. Instead, he played another game and lost, and invited Banning back the following week.

The very next day he dressed up and went down to visit Mary and her father.

"I wondered why you hadn't been down before," Mary said, standing beside the wheelchair in which sat a withered old man with sly eyes. For some reason, she seemed more amiable here than at the store, and Chronister remembered what Banning had said about the housecoat. Now she was wearing a kind of muu-muu which concealed all but her head and hands.

Aware of his scrutiny, she colored and excused herself, and the old man began talking about the First World War.

"If I hadn't got shrapnel in my spine," he whined, "I'd have taken up the Army as a profession. You been in the service yet, sonny?"

Chronister winced. "No, sir. My father was a colonel in the First World War, and he wanted me to go into the Army, too, but I guess I wasn't cut out for it."

"Good life for a red-blooded man!"

"My father thought so, too."

Mary returned shortly wearing jeans and a tight-fitting sweater, and Chronister saw what Banning had meant.

"My chess partner said he enjoyed a visit with you," Chronister said, following the line of least resistance.

"Oh, Mr. Banning, yes. He's quite delightful."

Chronister felt a stab of jealousy. "I guess he talks a little more easily than I do," he admitted. "Social situations have always been pretty hard going for me."

"It mustn't be that you're antisocial; you just don't like crowds. Well, neither do we. That's why Papa and I live in the woods. I see your light up there sometimes."

"And I see yours."

It went like that for perhaps an hour. Mary served tea and some cookies she'd made, and he departed, not sure what kind of impression he'd created. But he knew that Mary attracted him, and that he felt the need of her, because when he returned to his cabin that night he was aware for the first time of its emptiness.

Through the rest of the week he continued playing over the master games, but no matter how hard he tried to concentrate, thoughts of Mary interfered. Finally, on a Thursday, in the middle of a game, he threw the chess book aside in disgust, put on his hiking boots, and went walking in the sunny woods.

As he sat resting under a yellow pine, he heard voices, a man's and a woman's, which presently he recognized as Banning's—and Mary's.

He wanted to run, but he felt paralyzed, and as he sat they came close enough for him to hear what they were saying.

". . . spring is the time for a walk," Banning was saying. "I don't get out half enough."

"Nor do I," Mary replied. "It's so lovely."

The two had stopped a few yards off, and Chronister prayed that the chaparral concealed him sufficiently.

"Look," Mary said, "you can see a roof from here. It must be Mr. Chronister's."

"Does he ever take you for a walk?"

"Mr. Chronister? Oh, never. He's been to see me only once in two years! Besides, I don't get out much."

"You should. Your father can do a little for himself, can't he?"

"Not much, and he's getting worse every day, so I like to be around when he calls."

"If you ever need help, Mary—I mean, with your father . . ."

"Thank you."

A silence followed, and Chronister, straining his ears, thought he heard them kiss. Then there was a sudden movement and quick footsteps sounded down the leafy trail.

"Mary!" Banning called, and then he, too, was gone.

Chronister continued to sit, his fear giving way to anger, then to rage. Finally he rose and pounded through the brush, not caring whether he was seen or heard, and by the time he reached his cabin his mind was made up. Mary was going to be his. He was going to kill Banning—tomorrow night . . .

The zero hour had come.

Banning, sure of himself tonight as ever, sat down in his usual chair, took out his tobacco pouch and loaded his pipe.

"Been doing some changing around, eh?" he asked, looking up to where Chronister had hung his father's portrait to hide the hole in the wall.

"I like a change every once in a while," Chronister said. He sat down opposite Banning, casually leaned over and picked up the twine, laying the loose end across his lap. Banning was staring at the picture.

"Would that be your father? He was an Army man, wasn't he?"

"Yes."

"You know, he looked familiar. I see he lost his left arm, too."

"In the Argonne. He led his own battalion."

"Must have been quite a man." Banning's eyes seemed to hold a taunt. "Well, it's your turn, Martin, I think with the white."

Chronister played pawn to King's fourth, and as the opening game developed in a conventional pattern, his hands upon the twine began to sweat.

In fifteen minutes, however, the game took an unexpected turn, and Chronister concentrated on the problems so avidly that he forgot the string, the gun, even his intent to murder. At the back of his mind he knew he was playing superbly well, with a freedom and dash that he had never before achieved. His moves seemed to flow, to dovetail, shaping themselves into a pattern that was a sheer work of art. Time and again he heard exasperated sighs from his chess companion that ignited his ingenuity further until finally, in the end game, he played simple cat and mouse, certain of victory.

"I concede the game," Banning said at last, leaning back in his chair. Chronister, looking up like one coming out of a dream, was surprised to see a new Banning, one divested of pride, humble and human.

In the objectivity of the moment he saw, too, that Banning had never deliberately meant to make him feel inferior. The guy had just been elated by winning a *game*.

"You played better tonight than I ever could," Banning said, smiling warmly. "But I guess it's just your lucky night." He put his hand into his coat pocket and pulled out a folded piece of paper. "I met Mary in town this morning, and she gave me this to give to you. I won't say I didn't read it, so I happen to know she prefers you to me."

Chronister took the note in a daze, letting the twine fall lightly to the floor.

DEAR MR. CHRONISTER:

Papa had a bad spell last evening, and since we are without a telephone, and you are the closest person to me, I wonder if you'd mind my coming up to see you if I have need of your help?

I'd rather call on you than anyone.

MARY

When Chronister looked up, Banning was staring at the portrait again.

"Now I know who your father looks like," he said. "He looks like *me*—even if his arm weren't missing!"

Chronister's mouth felt dry as he rose. "Let's go into the kitchen and have a beer," he said through stiff lips. He took a step forward then, and felt the tug upon his hiking boot where the twine had caught in a lace hook. Before he knew what happened, the explosion filled the room, making the lamps wink in their sockets.

The echoes seemed a long time drying away, and the blood upon the floor grew into a pool beside the dead man.

There came a timid tapping at the cabin door.

Knowing at last the meaning of utter involvement, Martin Chronister went to answer it.

Henry Slesar

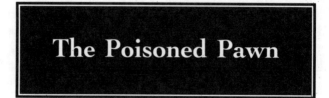

The Poisoned Pawn

Even if you know nothing about chess, you can play against two world champions at the same time and be certain of ending up with an even score—either a draw with both opponents or a win and a loss. Here's the trick: Play Black against one and White against the other, and copy the moves from game to game. When Opponent A, as White, plays the first move against you, use that move as White against Opponent B; when Opponent B replies, use that move in reply to Opponent A's first move; and so on. In effect, your two opponents unknowingly play each other while you passively relay the moves between them.

The venerable age and familiarity of this very simple trick would seem to obviate it as a plausible plot device in modern fiction. Yet Henry Slesar makes excellent use of it in this clever story of revenge.

If it weren't for the state of his own health (his stomach felt lined with broken green bottle glass), Milo Bloom would have giggled at the sight of his roommate in the six-bed ward on the third floor of Misericordia Hospital. Both of his arms were in casts, giving them the appearance of two chubby white sausages; the left arm dangled from a pulley in a complex traction arrangement that somehow included his left leg. Later, he learned that his companion (Dietz was his name), had fallen from a loading platform. Milo's hospital admittance record told a far more dramatic story. He had been poisoned.

"And I'll tell you something," Milo said, shaking his head sadly and making the broken glass jiggle, "I learned a lesson from it. I was lying under my own dining table, and my whole life flashed in front of my eyes, and you know what it looked like? One long chess game. I saw myself born on QB4, a white pawn wrapped in a baby blanket, and here I was, dying, caught in a zugzwang and about to be checkmated . . ."

Of course, Milo was still under sedation and wasn't expected to talk coherently. An hour later, however, he was able to express himself more clearly.

"Never again," he said solemnly. "Never, never again will I play another game of chess. I'll never touch another piece, never read another chess column. You say the name 'Bobby Fischer' to me, I'll put my hands over my ears. For thirty years I was a prisoner of that miserable board, but now I'm through. You call that a game? That's an obsession! And look where it got me. Just look!"

What he really meant, of course, was "listen," which is what Dietz, who had no other plans that day, was perfectly willing to do.

My father cared very little about chess. When he proudly displayed me to the membership of the Greenpoint Chess Club, and mockingly promoted a match with Kupperman, its champion, it wasn't for love of the game; just hate for Kupperman. I was eleven years old, Kupperman was forty-five. The thought of my tiny hands strangling Kupperman's King filled him with ecstasy.

I sat opposite Kupperman's bulking body and ignored the heavy-jowled sneer that had terrified other opponents, confident that I was a prodigy, whose ability Kupperman would underestimate. Then zip! wham! thud! the pieces came together in the center of the board. Bang! Kupperman's Queen lashed out in an unorthodox early attack. *Whoosh!* came his black Knights in a double assault that made me whimper. Then *crash!* my defense crumpled and my King was running for his life, only to fall dead ignobly at the feet of a Rook Pawn. Unbelievable. In seventeen moves, most of them textbook defying, Kupperman had crushed me. Guess who didn't get ice cream that night?

Of course, I was humiliated by Kupperman's victory. I had bested every opponent in my peer group, and thought I was ready for prodigy-type encounters. I didn't realize at the time how very good Kupperman was. The fact that he was Number One in a small Brooklyn chess club gave no real measure of the man's talent, his extraordinary, Petrosian-like play.

I learned a great deal more about that talent in the next two decades, because that wasn't the last Bloom-Kupperman match; it was only the first of many.

Kupperman refused to play me again until four years later, when I was not only a ripe fifteen, but had already proved my worth by winning the Junior Championship of Brooklyn. I was bristling with self-confidence then, but when I faced the forty-nine-year-old Kupperman across the table, and once again witnessed the strange, slashing style, the wild romping of his Knights, the long-delayed castling, the baffling retreat of well-developed pieces, surprising *Zwischenzuge*—in-between moves with no apparent purpose—and most disturbing of all, little stabbing moves of his Pawns, pinpricks from both sides of the board, nibbling at my presumably solid center, panic set in and my brain fogged over, to say nothing of my glasses from the steam of my own accelerated breathing. Yes, I lost that game, too; but it wasn't to be my last loss to Kupperman, even though he abruptly decided to leave not only the Greenpoint Chess Club, but the East Coast itself.

I never knew for certain why Kupperman decided to leave. My father theorized that he was an asthma victim who had been advised to bask in the drying sunshine of Arizona or some other western state. Actually, the first postmark I saw from a Kupperman correspondence was a town called Kenton, Illinois. He had sent a letter to the Greenpoint Chess Club, offering to play its current champion by mail. I suppose he was homesick for Brooklyn. Now, guess who was current champion? Milo Bloom.

I was twenty-two then, past the age of prodigy, but smug in my dominance of the neighborhood *potzers*, and pantingly eager to face the Kupperman unorthodoxy again, certain that nobody could break so many rules and still come out on top consistently. I replied to Kupperman at once, special delivery no less, and told him with becoming modesty of my ascension in the club and my gracious willingness to play him by mail.

A week later, I received his reply, a written scowl is what it was, and an opening move—N-KB3! Obviously, Kupperman hadn't changed too much in the intervening seven years.

Well, I might as well get it over with and admit that Kupperman defeated me in that game and, if anything, the defeat was more shattering than the head-to-head encounters of the past. Incredibly, Kupperman posted most of his pieces on the back rank. Then came a Knight sacrifice, a pinned Queen, and a neatly executed check.

Foreseeing the slaughter ahead, I resigned, despite the fact that I was actually ahead by one Pawn.

Obviously, my early resignation didn't fully satisfy Kupperman (I could just visualize him, his unshaven cheeks quivering in a fleshy frown, as he tore open my letter and growled in chagrin at my reply). Almost the next day, I received a letter asking me why I hadn't sent my White opening for the next game.

I finally did: P-Q4. He replied with N-KB3. I moved my own Knight. He responded by moving his Pawn to the Queen's third square. I moved my Knight to the Bishop's third square, and he promptly pinned it with *his* Bishop, contrary to all common sense. Then he proceeded to let me have both Bishops and bring up my Queen. I should have known that I was doomed then and there. He smothered my Bishops, made an aggressive castling move, and needled me with Pawns until my position was hopeless.

A month went by before Kupperman sent me the next opening move (this time, his letter was postmarked Tyler, Kansas) and we were launched into the third game of what was to become a lifetime of humiliating encounters.

Yes, that's correct. *I never won a game from Kupperman.* Yet, despite my continuing chagrin and, one might think, despite Kupperman's boredom, our games-by-mail were played for a period of *nineteen years*. The only real variations were in Kupperman's postmarks; he seemed to change his residence monthly. Otherwise the pattern remained the same: Kupperman's unorthodox, Petrosian-like style invariably bested my solid, self-righteous, textbook game. As you can imagine, beating Kupperman became the primary challenge, then, of my life.

Then he sent me The Letter.

It was the first time Kupperman's correspondence consisted of anything but chess notations. It was postmarked from New Mexico, and the handwriting looked as if it had been scrawled out with a screwdriver dipped in axle grease.

"*Dear Grand Master,*" it said, with heavy irony. "*Please be advised that the present score is ninety-seven games to nothing. Please be advised that upon my hundredth victory, we play no more. Yours respectfully, A. Kupperman.*"

I don't know how to describe the effect of that letter upon me. I couldn't have been more staggered if my family doctor had diagnosed a terminal illness. Yes, I knew full well that the score was 97 to 0, although I hadn't realized that Kupperman kept such scrupulous records; but the humiliation that lay ahead of me, the hundredth defeat, the *final* defeat, was almost too much for me to bear. Suddenly, I knew that if I didn't beat Kupperman at least *once* before that deadline, my life would be lived out in shame and total frustration.

It was no use returning to the textbooks; I had studied thousands of games (*all* of Petrosian's, until I knew each move by rote) without finding the secret of overcoming Kupperman's singular style. If anything, his use of Knights and Pawns was even wilder and more distinctive than Petrosian's. It was no use hoping for a sudden failure of Kupperman's play; not with only three games left. In fact, it was no use believing in miracles of any kind.

I walked about in a daze, unable to decide whether to send Kupperman the opening move of the ninety-eighth game. My employer (the accounting firm of Bernard & Yerkes) began to complain bitterly about frequent errors in my work. The young woman I had been dating for almost two years took personal affront at my attitude and severed our relationship.

Then, one day, the solution to my problem appeared almost magically before my eyes.

Strangely enough, I had seen the very same advertisement in *Chess Review* for almost a dozen years, and it never assumed the significance it did that evening.

The advertisement read: "*Grand Master willing to play for small fee, by mail. Guaranteed credentials. Fee returned in case of draw or mate. Yankovich, Box 87.*"

I had never been tempted to clash with any other player by mail except Kupperman; I had certainly never been willing to lose money in such encounters.

I stared at the small print of the advertisement, and my brain seemed flooded with brilliant light. It was as if a voice, a basso profundo voice, was speaking to me and saying: Why not let someone *else* beat Kupperman?

The simple beauty of the idea thrilled me, and completely obliterated all ethical doubts. Who said chess was a game of ethics, anyway? Chess players are notorious for their killer instincts. Half the sport lay in rattling your opponent. Who can deny the malevolent effects of Fischer's gamesmanship on Boris Spassky? Yes, this would be different; this would be a blatant falsehood. If I gained a victory, it would be a false one; but if I could beat Kupperman, even a phantom victory would do.

That night I addressed a letter to the Grand Master's box number, and within two days received a reply. Yankovich's fee was a mere twenty-five dollars, he wrote. He required the money in advance, but promised to return it after the conclusion of the game, in the event of a draw or a defeat. He wished me luck, and on the assumption that I would be interested, sent me his opening move: P-Q4.

With a feeling of rising excitement, I sent off two letters that day. One to Yankovich, Box 87, and one to A. Kupperman in New Mexico. The letter to Yankovich contained twenty-five dollars, and a brief note explaining that I would send my countermove by return mail. The letter to Kupperman was briefer. It merely said: "*P-Q4.*"

Within two days, I had Kupperman's reply: "*N-KB3.*"

I wasted no time in writing to Yankovich. "*N-KB3,*" my letter said.

Yankovich was equally prompt. "*N-KB3,*" he said.

I wrote Kupperman: "*N-KB3.*"

Kupperman replied: "*P-B4.*"

I wrote Yankovich: "*P-B4.*"

By the sixth move, Yankovich-Bloom's Bishop had captured Kupperman's Knight, and Kupperman's King's Pawn took possession of our Bishop. (I had begun to think of the White forces as *ours.*) True to form, Kupperman *didn't* capture toward the center. This fact seemed to give Yankovich pause, because his next letter arrived two days later than usual. He responded with a Pawn move, as did Kupperman, who then gave up a Pawn. I felt a momentary sense of triumph, which was diminished a dozen moves later when I realized that Kupperman, once again poising his pieces on the *back* rank, was up to his old tricks. I fervently hoped that Grand Master Yankovich wouldn't be as bemused by this tactic as I was.

Unfortunately, he was. It took Kupperman forty moves to beat him into submission, but after battering at Yankovich-Bloom's King side, he suddenly switched his attack to the Queen's, and . . . *we* had to resign.

Believe me, I took no pleasure in the letter Yankovich sent me, congratulating me on my victory and returning my twenty-five dollars.

Nor was there much pleasure in the grudging note that Kupperman penned in his screwdriver style to the bottom of his next missive, which read: "*Good game. P-K4.*"

I decided, however, that the experiment was worth continuing. Perhaps Yankovich had simply been unprepared for so unorthodox a style as Kupperman's. Surely, in the next round he would be much warier. So I returned the twenty-five dollars to Box 87, and sent Yankovich my opening move: "*P-K4.*"

Yankovich took an extra day to respond with P-K3.

I don't know how to describe the rest of the game. Some chess games almost defy description. Their sweep and grandeur can only be compared to symphonies, or epic novels. Yes, that would be more appropriate to describe my ninety-ninth game with Kupperman. (By the fourteenth move, I stopped calling it Yankovich-Bloom, and simply thought of it as "mine.")

The game was full of plots and counterplots, much like the famous Bogoljubow-Alekhine match at Hastings in 1922. As we passed the fortieth move, with neither side boasting a clear advantage, I began to recognize that even if my next-to-last game with Kupperman might not be a victory, it would be no less than a Draw.

Finally, on the fifty-first move, an obviously admiring Yankovich offered the Draw to Kupperman-Bloom. In turn, I offered it to Kupperman, and waited anxiously for his rejection or acceptance.

Kupperman wrote back: "*Draw accepted.*" He added, in a greasy postscript, "*Send opening move to new address—Box 991, General Post Office, Chicago, Ill.*"

My heart was pounding when I addressed my next letter to Yankovich, asking him to retain the twenty-five dollars, and to send me *his* White move for what was to be my final match—with Yankovich, with Kupperman, or with anyone else.

Yankovich replied with a P-K4.

I wrote to Kupperman, and across the top of the page, I inscribed the words: "*Match No. 100—P-K4.*"

Kupperman answered with an identical move, and the Last Battle was joined.

Then a strange thing happened. Despite the fact that I was still the intermediary, the shadow player, the very existence of Yankovich began to recede in my mind. Yes, the letters continued to arrive from Box 87, and it was Yankovich's hand still inscribing the White moves, but now each move seemed to emanate from my own brain, and Yankovich seemed as insubstantial as Thought itself. In the Chess Journal of my mind, this one-hundredth match would be recorded forever as Bloom vs. Kupperman, win, lose, or draw.

If the previous match had been a masterpiece, this one was a monument.

I won't claim it was the greatest chess game ever played, but for its sheer wild inventiveness, its incredible twists and turns, it was unmatched in either my experience or my reading.

If anything, Kupperman was out-Petrosianing Petrosian in the daring mystery of his maneuvers. Like a Petrosian-Spassky game I particularly admired, it was impossible to see a truly decisive series of moves until thirty plays had been made, and suddenly, two glorious armies seemed opposed to each other on the crest of a mountain. With each letter in my mailbox, the rhythm of my heartbeats accelerated, until I began to wonder how I could bear so much suspense—suspense *doubled* by virtue of receiving both sides of the game from the two battling champions, one of whom I had completely identified as myself. Impatiently, I waited to see how *I* was going to respond to Kupperman's late castling, how *I* was going to defend against his romping Knights, how *I* was going to withstand the pinpricks of his Pawns.

Then it happened.

With explosive suddenness, there were four captures of major pieces, and only Pawns and Rooks and Kings remained in action. Then, my King moved against both Kupperman's Rook and Pawn, and Kupperman saw the inevitable.

He resigned.

Yes, you can imagine my sense of joy and triumph and fulfillment. I was so elated that I neglected to send my own resignation to Yankovich; not that he required formal notification. Yankovich, however, was gracious to his defeated foe, not realizing that my defeat was actually victory. He wrote me a letter, congratulating me on the extraordinary game I had played against him, and while he could not return the twenty-five-dollar fee according to the rules of our agreement, he *could* send me a fine bottle of wine to thank me for a most rewarding experience.

The wine was magnificent. It was a Chateau Latour, '59. I drank it all down with a fine dinner-for-one in my apartment, not willing to share this moment with anyone. I recall toasting my invisible chess player across the table, and that was the last thing I recalled. The next thing I saw was the tube of a stomach pump.

No, there wasn't any way I could help the police locate Yankovich. He was as phantomlike as I had been myself. The name was a pseudonym, the box number was abandoned after the wine had been dispatched to me, and the *Review* could provide no clues to the identity of the box holder. The reason for his poisoning attempt was made clear only when Kupperman himself read that I was hospitalized, and wrote me a brief letter of explanation.

Yankovich's real name was Schlagel, Kupperman said. Forty years ago, Schlagel and Kupperman (his name, too, was an alias) had been cell mates in a Siberian prison. They had made five years pass more swiftly by playing more than two thousand games of chess. Schlagel had the advantage when the series ended with Kupperman's release.

Kupperman then took a different kind of advantage. Schlagel had charged him with seeking out the beautiful young wife Schlagel had left behind. Kupperman found her, and gave her Schlagel's best. He also gave her Kupperman's best. Six months later, she and Kupperman headed for the United States.

Like so many romances, the ending was tragicomic. Schlagel's wife developed into a fat shrew who finally died of overweight. No matter; Schlagel still wanted revenge, and came to the States to seek it after his release. He knew Kupperman would have changed his name, of course, but he wouldn't change his chess style.

Consequently, year after year, Schlagel-Yankovich ran his advertisement in the chess journals, hoping to find the player whose method Schlagel would recognize in an instant . . .

"Well, that's what happened," Milo Bloom told his roommate at Misericordia Hospital. "Believe me, if I didn't have a nosy landlady, I would be dead now. Luckily, she called the ambulance in time.

"Sure, it was a terrible thing to happen to anybody. But at least I've learned my lesson. Life wasn't meant to be spent pushing funny-looking pieces around a checkered board. But maybe you've never even tried the game . . ."

The man in traction mumbled something.

"What was that?" Milo asked.

"I play," Dietz said. "I play chess. I've even got a pocket set with me."

Milo, merely curious to see what the set looked like, eased himself out of bed and removed it from the bedside table. It was a nice little one, all leather and ivory.

"It's not a bad way to pass the time," Dietz said cautiously. "I mean, I know you said you'd never play anymore, but—if you wanted to try just *one* game . . ."

Milo looked at his casts, and said, "Even if I wanted to play— how could *you?*"

Dietz smiled shyly, and showed him. He picked up the pieces with his teeth. In the face of a dedication matching his own, how could Milo refuse? He moved the Pawn to P-K4.

Harry Kemelman

End Play

In Harry Kemelman's "End Play," the reconstruction of a chess position is the key to solving the murder of a college professor. Incidentally, there is no such opening as the Logan–Asquith Gambit and no such book as Lowenstein's End Games.

It was Friday, my regular evening for chess with Nicky, a custom begun when I had first joined the Law Faculty at the university and continued even after I had given up teaching to become County Attorney. I had just announced a mate in three more moves to win the rubber game of our usual three-game match.

Nicky's bushy white eyebrows came together as he scrutinized the corner of the board where my attack was focused. Then he nodded briskly in admission of defeat.

"You might have prevented it," I offered, "if you had advanced the pawn."

"I suppose so," he replied, his little blue eyes glittering with amusement, "but it would only have prolonged the game and the position was beginning to bore me."

I was on the point of retorting that he was most apt to be bored by the position when he was losing, when the doorbell rang and I rose to answer it. It seemed as if I was always being interrupted whenever I had a chance to answer Nicky in kind.

My caller proved to be Colonel Edwards of Army Intelligence who was collaborating with me on the investigation of the death of Professor McNulty. Perhaps it would be fairer to say that we were both investigating the same case rather than that we were collaborating, for there had been an ill-concealed rivalry in our association from the beginning, and we had both gone our separate ways, each working on that phase of the problem that seemed to him most likely to bear fruit. True, we had agreed to meet in my office every morning and discuss our progress, but there was no doubt that each of us was as much concerned with being the first to solve the case as to bring it to a successful conclusion. Since I had had a conference with Colonel Edwards that morning and expected to have another the following morning, his appearance now gave me a vague feeling of uneasiness.

He was a young man, little more than thirty, entirely too young in my opinion to sport eagles. He was short and stocky with something like a strut in his walk, not uncommon in men of that build, and not necessarily indicating conceit. He was a decent chap, I suppose, and probably good at his job, but I did not warm to him and had not from the beginning of our association some two days before. In part, this was due to his insistence, when we had first met, that he should have full charge of the investigation inasmuch as Professor McNulty had been engaged in research for the Army; in part, it was due to his insufferable arrogance. Although he was half a head shorter than I, he somehow contrived to look down his pudgy nose at me.

"I saw a light in your study as I was passing," he explained.

I nodded.

"I thought I'd like to go over certain points with you and get the benefit of your experience," he continued.

That was his usual style and it annoyed me because I was never quite sure whether this seeming deference was his idea of politeness or whether it was his downright impudence, said with tongue in cheek. In any case, I did not take it at face value.

I nodded again and led him into the study where Nicky was putting the chessmen back in the box. After I had introduced the two men and we were all seated again, Edwards asked, "Have you uncovered anything important since this morning?"

It flitted across my mind that it was customary for the visiting team to go to bat first, but to have said so would have been to bring our antagonism out into the open.

"Well, we caught Trowbridge," I said. "We found him in Boston and brought him back."

"That was quick work," he said patronizingly, "but I'm afraid you're barking up the wrong tree."

I should have answered that with a shrug of the shoulders, but I felt that I had a strong case, so I said quietly, "He quarreled with McNulty some few hours before he was shot. McNulty had flunked him in his physics course because he had not had his experiments for the semester done in time. He came to see him to explain that he had been handicapped because he had sprained his wrist and so had been unable to write. McNulty was upset and out of sorts that day. Never a very amiable man, he was downright nasty during the interview. I got that from his secretary who was sitting right outside the door of his office and heard most of it. She reported that McNulty had said point-blank that he thought Trowbridge was exaggerating his injury, and even suggested that the young man had managed to get a medical discharge from the Army by the same trick. Parenthetically, I might say, I checked the young man's Army record and found it excellent. He did not get his discharge until after he had been wounded in action twice. Naturally, Trowbridge did not take McNulty's sneer in silence. There was quite a row and the young man was heard by the secretary to say, 'You deserve to be shot.' " I paused impressively.

"Very well," I went on, "we know that Trowbridge took the eight-ten train to Boston. He had to pass McNulty's house on his way to the station and that was no later than eight-five. According to Professor Albrecht, McNulty was shot at a minute or two after eight." I paused again to give added weight to the highly suggestive significance of the time elements. Then I said in quiet triumph, "Under the circumstances, I would say that Trowbridge was a logical suspect." I counted off the points on my fingers. "He quarreled with him and threatened him—that's motive; he had been in the Army and had fought overseas and was likely to have a German Luger as a war trophy—that's weapon; he was near the house at the time—that's opportunity; and finally, he ran off to Boston—that's indication of guilt."

"But you don't shoot a professor because he flunks you in a course," Edwards objected.

"No, you don't ordinarily," I admitted. "But values change.

Trowbridge had fought overseas. I fancy he saw a lot of killing and came to have a much lower opinion of the sanctity of human life. Besides, flunking this course meant dropping out of college. He claims, as a matter of fact, that he came up to Boston to see about the chances of transferring to one of the colleges there. A nervous, sensitive young man could easily convince himself that his whole future had been ruined."

Edwards nodded slowly as if to grant me the point, "You questioned him?" he asked.

"I did. I didn't get a confession, if that's what you're thinking. But I did get something. Knowing that he must have passed McNulty's house around eight-five, I told him that he had been seen there. It was just a shot in the dark, of course, and yet not too improbable. The Albany train pulls in around then and there are always two or three passengers who get off here. Going toward town, they'd be likely to pass him on his way to the station."

Edwards nodded again.

"It worked," I went on. "He got very red and finally admitted that he had stopped opposite McNulty's house. He said that he stood there for a few minutes debating whether to see him again and try to get him to change his mind. And then he heard the Albany train pulling in and knowing that the Boston train left soon after, he hurried off. I'm holding him as a material witness. I'll question him again tomorrow after he has spent a night in jail. Maybe I'll get some more out of him then."

Colonel Edwards shook his head slowly. "I doubt if you'll get any more out of him," he said. "Trowbridge didn't shoot him. McNulty shot himself. It was suicide."

I looked at him in surprise. "But we discarded the idea of suicide at the very beginning," I pointed out. "Why, it was you yourself who—"

"I was mistaken," he said coldly, annoyed that I should have mentioned it.

"But our original objections hold good," I pointed out. "Someone rang the doorbell and McNulty went to answer it. Professor Albrecht testified to that."

"Ah, but he didn't. We *thought* he did. What Albrecht actually said was that McNulty excused himself in the middle of their chess game with some remark about there being someone at the door. Here, let's go over the whole business and you'll see how we made our mistake. Professor Albrecht's story was that he was playing chess with McNulty. I take it that's a common thing with them."

"That's right," I said, "they play every Wednesday night, just as Nicky and I do every Friday evening. They dine together at the University Club and then go on to McNulty's place."

"Well, they didn't this Wednesday," said Edwards. "Albrecht was detained by some work in the lab and went on out to McNulty's house afterwards. In any case, they were playing chess. You recall the arrangement of furniture in McNulty's study? Here, let me show you." He opened the briefcase he had brought with him and drew out a photograph of the study. It showed a book-lined room with an opening in the form of an arch leading to a corridor. The chess table had been set up near the middle of the room, just to the right of the arch. The photograph had evidently been taken from just below the chess table so that it clearly showed the chess game in progress, the captured men, black and white, lying intermixed on one side of the board.

He pointed to a chair that was drawn up to the chess table.

"This is where Albrecht was sitting," Edwards explained, "facing the arch which is the entrance from the corridor. The vestibule and the front door beyond is down the corridor to the left—that is, Albrecht's left from where he was sitting.

"Now, his story was that in the middle of the game McNulty went to answer the door. Albrecht heard what he later decided was a pistol shot, but which at the time he thought was a car backfiring outside. That's reasonable because the evidence shows that the gun was pressed tightly against McNulty's body. That would muffle the sound, like firing into a pillow. In any case, Albrecht waited a couple of minutes and then called out. Receiving no answer, he went out to investigate and found his friend lying on the floor of the vestibule, shot through the heart, the still warm gun in his hand." He addressed himself to me. "Is that the way Albrecht told it? Did I leave out anything?"

I shook my head, wondering what was coming.

He smiled with great satisfaction. "Naturally, on the basis of that story we immediately ruled out suicide. We assumed that the man who rang the doorbell had shot him, and then thinking that McNulty was alone, had put the gun in his hand to make it look like suicide. If the doorbell rang, it had to be murder and could not be suicide. That's logical," he insisted firmly as though still annoyed that I had attributed the discarding of the suicide theory to him. "Even if the man who rang the doorbell had been a total stranger inquiring the way to the railroad station, say, it still could not have been suicide because it would have happened almost before the stranger could shut the door behind him and he would immediately have opened it again to see what the trouble was. It would have meant that McNulty had a loaded gun in his pocket all the time that he was playing chess with Albrecht. It would have meant—"

"All right," I interrupted, "the suicide theory was untenable. What made you change your mind?"

He showed some annoyance at my interruption, but suppressed it immediately. "The doorbell," he said solemnly. "There was something about Albrecht's story that didn't quite click. I took him over it several times. And then it came to me that at no time did he say he had *heard* the doorbell—only that McNulty had excused himself with some remark about someone at the door. When I asked him point-blank if he had heard the bell, he became confused and finally admitted that he hadn't. He tried to explain it by saying that he was absorbed in the game, but it's a loud bell and if it had rung, I was sure he would have heard it. And since he didn't hear it, that meant it hadn't rung." He shrugged his shoulders. "Of course, if there were no third person at the door, the suicide theory had to be considered again."

He broke off suddenly. He blushed a little. "You know," he said in great earnestness, "I haven't been completely frank with you. I'm afraid I misled you into thinking that I came down here solely to investigate McNulty's death. The fact of the matter is that I arrived in the morning and made an appointment by phone to meet him at his home at half-past eight that night. You see, the research project on which McNulty and Albrecht have been working hasn't been going too well. There were strange mishaps occurring all too frequently. Delicate apparatus that would take weeks and months to replace was damaged. Reports had been late coming in and frequently contained errors. Army Ordnance, which was sponsoring the project, asked us to check on the work and I was sent down to make the preliminary investigation.

"Having in mind now the possibility of suicide, I asked Albrecht about sabotage on the project. That broke it. He admitted that he had been suspicious of McNulty for some time and had conducted a little investigation of his own. Though he was certain that McNulty was guilty, he had hesitated to accuse him openly. But he had hinted. All through the game he had hinted that he knew what McNulty had been up to. I gathered that he couched his hints in the terms of the game. I don't play chess, but I imagine that he said something like, 'You will be in great danger if you continue on this line'—that kind of thing. After a while, McNulty got the idea and became very upset. Albrecht said he murmured over and over again, 'What shall I do?' Then Albrecht made a move and said, 'Resign!'—which I understand is the regular chess term for 'give up.' " Edwards spread his hands as though presenting us with the case all nicely gift-wrapped. "It was then that McNulty muttered something about there being someone at the door and got up from the table."

"Albrecht saw him shoot himself?" I demanded.

"All but. He saw McNulty go through the arch. Instead of going to the left to the vestibule, he went to the right, and that's where his bedroom is. I submit that he went to get his gun. Then he came back and walked past the arch to the vestibule."

"Why didn't he wait until after Albrecht left?" I asked.

"I suppose because he knew that I would be along presently."

There was little doubt in my mind that Edwards had arrived at the correct solution. But I hated to admit it. It was no longer a question of beating Edwards to the finish. I was thinking of McNulty now. He was not a friend, but I had played chess with him at the University Club a number of times. I had not cared too much for the man, but I did not like to think of him taking his own life, especially since it implied that he had been guilty of treason. I suppose my uneasiness and my doubts were patent in the very vehemence with which I tried to conceal them. "And that's your case?" I demanded scornfully. "Why, a freshman law student could pick it to pieces! It's as full of holes as a sieve."

He reddened, a little taken aback at the belligerence in my tone. "Such as?" he asked.

"Such as the gun. Have you traced it to him? Such as why did Albrecht lie in the first place? Such as the choice of the vestibule. Why should a man with a house full of rooms choose to shoot himself in the vestibule?"

"Albrecht lied because McNulty was his friend," Edwards replied. "He could no longer affect the research project—why should he make him out a suicide and a traitor if he could avoid it? Besides, I guess he felt a little guilty about McNulty's taking his own life.

Remember? He called on him to resign. I imagine he must have been pretty upset to find that his friend took his advice so thoroughly."

"And the gun?"

Edwards shrugged his shoulders. "You yourself pointed out that the gun was a war trophy. The country is flooded with them and very few of them have been registered. A former student might have given it to him. As a matter of fact, Albrecht admitted that McNulty had mentioned something of the sort some months back. No, the gun didn't bother me. I found the business of the vestibule a lot harder to understand—until I made a thorough check of the house. It appears that since the death of his wife some years ago, McNulty has practically closed up all the upper part of the house and part of the lower. So although there are six rooms in the house, he actually occupies what amounts to a small apartment on the first floor consisting of the study which was formerly the dining room, a bedroom, and the kitchen. He couldn't shoot himself in the study since Albrecht was there and would stop him. The kitchen leads off the study and I suppose he would not want to pass Albrecht if he could help it. That leaves only the bedroom, which I would consider the most likely place were it not for one thing: there's a large portrait of his wife hanging there. It was taken full view so that the eyes seem to follow you no matter from what angle you look at it. It occurred to me that it was that which deterred him. He wouldn't want to shoot himself under the very eyes of his wife, as it were. That's only a guess, of course," he added with something of a smirk which implied that in his opinion it was a pretty good guess.

"It's a theory," I admitted grudgingly, "but it's no more than that. You have no proof."

"As a matter of fact," he said slowly, a malicious little smile playing about the corners of his mouth, "I have proof—absolute proof. We're pretty thorough in the Army and some of us have had quite a bit of experience. You see, I did a paraffin test on McNulty— and it was positive."

I should have known that he had an ace up his sleeve. This time I made no effort to conceal my disappointment. My shoulders drooped and I nodded slowly.

"What's a paraffin test?" asked Nicky, speaking for the first time.

"It's quite conclusive, Nicky," I said. "I'm not sure that I know the chemistry of it exactly, but it's scientifically correct. You see, every gun no matter how well fitted has a certain amount of backfire. Some of the gunpowder flashes back and is embedded in the hand of the man that fires. They coat his hand with hot paraffin and then draw it off like a glove. They then test it for gunpowder—for nitrates, that is—and if it's positive, it means that the man fired the gun. I'm afraid that winds it up for McNulty."

"So the oracle of the test tube has spoken?" Nicky murmured ironically.

"It's conclusive evidence, Nicky," I said.

"Evidence, eh? I was wondering when you would begin to examine the evidence," he remarked.

Edwards and I both looked at him, puzzled.

"What evidence have I neglected?" asked Edwards superciliously.

"Look at the photograph of the room," Nicky replied. "Look at the chess game."

I studied the photograph while Edwards watched uncertainly. It was not easy to see the position of the pieces because the ones nearest the camera were naturally greatly foreshortened. But after a moment I got the glimmering of an idea.

"Let's see what it looks like set up," I said, as I dumped the chessmen out of the box onto the table and then proceeded to select the necessary pieces to copy the position indicated in the photograph.

Nicky watched, a sardonic smile on his lips, amused at my inability to read the position directly from the photograph. Edwards looked uneasily from one to the other of us, half expecting to find the name of the murderer spelled out on the board.

"If there is some sort of clue in those chessmen," he essayed, "in the way they're set up, I mean, we can always check the position against the original. Nothing was moved and the house is sealed."

I nodded impatiently as I studied the board. The pattern of the pieces was beginning to take on a meaning in my mind. Then I had it.

"Why, he was playing the Logan-Asquith Gambit," I exclaimed. "And playing it extremely well."

"Never heard of it," said Nicky.

"Neither had I until McNulty showed it to me about a week ago at the University Club. He had come across it in Lowenstein's *End Games*. It's almost never used because it's such a risky opening. But it's interesting because of the way the position of the bishops is developed. Were you thinking, Nicky, that a man who was upset and about to shoot himself would not be playing so difficult a game, nor playing it so well?"

"As a matter of fact, I was thinking not of the position of the pieces on the board," said Nicky mildly, "but of those *off the board*—the captured men."

"What about them?" I demanded.

"They're all together on one side of the board, black and white."

"Well?"

Nicky's face was resigned, not to say martyred, and his tone was weary as he strove to explain what he thought should have been obvious.

"You play chess the way you write, or handle a tennis racket. If you're right-handed, you move your pieces with your right hand, and you take off your opponent's pieces with your right hand, and you deposit them on the table to your right. When two right-handed players like McNulty and Albrecht are engaged, the game ends with the black pieces that White has captured at his right and diagonally across the board are the white pieces that Black has captured."

There flashed through my mind the image of Trowbridge as I had seen him that afternoon, awkwardly trying to light a cigarette with his left hand because his right arm hung in a black silk sling.

"When a left-handed player opposes a right-handed player," Nicky went on, almost as though he had read my mind, "the captured men are on the same side of the board—but, of course, they're separated, the black chessmen near White and the white chessmen near Black. They wouldn't be jumbled together the way they are in the photograph unless—"

I glanced down at the board I had just set up.

Nicky nodded as he would to a stupid pupil who had managed to stumble onto the right answer. "That's right—not unless you've dumped them out of the box and then set up only the men you need in accordance with the diagram of an end game."

"Do you mean that instead of playing a regular game, McNulty was demonstrating some special kind of opening?" asked Edwards. He struggled with the idea, his eyes abstracted as he tried to fit it into the rest of the picture. Then he shook his head. "It doesn't make sense," he declared. "What would be the point of Albrecht's saying that they were playing a game?"

"Try it with Albrecht," Nicky suggested. "Suppose it was Albrecht who set up the board?"

"Same objection," said Edwards. "What would be the point of lying about it?"

"No point," Nicky admitted, "if he set it up before McNulty was shot. But suppose Albrecht set up the game *after* McNulty was shot."

"Why would he do that?" demanded Edwards, his belligerence growing with his bewilderment.

Nicky gazed dreamily at the ceiling. "Because a game of chess partly played suggests first, that the player has been there for some time, at least since the beginning of the game, and second, that he was there on friendly terms. It is hardly necessary to add that if a deliberate attempt is made to suggest both ideas, the chances are that neither is actually true."

"You mean—"

"I mean," said Nicky, "that Professor Luther Albrecht rang McNulty's doorbell at approximately eight o'clock and when McNulty opened the door for him, he pressed a gun against his breast and pulled the trigger, after which he put the gun in the dead man's hand and then stepped over his fallen body and coolly set up the ever-present chessmen in accordance with the diagram of an end game from one of McNulty's many books of chess. That's why the game was so well played. It had been worked out by an expert, by Lowenstein probably in the book you mentioned."

We both, the Colonel and I, sat back and just stared at Nicky. Edwards was the first to recover.

"But why should Albrecht shoot him? He was his best friend."

Nicky's little blue eyes glittered with amusement. "I suspect that you're to blame for that, Colonel. You called in the morning and made an appointment for that evening. I fancy that was what upset McNulty so. I doubt if he was directly to blame for the difficulties encountered on the project, but as head of the project he was responsible. I fancy that he told his good friend and colleague, Albrecht, about your call. And Albrecht knew that an investigation by an outsider meant certain discovery—unless he could provide a scapegoat, or what's the slang expression?—a fall guy, that's it, a fall guy."

I glanced at Edwards and saw that he was pouting like a small boy with a broken balloon. Suddenly he remembered something. His eyes lit up and his lips parted in a smile that was almost a sneer.

"It's all very pretty," he said, "but it's a lot of hogwash just the same. You've forgotten that I have proof that it was suicide. The paraffin test proved that McNulty had fired the gun."

Nicky smiled. "It's your test that is hogwash, Colonel. In this case it proves nothing."

"No, really," I intervened. "The test is perfectly correct."

"The test proves only that McNulty's hand was behind the gun," said Nicky sharply.

"Well?"

"Suppose someone rang your doorbell," Nicky addressed me, the same martyred look in his face, "as the Colonel did this evening, and when you opened the door, he thrust a gun against your breast. What would you do?"

"Why, I—I'd grab his hand, I suppose."

"Precisely, and if he fired at that instant, there would be nitrates backfired into your hand as well as into his."

The Colonel sat bolt upright. Then he jumped up and grabbed his briefcase and made for the door.

"You can't wash that stuff off too easily," he said over his shoulder. "And it's even harder to get it off your clothes. I'm going to get hold of Albrecht and do a paraffin on him."

When I returned to the study from seeing the Colonel to the door, Nicky said, "There was really no need for our young friend's haste. I could have offered him other proof—the chessmen. I have no doubt that the last fingerprint made on each chessman, black as well as white, will be found to be Albrecht's. And that would be a hard thing for him to explain if he persists in his story that it was just an ordinary game of chess."

"Say, that's right, Nicky. I'll spring that one on Edwards in the morning." I hesitated, then I took the plunge. "Wasn't Albrecht taking an awful chance though? Wouldn't it have been better if he had just walked away after shooting McNulty instead of staying on and calling the police and making up that story and—"

Nicky showed his exasperation. "Don't you see it? He couldn't walk off. The poor devil was stuck there. He had got McNulty's lifeless hand nicely fitted onto the gun. He was ready to leave. Naturally, he looked through the door window up and down the street, normally deserted at that hour, to make sure the coast was clear. And he saw Trowbridge trudging along. He waited a minute or two for him to pass and then looked out again to find that the young man had stopped directly across the street and gave no indication of moving on. And in a minute or two the passengers from the Albany train would be along. And after that, perhaps our friend the Colonel, early for his appointment."

"So my investigation of Trowbridge wasn't entirely fruitless, eh?" I exclaimed, rubbing my hands together gleefully. "At least, that puts me one up on the Colonel."

Nicky nodded. "A brash young man, that. What branch of the service did he say he was connected with?"

"Intelligence."

"Indeed!" Nicky pursed his lips and then relaxed them in a frosty little smile. "I was infantry, myself, in the last war."

IX. Confronting the Enemy

When it comes to confrontational drama, there's nothing like a world championship chess match: the two mightiest players in the world go head-to-head—I should say mind-to-mind—in a months-long all-out struggle for supremacy that only one of them can win. From a sporting standpoint, the stakes could not be higher.

But when the two players are enemies as well as rivals, the struggle takes place on another plane where the stakes are *much* higher. Fernando Arrabal knows this well. Arrabal, an avant-garde Spanish-born playwright, filmmaker, and poet now living in Paris, played a significant role in *The Great Chess Movie*, a Canadian documentary about the 1981 world championship match between two bitter personal and political enemies, Anatoly Karpov and Viktor Korchnoi. His 1988 novel, *The Tower Struck by Lightning*, focuses on the twenty-fourth and decisive game of a championship match between two antagonists who, not coincidentally, are personally and politically poles apart: Marc Amary (White), a Swiss physicist who may be involved in the terrorist kidnapping of a Soviet politician; and Elias Tarsis, an apolitical Spanish machine operator whose twin passions, aside from chess, are religion and sex. Their match, wrote Walter Goodman in his review of the novel in *The New York Times* (July 20, 1988), "pits anarchism against Marxism, intuition against icy ideology, human vagaries against scientific fanaticism." And it gives Arrabal the opportunity to comment on a few of the cherished customs and taboos of chess competition.

Not mentioned anywhere in the novel is the fact that the Amary-Tarsis game was based on Capablanca's draw with Tartakower in the London International Tournament of 1922. Arrabal, however, has slightly altered the opening and has created a fictional conclusion that suited his purposes better than that of the actual game. The moves of the Capablanca-Tartakower game are: 1 d4 Nf6 2 Nf3 d5 3 c4 e6 4 Nc3 Be7 (Amary-Tarsis reaches this position by a different order of moves) 5 Bg5 0-0 6 e3 h6 7 Bh4 b6 8 cxd5 exd5 9 Qb3 Be6 10 Rd1 c6 11 Qc2 Ne4 12 Bxe7 Qxe7 13 Nxe4 dxe4 14 Qxe4 Qb4+ 15 Nd2 Qxb2 16 Bd3 g6 17 Qf4 Kg7 18 h4 Nd7 19 Ne4 Qxa2 20 h5 g5 21 Qg3.

Amary-Tarsis continues from this point: 21 . . . f5 22 Nxg5 hxg5 23 Qxg5+ Kf7 24 Bxf5 Qa5+, and Amary resigned by repeatedly smashing the chess clock on the board "and then furiously attacked the black king as if he were trying to open up its head and dash its brains out."

The Capablanca-Tartakower game proceeded: 21 . . . Qa5+ 22 Ke2 f5 23 Nxg5 hxg5 24 Qxg5+ Kf7 25 h6 Rg8 26 Qh5+ Ke7 27 h7 Rxg2 28 Kf1 Qd5 29 h8Q Rxh8 30 Qxh8 Qf3 31 Rd2 Bd5 32 Ke1 Rg8 33 Qh4+ Kd6 34 Rf1 Be6 35 Rc2 a5 36 Qh2+ Ke7 37 Be2 Qe4 38 Kd2 c5 39 Bd3 Qg2 40 Qh4+ Qg5 41 Qxg5+ Rxg5 42 Rb1, draw.

Fernando Arrabal

The Tower Struck by Lightning

At the end of two minutes and five seconds of study and analysis, Amary accepts Tarsis's challenge and plays 2. d2-d4, thus occupying the center, controlling e5 and c5, and demonstrating that he is venturing on the Queen's Gambit, an opening which does not suit him in principle.

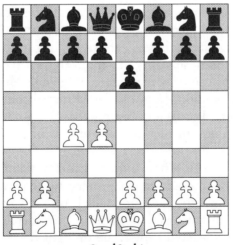

2. d2-d4

Immediately afterward he stops his clock and thereby automatically sets Tarsis's clock in motion; he scrupulously marks down his move and fixes his gaze between his adversary's eyebrows—a ritual with him.

Tarsis begins his reflections under the heavy weight of his rival's unbearable stare. But if he should look up, he will only provoke an incident that would disconcert him, as Amary hopes will happen. Nevertheless, it may be that Amary is contemplating him with real curiosity, even with a certain admiration, as he would a wild horse, or a jailer.

On his worksheet, Tarsis grudgingly notes Amary's move. Two types of writing appear on this sheet: the first, detailing his own moves, is not only legible but even polished; the other, an account of the moves made by the "assassin," is a series of scrawls or furious strokes. For Tarsis, to call Amary an "assassin" or a "robot" is to assimilate him, to appropriate him; and to write out his name with any care would be as repugnant as to caress him.

The most well-established taboo in chess is the one forbidding touching. "A piece touched is a piece played," according to the rules. Thus we see the irrevocable nature of the act of touching. If a player's fingers graze a piece, he is obliged to declare "*J'adoube*," a French term originating in the Middle Ages used in solemnly dressing a knight in his armor, and which today may signify "Pardon!" or, more precisely, "I am arranging," or "I am disposing." For some psychologists, among them the American ex-champion Fine, this taboo against touching masks the two threats menacing every champion: masturbation (according to these experts, the figure being touched is a penis, which is why, after touching it, the player excuses himself) and the homosexuality "latent in chess players." Tarsis finds these theories as absurd as they are outrageous. Most chess players are of the same opinion. [During the Montreal tourney a Canadian woman poet asked Portisch his opinion of Fine's thesis; in reply the Hungarian champion turned his back and went off in a huff; he did not strike her, because she was a woman.]

As things went, the first public "hand to hand" encounter between our two rivals could not have been more exemplary. The occasion was the draw to determine which player would use white in the first game. For reasons that might be considered either mythical or magical, Tarsis wanted to win: he thought that it would demonstrate that he had Luck (or Nature? or Fortune? or God?) on his side.

With equal zeal, Amary wished to win the first skirmish for quite reasonable motives: to be able to count on the small advantage given by possession of whites would provide the initial benefit, which he would know how to exploit to deliver a telling blow. After the official speeches and the patriotic hymns, the two players faced each other: Amary was ashen, while Tarsis's face was inflamed. Amary accepted the pawn offered him by the president of the federation, whipped it behind his back, and then extended two closed hands in front of his rival: one fist held the fateful pawn. Tarsis was about to tap one of the hands, but suddenly held back, raised his index finger, and made a pass at the other's left fist, which was precisely where the white pawn lay hidden. This gesture—a symbolic victory for Tarsis—would have been enough to justify the theoreticians who see in chess a playing out of narcissistic conflicts, but it went unnoticed. Perhaps Fine might have maintained that Tarsis had brandished the phallus of triumph during the above ceremony in mock-sodomy of his competitor, but that at the last moment, in fear of being masturbated by Amary, he managed to wave his finger so close to his enemy's hand that everyone thought he had touched it when in reality he had not even grazed it. . . .

Tarsis believes that to play chess is to enter into the realm of order, the secret and inexplicable calligraphy of precision. For Amary, on the other hand, everything in chess can be explained: each problem has its rational solution, and so he moves his queen (17. Qe4-f4) as he tells himself that an analysis of the lessons of history is always instructive. His chess piece at the vital center position is dominating the board and attacking one of the ramparts of the adversary's defense: h6. Tarsis believes that the most decisive results come about after much useless planning and that in history, moreover, the most lofty endeavors may be the result of chance and the most mediocre causes may provoke the moist fabulous effects.

Tarsis plays 17. . . . Kg8-g7. For a quarter of an hour he has weighed the two ways of protecting his parapet: h6. At length he discards King-h7. He decides by intuition . . . after long reflection. He thinks he is recalling certain moments before his birth . . . and that his intuition comes from a knowledge gained before he came into the world.

Amary is convinced that the encounter between himself and

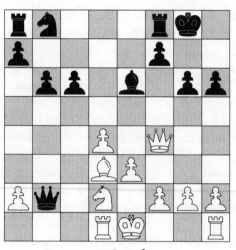

17. Qe4-f4

Tarsis represents a historic and apocalyptic combat between Good and Evil, between the Proletarian and the Bourgeois (the bourgeoisie represented by the workman Tarsis and the proletariat by himself).

This world chess championship match in reality opposes precision allied to intelligence against grace crowned by talent (reason vis-à-vis the mystery). When Fischer learned that his rival Spassky had declared, "Chess is like life," he corrected the statement to "Chess is life."

Korchnoi and Karpov, the two players who for years competed for the crown which the federation usurped from the American genius Fischer, each wrote books, years later; two different books with the same Fischerian title: *Chess Is My Life.* The history of chess is most exemplary in its own way: in the sixteenth century the Castilian monk Ruy López de Sigura reigned, and he was the inventor of the Spanish game, with the most audacious and daring attack, like that of the Conquistadores, while in the same epoch the southern Italian Giochino Greco exemplified the Italian Renaissance. The French Revolution of 1789 was preceded by Philidor, the French player who discovered that "the pawns are the soul of chess," thereby guillotining anterior monarchic dogmas based on the omnipotence of the king and queen. In the epoch of Romanticism, the German Anderssen played to win with splendor; the games bore the names of sonnets ("the immortal," "the eternally young," etc.) and prizes for Beauty

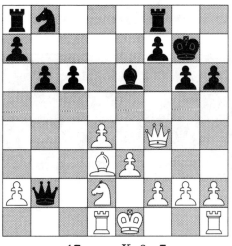

17. . . . Kg8-g7

flourished. Lasker, like Freud, adduced the importance of psychology early in the century. Alekhine, moving between his roots and exile, traveled the world with his cat, Chess, illustrating the painful road of expatriation . . . But the real confrontation between dissidence and power culminated in the encounter between Korchnoi and Karpov. Fischer, the solitary, anticipated today's spiritual renaissance, and the blind mullahs of the bureaucracy wrested his crown from him to underline the fact that his kingdom could not be of this world. Why should it be surprising that now the man of science is locked in combat with the man of intuition?

Martin Amis

Money: A Suicide Note

The chief character of Money, *Martin Amis's acidly funny novel, tells us at one point, "I'm called John Self. But who isn't?" And at that very point he meets, as if in a mirror, a character named Martin Amis. Self, an English director of television commercials, has been hired by producer Fielding Goodney to direct an American feature film, but he is unhappy with the screenplay turned out by Goodney's screenwriter, Doris Arthur, and hires Amis to rewrite it. At the end, it becomes clear that Goodney's intention was not to make a film at all, and that Self, driven by greed, is the main victim of an elaborate swindle. Unable to pay Amis what he had promised, Self challenges him to a high-stakes chess game, during which Amis explains all.*

Selina is Self's former girlfriend. The Fiasco is his car, which, he reports, "nearly always screws things up when it comes to getting you anywhere. . . . What it likes—what it's really incredibly good at—is staying put."

I feel better now, funnily enough. No, I do. I feel better for the whole experience. I feel a solid and stately calm. Now I know I'm perfectly capable of dealing with my life. Yes, everything is coming up roses. In fact the future looks really bright, now that I've decided to kill myself. I've decided. I have decided. Ah, it's so simple. Deciding is the hard part, and life has decided for me. Tonight. I've got the doings, here in my sock. Tonight, alone. Last thing.

"Thanks again for coming over," I said.

Martin stirred. "I suppose I ought to run," he said, "and let you get on with it."

"No, stay! . . . Go on, stick around. Just for a couple of hours."

He sighed, and tilted his head.

"Go on. Just for a couple of hours. I know I don't owe you any favours. Okay, I fucked you around. But I'll never ask for another. Go on, be a pal."

Martin stared dully round the room. He looked at his watch.

"I just, I've just been reading this book about Freud. What have you been reading?"

"Reading's overrated," he said. "As overrated as Shakespeare's women. I shouldn't bother your pretty little head with it if I were you . . . What's that? A set of skittles or something?"

"That? It's a chess set, for Christ's sake. Onyx," I said.

He selected a piece at random from the jade box. "What's this? A king or a queen?"

"It's a pawn. What's wrong with it?"

"You play much?"

"Yeah. I used to. You play, do you? Are you good?"

"Naturally," he said. "How about a game? It'll pass the time."

"Okay, sure," I said, and felt the heat of sudden excitement. What was it? The prospect of exoneration, revenge? I'll fucking show him, I thought, the little smirkbag, the student, the abstainer, with his facetiousness and his degrees. He's got me down for a know-nothing. But *he* doesn't know I'm a chess artist. I'll show him. "Right," I said. "We're playing for money."

"*Money*? What do you think this is, a game of darts in the Jack the Ripper? You can't play chess for money."

"Ten quid. With doubling. We're playing for money."

". . . But you haven't *got* any money."

"Oh yeah? This set alone is worth five hundred quid. I've got a cashmere overcoat in there that's worth a thousand easy. And," I said, straightening a finger, "*and*, I've got the Fiasco. Okay, what's so bloody funny?"

"Nothing. I'm sorry. Look, are you sure you wouldn't rather a game of snap or noughts-and-crosses? No? All right. But it's serious. Yes?"

"Oh it's serious, mate. And you're in for a nasty surprise. Come on, let's do it."

I took the numbered dice from my backgammon set. I adjusted the two-faced clock: one hour each. Amis drew white.

"Hah!" I said. 1. P-QN3. I ask you. "Where'd you learn that. Some book?"

You won't catch me playing by the rules but most of the opening lines have by now been embossed on my repertoire. I didn't think any player could really disconcert me before the middle-game: as early as the fifth move, though, little Martin here drove right out of lane. He went on a meaningless sortie with his knight, prancing round the centre of the board while I jabbed him with my evolving front line. There *is* an opening like that, but it's a defence, not an attack. He's a total rabbit, I thought, and doubled him. Then he beavered me! I stared down at the redoubled dice . . . Chess is a meeting of minds, a shock of private cultures, and there's a rich seam of shame in it somewhere. I ottered him. He raccooned me. I moled him. The doubling dice read 32. That was it for now.

"I've been thinking about your little adventure in New York," he said, as his knight scuttled back to the second rank. "I think I've got it all worked out. Do you want to hear my theory?"

"Shut up a minute. I'm concentrating."

Now I was way ahead on development but my pawn structure looked distinctly ragged. The game went quiet for a couple of moves as we tended our own gardens, both briskly castling, kingside. I was searching for blueprints, for forms and patterns, when he launched into a tedious series of pokes and prods at my extended pawns. This was no sweat to counter in itself, but I had to wheel my guns away from his sparse kingside, back from the centre too, where Martin was beginning to establish a couple of minor pieces—that knight again, a useful black-square bishop . . . Oh Christ, I thought, it's turning into one of those games. Within the space of three moves I had been nudged into a position of intricate inertia, my pieces cramped and clustered, misled, cross-purposed. It would take at least two tempos to find any freedom and I never seemed to have a beat to spare. My every touch was a bit of fine-tuning, delicate repair-work in shrinking space.

"Fielding Goodney," he said, "—everything went his way until I entered the picture. *I* was the joker in the pack. I don't know how—how realistic his scheme was, but it might have gone something like this. Double," he said, and moved.

His second bishop lanced out, trapping my knight against a queen already smothered by her paranoid underlings. Oh, this was hell, an awful dream of constriction, of pins and forks and skewers. I gulped scotch and looked for exchanges. There were two on offer, each with its strong disincentive—a doubled pawn, an opened file giving gangway to his centralized rook, which would then . . . Man, I could lose right away! This is really *serious*, I thought, and raised a hand to my damaged face.

"Given the stars he'd signed up, given their neuroses and delusions, the Doris Arthur script was designed to be absolutely unworkable. Watching you trying to coax them into it would have made quite a spectacle. But you held out. You weren't as wasted as he thought you were. You had some strength he couldn't undermine."

"Go on," I said. Suddenly I was seeing light and smelling air. If I could inch my queen on to the third rank, then I could cover the knight and release the bishop *and* threaten his . . . yeah. All I needed was a tempo. Leave me alone, you son of a bitch. God damn it, stay off my case for a single move. Keep talking. With a glance at the clock and a show of flurry or dither I edged my queen out of her hive. Martin considered, then tamely pushed a pawn.

"Go on."

"Those girls you said were chasing you last time out. They were on the payroll too. Either that or they were—they were auditioning. But you weren't as dumb and drunk as he hoped you'd be. You held out. That girlfriend of yours, the one with the degrees. Maybe she was a joker, just like me. Maybe she was the second joker in the pack."

At last I was back on terms with a glimpse of some counterplay. And, well, it's hard to describe, but the other end of the board just turned all limp on me. I seemed to have tempos to burn—it was like playing *Selina*, with white forming pretty patterns on distant squares. There was no, there was no opposition any more. Idly Martin continued to push his queenside pawns, apparently unmoved by the bursting arsenal I was amassing to his left. Now my linked bishops threw out their searchlights towards his king, and my chubby rooks were all set to gun it down the single open file. Time, too, was on my side.

"Fielding's original notion might have gone as follows. Did you study the paperwork? Obviously not. Hogtied by the Arthur screenplay, which is little more than a witty, four-pronged character assassination, the stars renege on you. Fielding comes down on them for breaking contract. No big deal. Nuisance claims. Happens all the time. The stars are all insured for this so there's no real loser, except John Self. Fielding had non-completion insurance too. But then you screwed it up by bringing *me* in."

"Double," I said. I turned the dice from 64 to 16—the usual highrolling practice. "Sixteen hundred quid. Okay?"

He just wasn't interested, I thought. His moves are waiting moves—but waiting for what? I had it all my own way now on this squared field of power. Martin could wait as long as he liked: he'll have black in his pants before he knows it. When the knight is poised I'll go straight for the crotch of his defence. Yes, me and my rooks, we'll tear the joint to shreds. I haven't got him good. I've got him beautiful.

"How he managed the money, well, that's another story. What's the phrase? 'The mad agility of compound deceit.' You said he had a lot of computer equipment in his room. Clearly he was hacking—you know, a spool artist, riding the software and the memory circuits of banks and conglomerates. He couldn't keep the balls in the air for ever. But he had his hands on money at some point. He could make money. But he didn't care about money. Not as *money*. Double."

And neither does this guy. Am I missing something? Quickly I reviewed the disposition of his pieces and their possible flarepaths. Zero—no bookish sacrifice or swingeing combination, no discovered brilliancy. The advanced queenside pawns might give me a few headaches later on, but . . . Later on? Jesus. They say that pawns are the soul of chess. This might explain why I never pay them much mind, not until the endgame anyway, when you can't help but think about your soul. Those four white skinheads were coming down toward me like space invaders on a churning screen. Black's broken battlements just stood there, gaping, as once again my forces entered turnaround.

"The wonder is," said Martin musingly, "the wonder is that Fielding didn't cut and run at an earlier stage. Probably he was too deep into his themes and forms, his own artwork. The illusionist, the lie artist, the storyboard—they have a helplessness. And then of course there was the underside of his character. All that had to have its play. Why didn't he let you walk out of the door at the Carraway? Because he was hooked. On the fiction, the art. He wanted to get to the end. We all do. A failed actor, he wanted an actor's revenge. He took it out on real life."

Now there was some warm work out on the flank as the pawns began to strut their stuff. This must have given us a taste for carnage because the central bloodbath, when it came, was all smash and grab. Those vanished pawns breathed new powers into his sleeping pieces: I watched it all come down, nabbed what I could, and huddled whimpering on my own back lines. The wound dispatches were telling me that I was only a pawn to the bad, but I had two pieces under threat and this fat rook lurking on my second rank. If I can just survive, I thought, if I can just survive. I don't expect to beat this guy. I won't let him beat me, though—I won't take another loss.

"Can you remember," he asked, "can you remember what Fielding said, in the alley, after the fight? He said something. Can you remember what it was?"

"I don't know. You—new man dog. Something like that. It didn't make any sense."

"Could it have been *inhuman dog*? . . . Fascinating. Pure transference. Oh damned Iago. Tell you what. You're better than I thought but this is still money for jam. If you win, I pay up. If we draw, you win—I'll give you the game. If I win—I just take something from you. Anything I want, but just one thing." He pointed to the dice. "The money's sort of a joke by now anyway, or a symbol. Sex, status, phallic. Have I left any out?"

The cunning bastard, I thought. Oh, I caught that reference to his own little rattletrap. He's definitely after my Fiasco.

"Okay?"

"Okay."

And I did survive, more or less. All right, so I lost the exchange—knight for rook—but I regained my lost pawn and tiptoed into the endgame like a street dog heading for home—and food, warmth, shelter. It was this way. White king, pawn, rook: black king, pawn, knight. Pawns opposed on the queen's bishop file. Now theoretically he might have had winning chances—but I had something else: I had the clock on my side. Martin, *he'd* done all the talking, and he'd done it in his own good time. There were nineteen

minutes on my clock, and less than seven on his . . . Our pawns met
head on, escorted by their kings. His rook made broad sweeps, came
in close, backed off again. My knight held its ground. It was gridlock,
diversion, no thoroughfare: all his decisive moves seemed to lay him
open to a king-rook fork. Time ticked. I even ventured out with my
knight, innocuously splitting his rook and his pawn.

"This is exquisite," he said—and made a waiting move with the
king.

Greedily I stared at the board. His rook was there for the taking.
Exchange, then locked pawns: a draw. All over. I think I even incurred a minor hard-on as I leaned across the table and said, "I hope
you mean that, pal, because you're not having it back. Double."

"Double."

"Double."

"Double."

I sank back in the chair and feasted on my drink. Ah, such
luxury, in this clubbed face, in this hired sock, even in this extremity.
I wanted Martin to see it all coming. I would take his rook with my
knight. He would recapture—or resign. That would leave the opposed foursome, his king to the left of my pawn, my king to the right
of his. When I had his cheque in my hands I was going to tear it up
and throw it back in his face. "There's your payment," I would say,
and point towards the door.

"Sixty-four thousand pounds," he said. "I don't think you'll
quite run to that. But I'm going to take what I'm going to take. You
won't miss it. You never even knew you had it."

"What were you after? It was the Fiasco, wasn't it?"

"You don't understand. Your car's just a joke. I think I've
worked out how Fielding did it, moneywise. How much are you out
on the whole deal? Personally?"

"I don't know. Not that much. He paid for nearly everything."

"Wrong. It's finally come to me. And it *is* beautiful. You signed
a lot of documents. My guess is that you signed them all twice. Once
under *Co-signatory*, once under *Self*. It was your *name*. The company you formed wasn't Goodney & Self. It was Self & Self. It was
Self. The hotels, the plane tickets, the limousines, the wage bill, the
studio rental. You were paying. It was you. It was you."

I shrugged, dead cool, and just said, "Let's play."

I captured his rook. He captured my knight. The four pieces
stood locked in their formal pose. We climbed to our feet, and

stretched, facing each other over the square table. I offered him my hand and said,

"A draw."

"No. I'm afraid you lose."

"Come on, there's nothing doing." I gestured airily at the board. And saw that he was right. My only moves were king moves, and they were suicide. He could capture, and keep his own pawn in range.

"Zugzwang," he said.

"What the fuck does that mean?"

"Literally, *forced to move*. It means that whoever has to move has to lose. If it were my turn now, you'd win. But it's yours. And you lose."

"Pure fucking jam, in other words. Dumb luck."

"Hardly," he said. "The opposition itself is a kind of zugzwang in which the relationship between the kings assumes a regular pattern. There is such a thing, though, as the heterodox opposition. In composed positions you could call them conjugated square studies. You see, the—"

I clamped my hands over my ears. Martin talked on, shadowy, waxy, flicker-faced. I don't know if this strange new voice of mine carried anywhere when I said, *"I'm the joke. I'm it! It was you. It was you."*

I didn't see my first swing coming—but he did. He ducked or shied or stood swiftly aloof and my fist slammed into the light bracket above his head. I wheeled sideways with a wide backhander, fell against the low chair and caught its shoulder-spike deep in the ribs. I came up flailing. I hurled myself round that room like a big ape in a small cage. But I could never connect. Oh Christ, he just isn't here, he just isn't there. My last shot upended me by the rhino-hide sofa, which kicked me full in the face with its square steel boot. The boil in my head now broke or burst. The room tipped and tunnelled and fled screaming in to the night.

When I awoke, Martin was still in the room, and still talking.

When I awoke, Martin was gone and there was no sound anywhere.

Kurt Vonnegut, Jr.

All the King's Horses

In Kurt Vonnegut's 1953 story, Colonel Kelly, his crew, and his family have been captured by the sadistic Pi Ying, who forces them to represent the pieces of a living chess game played for drastically high stakes: Whenever one of Kelly's pawns or pieces is captured, the person who represents it is to be immediately executed. Chessplaying readers may enjoy working out why Colonel Kelly's opening moves are logically defective, given the special conditions under which the game is played. (A detailed analysis appears in the book Timid Virgins Make Dull Company *by Dr. Crypton, a.k.a. Paul Hoffman [Viking, 1984].)*

Colonel Bryan Kelly, his huge figure blocking off the light that filtered down the narrow corridor behind him, leaned for a moment against the locked door in an agony of anxiety and helpless rage. The small Oriental guard sorted through a ring of keys, searching for the one that would open the door. Colonel Kelly listened to the voices inside the room.

"Sarge, they wouldn't dare do anything to Americans, would they?" The voice was youthful, unsure. "I mean, there'd be hell to pay if they hurt—"

"Shut up. Want to wake up Kelly's kids and have them hear you running off at the mouth that way?" The voice was gruff, tired.

"They'll turn us loose pretty quick, whaddya bet, Sarge?" insisted the young voice.

"Oh, sure, kid, they love Americans around here. That's probably what they wanted to talk to Kelly about, and they're packing the beer and ham sandwiches into box lunches for us right now. All that's holding things up is they don't know how many with mustard, how many without. How d'ya want yours?"

"I'd just like to—"

"Shut up."

"Okay, I'd just—"

"Shut up."

"I'd just like to know what's going on, is all." The young corporal coughed.

"Pipe down and pass the butt along," said a third voice irritably. "There's ten good puffs left in it. Don't hog the whole thing, kid." A few other voices muttered in agreement.

Colonel Kelly opened and closed his hands nervously, wondering how he could tell the fifteen human beings behind the door about the interview with Pi Ying and the lunatic ordeal they were going to have to endure. Pi Ying said that their fight against death would be no different, philosophically, from what all of them, except Kelly's wife and children, had known in battle. In a cold way, it was true—no different, philosophically. But Colonel Kelly was more shaken than he had ever been in battle.

Colonel Kelly and the fifteen on the other side of the door had crash-landed two days before on the Asiatic mainland, after they had been blown off course by a sudden storm and their radio had gone dead. Colonel Kelly had been on his way, with his family, to a post as military attaché in India. On board the Army transport plane with them had been a group of enlisted men, technical specialists needed in the Middle East. The plane had come to earth in territory held by a Communist guerrilla chief, Pi Ying.

All had survived the crash—Kelly, his wife Margaret, his ten-year-old twin sons, the pilot and copilot, and the ten enlisted men. A dozen of Pi Ying's ragged riflemen had been waiting for them when they climbed from the plane. Unable to communicate with their captors, the Americans had been marched for a day through rice fields and near-jungle to come at sunset to a decaying palace. There they had been locked in a subterranean room, with no idea of what their fates might be.

Now, Colonel Kelly was returning from an interview with Pi Ying, who had told him what was to become of the sixteen American prisoners. *Sixteen*—Kelly shook his head as the number repeated itself in his thoughts.

The guard prodded him to one side with his pistol and thrust the key into the lock, and the door swung open. Kelly stood silently in the doorway.

A cigarette was being passed from hand to hand. It cast its glow for an instant on each expectant face in turn. Now it lighted the ruddy face of the talkative young corporal from Minneapolis, now cast rugged shadows over the eye sockets and heavy brows of the pilot from Salt Lake, now bloomed red at the thin lips of the sergeant.

Kelly looked from the men to what seemed in the twilight to be a small hillock by the door. There his wife Margaret sat, with the blond heads of her sleeping sons cradled in her lap. She smiled up at him, her face misty white. "Darling—you're all right?" Margaret asked quietly.

"Yes, I'm all right."

"Sarge," said the corporal, "ask him what Pi Ying said."

"Shut up." The sergeant paused. "What about it, sir—good news or bad?"

Kelly stroked his wife's shoulder, trying to make the right words come—words to carry courage he wasn't sure he had. "Bad news," he said at last. "Rotten news."

"Well, let's have it," said the transport pilot loudly. Kelly supposed he was trying to reassure himself with the boom of his own voice, with brusqueness. "The worst he can do is kill us. Is that it?" He stood and dug his hands into his pockets.

"He wouldn't dare!" said the young corporal in a threatening voice—as though he could bring the wrath of the United States Army to bear on Pi Ying with a snap of his fingers.

Colonel Kelly looked at the youngster with curiosity and dejection. "Let's face it. The little man upstairs has all the trumps." An expression borrowed from another game, he thought irrelevantly.

"He's an outlaw. He hasn't got a thing to lose by getting the United States sore at him."

"If he's going to kill us, say so!" the pilot said explosively. "So he's got us cold! What's he going to do?"

"He considers us prisoners of war," said Kelly, trying to keep his voice even. "He'd like to shoot us all." He shrugged. "I haven't been trying to keep you in suspense, I've been looking for the right words—and there aren't any. Pi Ying wants more entertainment out of us than shooting us would provide. He'd like to prove that he's smarter than we are in the bargain."

"How?" asked Margaret. Her eyes were wide. The two children were waking up.

"In a little while, Pi Ying and I are going to play chess for your lives." He closed his fist over his wife's limp hand. "And for my four lives. It's the only chance Pi Ying will give us." He shrugged, and smiled wryly. "I play a better-than-average game—a little better than average."

"Is he nuts?" said the sergeant.

"You'll all see for yourselves," said Colonel Kelly simply. "You'll see him when the game begins—Pi Ying and his friend, Major Barzov." He raised his eyebrows. "The major claims to be sorry that, in his capacity as a military observer for the Russian army, he is powerless to intervene in our behalf. He also says we have his sympathy. I suspect he's a damn liar on both counts. Pi Ying is scared stiff of him."

"We get to watch the game?" whispered the corporal tensely.

"The sixteen of us, soldier, are the chessmen I'll be playing with."

The door swung open. . . .

"Can you see the whole board from down there, White King?" called Pi Ying cheerfully from a balcony overlooking the azure-domed chamber. He was smiling down at Colonel Bryan Kelly, his family, and his men. "You must be the White King, you know. Otherwise, we couldn't be sure that you'd be with us for the whole game." The guerrilla chief's face was flushed. His smile was one of mock solicitousness. "Delighted to see all of you!"

To Pi Ying's right, indistinct in the shadows, stood Major Barzov, the taciturn Russian military observer. He acknowledged Kelly's stare with a slow nod. Kelly continued to stare fixedly. The arrogant, bristle-haired major became restless, folding and unfolding his arms, repeatedly rocking back and forth in his black boots. "I wish I could help you," he said at last. It wasn't an amenity but a contemptuous jest. "I am only an observer here." Barzov said it heavily. "I wish you luck, Colonel," he added, and turned his back.

Seated on Pi Ying's left was a delicate young Oriental woman. She gazed expressionlessly at the wall over the Americans' heads. She and Barzov had been present when Pi Ying had first told Colonel Kelly of the game he wanted to play. When Kelly had begged Pi Ying to leave his wife and children out of it, he had thought he saw a spark of pity in her eyes. As he looked up at the motionless, ornamental girl now, he knew he must have been mistaken.

"This room was a whim of my predecessors, who for generations held the people in slavery," said Pi Ying sententiously. "It served nicely as a throne room. But the floor is inlaid with squares, sixty-four of them—a chessboard, you see? The former tenants had those handsome, man-sized chessmen before you built so that they and their friends could sit up here and order servants to move them about." He twisted a ring on his finger. "Imaginative as that was, it remained for us to hit upon this new twist. Today, of course, we will use only the black chessmen, my pieces." He turned to the restive Major Barzov. "The Americans have furnished their own chessmen. Fascinating idea." His smile faded when he saw that Barzov wasn't smiling with him. Pi Ying seemed eager to please the Russian. Barzov, in turn, appeared to regard Pi Ying as hardly worth listening to.

The twelve American soldiers stood against a wall under heavy guard. Instinctively, they bunched together and glared sullenly at their patronizing host. "Take it easy," said Colonel Kelly, "or we'll lose the one chance we've got." He looked quickly at his twin sons, Jerry and Paul, who gazed about the room, unruffled, interested, blinking sleepily at the side of their stunned mother. Kelly wondered why he felt so little as he watched his family in the face of death. The fear he had felt while they were waiting in their dark prison was gone. Now he recognized the eerie calm—an old wartime friend—that left only the cold machinery of his wits and senses alive. It was the narcotic of generalship. It was the essence of war.

"Now, my friends, your attention," said Pi Ying importantly. He stood. "The rules of the game are easy to remember. You are all to behave as Colonel Kelly tells you. Those of you who are so unfortunate as to be taken by one of my chessmen will be killed quickly, painlessly, promptly." Major Barzov looked at the ceiling as though he were inwardly criticizing everything Pi Ying said.

The corporal suddenly released a blistering stream of obscenities—half abuse, half self-pity. The sergeant clapped his hand over the youngster's mouth.

Pi Ying leaned over the balustrade and pointed a finger at the struggling soldier. "For those who run from the board or make an outcry, a special form of death can be arranged," he said sharply. "Colonel Kelly and I must have complete silence in which to concentrate. If the colonel is clever enough to win, then all of you who are still with us when I am checkmated will get safe transport out of my territory. If he loses—" Pi Ying shrugged. He settled back on a mound of cushions. "Now, you must all be good sports," he said briskly. "Americans are noted for that, I believe. As Colonel Kelly can tell you, a chess game can very rarely be won—any more than a battle can be won—without sacrifices. Isn't that so, Colonel?"

Colonel Kelly nodded mechanically. He was recalling what Pi Ying had said earlier—that the game he was about to play was no different, philosophically, from what he had known in war.

"How can you do this to children!" cried Margaret suddenly, twisting free of a guard and striding across the squares to stand directly below Pi Ying's balcony. "For the love of God—" she began.

Pi Ying interrupted angrily: "Is it for the love of God that Americans make bombs and jet planes and tanks?" He waved her away impatiently. "Drag her back." He covered his eyes. "Where was I? We were talking about sacrifices, weren't we? I was going to ask you who you had chosen to be your king's pawn," said Pi Ying. "If you haven't chosen one, Colonel, I'd like to recommend the noisy young man down there—the one the sergeant is holding. A delicate position, king's pawn."

The corporal began to kick and twist with new fury. The sergeant tightened his arms about him. "The kid'll calm down in a minute," he said under his breath. He turned his head toward Colonel Kelly. "Whatever the hell the king's pawn is, that's me. Where do I stand, sir?" The youngster relaxed and the sergeant freed him.

Kelly pointed to the fourth square in the second row of the huge chessboard. The sergeant strode to the square and hunched his broad shoulders. The corporal mumbled something incoherent and took his place in the square next to the sergeant—a second dependable pawn. The rest still hung back.

"Colonel, you tell us where to go," said a lanky T-4 uncertainly. "What do we know about chess? You put us where you want us." His Adam's apple bobbed. "Save the soft spots for your wife and kids. They're the ones that count. You tell us what to do."

"There are no soft spots," said the pilot sardonically, "no soft spots for anybody. Pick a square, any square." He stepped onto the board. "What does this square make me?"

"You're a bishop, Lieutenant, the king's bishop," said Kelly.

He found himself thinking of the lieutenant in those terms—no longer human, but a piece capable of moving diagonally across the board; capable, when attacking with the queen, of terrible damage to the black men across the board.

"And me in church only twice in my life. Hey, Pi Ying," called the pilot insolently, "what's a bishop worth?"

Pi Ying was amused. "A knight and a pawn, my boy; a knight and a pawn."

Thank God for the lieutenant, thought Kelly. One of the American soldiers grinned. They had been sticking close together, backed against the wall. Now they began to talk among themselves—like a baseball team warming up. At Kelly's direction, seeming almost unconscious of the meaning of their actions, they moved out onto the board to fill out the ranks.

Pi Ying was speaking again. "All of your pieces are in place now, except your knights and your queen, Colonel. And you, of course, are the king. Come, come. The game must be over before suppertime."

Gently, shepherding them with his long arms, Kelly led his wife and Jerry and Paul to their proper squares. He detested himself for the calm, the detachment with which he did it. He saw the fear and reproach in Margaret's eyes. She couldn't understand that he had to be this way—that in his coldness was their only hope for survival. He looked away from Margaret.

Pi Ying clapped his hands for silence. "There, good; now we can begin." He tugged at his ear reflectively. "I think this is an excellent way of bringing together the Eastern and Western minds, don't you, Colonel? Here we indulge the Americans' love for gambling with our appreciation of profound drama and philosophy." Major Barzov whispered impatiently to him. "Oh, yes," said Pi Ying, "two more rules: We are allowed ten minutes a move, and—this goes without saying—no moves may be taken back. Very well," he said, pressing the button on a stop watch and setting it on the balustrade, "the honor of the first move belongs to the white men." He grinned. "An ancient tradition."

"Sergeant," said Colonel Kelly, his throat tight, "move two squares forward." He looked down at his hands. They were starting to tremble.

"I believe I'll be slightly unconventional," said Pi Ying, half turning his head toward the young girl, as though to make sure that she was sharing his enjoyment. "Move my queen's pawn forward two squares," he instructed a servant.

Colonel Kelly watched the servant slide the massive carving forward—to a point threatening the sergeant. The sergeant looked quizzically at Kelly. "Everything okay, sir?" He smiled faintly.

"I hope so," said Kelly. "Here's your protection . . . Soldier," he ordered the young corporal, "step forward one square." There—it was all he could do. Now there was no advantage in Pi Ying's taking the pawn he threatened—the sergeant. Tactically it would be a pointless trade, pawn for pawn. No advantage so far as good chess went.

"This is very bad form, I know," said Pi Ying blandly. He paused. "Well, then again, I'm not so sure I'd be wise to trade. With so brilliant an opponent, perhaps I'd better play flawless chess and forget the many temptations." Major Barzov murmured something to him. "But it would get us into the spirit of the game right off, wouldn't it?"

"What's he talking about, sir?" asked the sergeant apprehensively.

Before Kelly could order his thoughts, Pi Ying gave the order. "Take his king's pawn."

"Colonel! What'd you do?" cried the sergeant. Two guards pulled him from the board and out of the room. A studded door banged shut behind them.

"Kill me!" shouted Kelly, starting off his square after them. A half-dozen bayonets hemmed him in.

Impassively, the servant slid Pi Ying's wooden pawn onto the square where the sergeant had stood. A shot reverberated on the other side of the thick door, and the guards reappeared. Pi Ying was no longer smiling. "Your move, Colonel. Come, come—four minutes have gone already."

Kelly's calm was shattered, and with it the illusion of the game. The pieces in his power were human beings again. The precious, brutal stuff of command was gone from Colonel Kelly. He was no more fit to make decisions of life and death than the rawest recruit. Giddily, he realized that Pi Ying's object was not to win the game quickly, but to thin out the Americans in harrowing, pointless forays. Another two minutes crept by as he struggled to force himself to be rational. "I can't do it," he whispered at last. He slouched now.

"You wish me to have all of you shot right now?" asked Pi Ying. "I must say that I find you a rather pathetic colonel. Do all American officers give in so easily?"

"Pin his ears back, Colonel," said the pilot. "Let's go. Sharpen up. Let's go!"

"You're in no danger now," said Kelly to the corporal. "Take his pawn."

"How do I know you're not lying?" said the youngster bitterly. "Now I'm going to get it!"

"Get over there!" said the transport pilot sharply.

"No!"

The sergeant's two executioners pinned the corporal's arms to his sides. They looked up expectantly at Pi Ying.

"Young man," said Pi Ying solicitously, "would you enjoy being tortured to death, or would you rather do as Colonel Kelly tells you?"

The corporal spun suddenly and set both guards sprawling. He stepped onto the square occupied by the pawn that had taken the sergeant, kicked the piece over, and stood there with his feet apart.

Major Barzov guffawed. "He'll learn to be a pawn yet," he roared. "It's an Oriental skill Americans could do well to learn for the days ahead, eh?"

Pi Ying laughed with Barzov, and stroked the knee of the young girl, who had been sitting, expressionless, at his side. "Well, it's been perfectly even so far—a pawn for a pawn. Let's begin our offensives in earnest." He snapped his fingers for the attention of the servant. "King's pawn to king three," he commanded. "There! Now my queen and bishop are ready for an expedition into white man's territory." He pressed the button on the stop watch. "Your move, Colonel." . . .

It was an old reflex that made Colonel Bryan Kelly look to his wife for compassion, courage. He looked away again—Margaret was a frightening, heartbreaking sight, and there was nothing he could do for her but win. Nothing. Her stare was vacant, almost idiotic. She had taken refuge in deaf, blind, unfeeling shock.

Kelly counted the figures still surviving on the board. An hour had passed since the game's beginning. Five pawns were still alive, among them the young corporal; one bishop, the nervy pilot; two rooks; two knights—ten-year-old frightened knights; Margaret, a rigid, staring queen; and himself, the king. The missing four? Butchered—butchered in senseless exchanges that had cost Pi Ying only blocks of wood. The other soldiers had fallen silent, sullen in their own separate worlds.

"I think it's time for you to concede," said Pi Ying. "It's just about over, I'm afraid. Do you concede, Colonel?" Major Barzov frowned wisely at the chessmen, shook his head slowly, and yawned.

Colonel Kelly tried to bring his mind and eyes back into focus. He had the sensation of burrowing, burrowing, burrowing his way through a mountain of hot sand, of having to keep going on and on, digging, squirming, suffocated, blinded. "Go to hell," he muttered. He concentrated on the pattern of the chessmen. As chess, the ghastly game had been absurd. Pi Ying had moved with no strategy other than to destroy white men. Kelly had moved to defend each of his chessmen at any cost, had risked none in offense. His powerful queen, knights, and rooks stood unused in the relative safety of the two rear rows of squares. He clenched and unclenched his fists in frustration. His opponent's haphazard ranks were wide open. A checkmate of Pi Ying's king would be possible, if only the black knight weren't dominating the center of the board.

"Your move, Colonel. Two minutes," coaxed Pi Ying.

And then Kelly saw it—the price he would pay, that they all would pay, for the curse of conscience. Pi Ying had only to move his queen diagonally, three squares to the left, to put him in check. After that he needed to make one more move—inevitable, irresistible—and then checkmate, the end. And Pi Ying would move his queen. The game seemed to have lost its piquancy for him; he had the air of a man eager to busy himself elsewhere.

The guerrilla chief was standing now, leaning over the balustrade. Major Barzov stood behind him, fitting a cigarette into an ornate ivory holder. "It's a very distressing thing about chess," said Barzov, admiring the holder, turning it this way and that. "There isn't a grain of luck in the game, you know. There's no excuse for the loser." His tone was pedantic, with the superciliousness of a teacher imparting profound truths to students too immature to understand.

Pi Ying shrugged. "Winning this game gives me very little satisfaction. Colonel Kelly has been a disappointment. By risking nothing, he has deprived the game of its subtlety and wit. I could expect more brilliance from my cook."

The hot red of anger blazed over Kelly's cheeks, inflamed his ears. The muscles of his belly knotted; his legs moved apart. Pi Ying must not move his queen. If Pi Ying moved his queen, Kelly would lose; if Pi Ying moved his knight from Kelly's line of attack, Kelly would win. Only one thing might induce Pi Ying to move his knight—a fresh, poignant opportunity for sadism.

"Concede, Colonel. My time is valuable," said Pi Ying.

"Is it all over?" asked the young corporal querulously.

"Keep your mouth shut and stay where you are," said Kelly. He stared through shrewd, narrowed eyes at Pi Ying's knight, standing in the midst of the living chessmen. The horse's carved neck arched. Its nostrils flared.

The pure geometry of the white chessmen's fate burst upon Kelly's consciousness. Its simplicity had the effect of a refreshing, chilling wind. A sacrifice had to be offered to Pi Ying's knight. If Pi Ying accepted the sacrifice, the game would be Kelly's. The trap was perfect and deadly save for one detail—bait.

"One minute, Colonel," said Pi Ying.

Kelly looked quickly from face to face, unmoved by the hostility or distrust or fear that he now saw in each pair of eyes. One by one he eliminated the candidates for death. These four lives were vital to the sudden, crushing offense, and these must guard the king. Necessity, like a child counting eeny, meeny, miney, moe around a circle, pointed its finger at the one chessman who could be sacrificed. There was only one.

Kelly didn't permit himself to think of the chessman as anything but a cipher in a rigid mathematical proposition: if x is dead, the rest shall live. He perceived the tragedy of his decision only as a man who knew the definition of tragedy, not as one who felt it.

"Twenty seconds!" said Barzov. He had taken the stop watch from Pi Ying.

The cold resolve deserted Kelly for an instant, and he saw the utter pathos of his position—a dilemma as old as mankind, as new as the struggle between East and West. When human beings are attacked, x, multiplied by hundreds and thousands, must die—sent to death by those who love them most. Kelly's profession was the choosing of x.

"Ten seconds," said Barzov.

"Jerry," said Kelly, his voice loud and sure, "move forward one square and two to your left." Trustingly, his son stepped out of the back rank and into the shadow of the black knight. Awareness seemed to be filtering back into Margaret's eyes. She turned her head when her husband spoke.

Pi Ying stared down at the board in bafflement. "Are you in your right mind, Colonel?" he asked at last. "Do you realize what you've just done?"

A faint smile crossed Barzov's face. He bent forward as though to whisper to Pi Ying, but apparently thought better of it. He leaned back against a pillar to watch Kelly's every move through a gauze of cigarette smoke.

Kelly pretended to be mystified by Pi Ying's words. And then he buried his face in his hands and gave an agonized cry. "Oh, God, no!"

"An exquisite mistake, to be sure," said Pi Ying. He excitedly explained the blunder to the young girl beside him. She turned away. He seemed infuriated by the gesture.

"You've got to let me take him back," begged Kelly brokenly.

Pi Ying rapped on the balustrade with his knuckles. "Without rules, my friend, games become nonsense. We agreed that all moves would be final, and so they are." He motioned to a servant. "King's knight to king's bishop six!" The servant moved the piece onto the square where Jerry stood. The bait was taken; the game was Colonel Kelly's from here on in.

"What is he talking about?" murmured Margaret.

"Why keep your wife in suspense, Colonel?" said Pi Ying. "Be a good husband and answer her question, or should I?"

"Your husband sacrificed a knight," said Barzov, his voice overriding Pi Ying's. "You've just lost your son." His expression was that of an experimenter, keen, expectant, entranced.

Kelly heard the choking sound in Margaret's throat, caught her as she fell. He rubbed her wrists. "Darling, please—listen to me!" He shook her more roughly than he had intended. Her reaction was explosive. Words cascaded from her—hysterical babble condemning him. Kelly locked her wrists together in his hands and listened dumbly to her broken abuse.

Pi Ying's eyes bulged, transfixed by the fantastic drama below, oblivious of the tearful frenzy of the young girl behind him. She tugged at his blouse, pleading. He pushed her back without looking away from the board.

The tall T-4 suddenly dived at the nearest guard, driving his shoulder into the man's chest, his fist into his belly. Pi Ying's soldiers converged, hammered him to the floor and dragged him back to his square.

In the midst of the bedlam, Jerry burst into tears and raced terrified to his father and mother. Kelly freed Margaret, who dropped to her knees to hug the quaking child. Paul, Jerry's twin, held his ground, trembled, stared stolidly at the floor.

"Shall we get on with the game, Colonel?" asked Pi Ying, his voice high. Barzov turned his back to the board, unwilling to prevent the next step, apparently reluctant to watch it.

Kelly closed his eyes, and waited for Pi Ying to give the order to the executioners. He couldn't bring himself to look at Margaret and Jerry. Pi Ying waved his hand for silence. "It is with deep regret—" he began. His lips closed. The menace suddenly went out of his face, leaving only surprise and stupidity. The small man slumped on the balustrade, slithered over it to crash among his soldiers.

Major Barzov struggled with the Chinese girl. In her small hand, still free of his grasp, was a slender knife. She drove it into her breast and fell against the major. Barzov let her fall. He strode to the balustrade. "Keep the prisoners where they are!" he shouted at the guards. "Is he alive?" There was no anger in his voice, no sorrow—only irritation, resentment of inconvenience. A servant looked up and shook his head.

Barzov ordered servants and soldiers to carry out the bodies of Pi Ying and the girl. It was more the act of a scrupulous housekeeper than a pious mourner. No one questioned his brisk authority.

"So this is your party after all," said Kelly.

"The peoples of Asia have lost a very great leader," Barzov said severely. He smiled at Kelly oddly. "Though he wasn't without weaknesses, was he, Colonel?" He shrugged. "However, you've won only the initiative, not the game; and now you have me to reckon with instead of Pi Ying. Stay where you are, Colonel. I'll be back shortly."

He ground out his cigarette on the ornamented balustrade, returned the holder to his pocket with a flourish, and disappeared through the curtains.

"Is Jerry going to be all right?" whispered Margaret. It was a plea, not a question, as though mercy were Kelly's to dole out or to withhold.

"Only Barzov knows," he said. He was bursting to explain the moves to her, to make her understand why he had had no choice; but he knew that an explanation would only make the tragedy infinitely more cruel for her. Death through a blunder she might be able to understand; but death as a product of cool reason, a step in logic, she could never accept. Rather than accept it, she would have had them all die.

"Only Barzov knows," he repeated wearily. The bargain was still in force, the price of victory agreed to. Barzov apparently had yet to realize what it was that Kelly was buying with a life.

"How do we know Barzov will let us go if we do win?" said T-4.

"We don't, soldier. We don't." And then another doubt began to worm into his consciousness. Perhaps he had won no more than a brief reprieve. . . .

Colonel Kelly had lost track of how long they'd waited there on the chessboard for Barzov's return. His nerves were deadened by surge after surge of remorse and by the steady pressure of terrible responsibility. His consciousness had lapsed into twilight. Margaret slept in utter exhaustion, with Jerry, his life yet to be claimed, in her arms. Paul had curled up on his square, covered by the young corporal's field jacket. On what had been Jerry's square, the horse's carved head snarling as though fire would burst from its nostrils, stood Pi Ying's black knight.

Kelly barely heard the voice from the balcony—mistook it for another jagged fragment in a nightmare. His mind attached no sense to the words, heard only their sound. And then he opened his eyes and saw Major Barzov's lips moving. He saw the arrogant challenge in his eyes, understood the words. "Since so much blood has been shed in this game, it would be a pitiful waste to leave it unresolved."

Barzov settled regally on Pi Ying's cushions, his black boots crossed. "I propose to beat you, Colonel, and I will be surprised if you give me trouble. It would be very upsetting to have you win by the transparent ruse that fooled Pi Ying. It isn't that easy any more. You're playing me now, Colonel. You own the initiative for a moment. I'll take it and the game now, without any more delay."

Kelly rose to his feet, his great frame monumental above the white chessmen sitting on the squares about him. Major Barzov wasn't above the kind of entertainment Pi Ying had found so diverting. But Kelly sensed the difference between the major's demeanor and that of the guerrilla chief. The major was resuming the game, not because he liked it, but because he wanted to prove that he was one hell of a bright fellow, and that the Americans were dirt. Apparently, he didn't realize that Pi Ying had already lost the game. Either that, or Kelly had miscalculated.

In his mind, Kelly moved very piece on the board, driving his imagination to show him the flaw in his plan, if a flaw existed—if the hellish, heartbreaking sacrifice was for nothing. In an ordinary game, with nothing at stake but bits of wood, he would have called upon his opponent to concede, and the game would have ended there. But now, playing for flesh and blood, an aching, ineradicable doubt overshadowed the cleancut logic of the outcome. Kelly dared not reveal that he planned to attack and win in three moves—not until he had made the moves, not until Barzov had lost every chance to exploit the flaw, if there was one.

"What about Jerry?" cried Margaret.

"Jerry? Oh, of course, the little boy. Well, what about Jerry, Colonel?" asked Barzov. "I'll make a special concession, if you like.

Would you want to take the move back?" The major was urbane, a caricature of cheerful hospitality.

"Without rules, Major, games become nonsense," said Kelly flatly. "I'd be the last to ask you to break them."

Barzov's expression became one of profound sympathy. "Your husband, madame, has made the decision, not I." He pressed the button on the stop watch. "You may keep the boy with you until the Colonel has fumbled all of your lives away. Your move, Colonel. Ten minutes."

"Take his pawn," Kelly ordered Margaret. She didn't move. "Margaret! Do you hear me?"

"Help her, Colonel, help her," chided Barzov.

Kelly took Margaret by the elbow, led her unresisting to the square where a black pawn stood. Jerry tagged along, keeping his mother between himself and Kelly. Kelly returned to the square, dug his hands into his pockets, and watched a servant take the black pawn from the board. "Check, Major. Your king is in check."

Barzov raised an eyebrow. "Check, did you say? What shall I do about this annoyance? How shall I get you back to some of the more interesting problems on the board?" He gestured to a servant. "Move my king over one square to the left."

"Move diagonally one square toward me, Lieutenant," Kelly ordered the pilot. The pilot hesitated. "Move! Do you hear?"

"Yessir." The tone was mocking. "Retreating, eh, sir?" The lieutenant slouched into the square, slowly, insolently.

"Check again, Major," Kelly said evenly. He motioned at the lieutenant. "Now my bishop has your king in check." He closed his eyes and told himself again and again that he had made no miscalculations, that the sacrifice *had* won the game, that there *could* be no out for Barzov. This was it—the last of the three moves.

"Well," said Barzov, "is that the best you can do? I'll simply move my queen in front of my king." The servant moved the piece. "Now it will be a different story."

"Take his queen," said Kelly to his farthest-advanced pawn, the battered T-4.

Barzov jumped to his feet. "Wait!"

"You didn't see it? You'd like to take it back?" taunted Kelly.

*　　*　　*

Barzov paced back and forth on his balcony, breathing hard. "Of course I saw it!"

"It was the only thing you could do to save your king," said Kelly. "You may take it back if you like, but you'll find it's the only move you can make."

"Take the queen and get on with the game," shouted Barzov. "Take her!"

"Take her," echoed Kelly, and the servant trundled the huge piece to the sidelines. The T-4 now stood blinking at Barzov's king, inches away. Colonel Kelly said it very softly this time: "Check."

Barzov exhaled in exasperation. "Check indeed." His voice grew louder. "No credit to you, Colonel Kelly, but to the monumental stupidity of Pi Ying."

"And that's the game, Major."

T-4 laughed idiotically, the corporal sat down, the lieutenant threw his arms around Colonel Kelly. The two children gave a cheer. Only Margaret stood fast, still rigid, frightened.

"The price of your victory, of course, has yet to be paid," said Barzov acidly. "I presume you're ready to pay now?"

Kelly whitened. "That was the understanding, if it would give you satisfaction to hold me to it."

Barzov placed another cigarette in his ivory holder, taking a scowling minute to do it. When he spoke, it was in the tone of the pedant once more, the wielder of profundities. "No, I won't take the boy. I feel as Pi Ying felt about you—that you, as Americans, are the enemy, whether an official state of war exists or not. I look upon you as prisoners of war.

"However, as long as there is no official state of war, I have no choice, as a representative of my government, but to see that all of you are conducted safely through the lines. This was my plan when I resumed the game where Pi Ying left off. Your being freed has nothing to do with my personal feelings, nor with the outcome of the game. My winning would have delighted me and taught you a valuable lesson. But it would have made no difference in your fates." He lighted his cigarette and continued to look at them with severity.

"That's very chivalrous of you, Major," said Kelly.

"A matter of practical politics, I assure you. It wouldn't do to precipitate an incident between our countries just now. For a Russian to be chivalrous with an American is a spiritual impossibility, a contradiction in terms. In a long and bitter history, we've learned and learned well to reserve our chivalry for Russians." His expression became one of complete contempt. "Perhaps you'd like to play another game, Colonel—plain chess with wooden chessmen, without Pi Ying's refinement. I don't like to have you leave here thinking you play a better game than I."

"That's nice of you, but not this evening."

"Well, then, some other time." Major Barzov motioned for the guards to open the door of the throne room. "Some other time," he said again. "There will be others like Pi Ying eager to play you with live men, and I hope I will again be privileged to be an observer." He smiled brightly. "When and where would you like it to be?"

"Unfortunately, the time and the place are up to you," said Colonel Kelly wearily. "If you insist on arranging another game, issue an invitation, Major, and I'll be there."

Vasily Aksyonov

The "Victory"—A Story with Exaggerations

Vasily Aksyonov (b. 1932), one of the leading Soviet writers of his generation, emigrated to the United States in 1980 after resigning from the Soviet Writers' Union to protest the expulsion of two of his colleagues. His chess story, first published in 1965, is a subtle commentary on the relationship between the artist and society in Soviet Russia. Interviewed during the preparation of this anthology, Aksyonov described his grandmaster as "an internal émigré" who deliberately loses the chess game because he understands that his opponent, who represents the Soviet masses, must be allowed to evince his power over the artist. In so doing, the grandmaster wins his artistic integrity while demonstrating the shallowness of his rival, who is delighted with the vulgar material evidence of his "victory": a gold trinket. The letters "G.B." tattooed on the stranger's hand are meant to suggest KGB.

In a compartment of an express train, a grandmaster played chess with a chance companion.

The man recognized the grandmaster as soon as he entered the compartment, and was immediately consumed by an unthinkable desire—the unthinkable defeat of a grandmaster. *Who knows?* he thought, glancing at him with sly, knowing looks. *Anything can happen. He looks pretty weak.*

The grandmaster realized immediately that he had been recognized and gloomily resigned himself: can't avoid at least two games. He knew this type of fellow. He sometimes saw their steep ruddy brows through the window of the Chess Club on Gogol Boulevard.

When the train started to move, the grandmaster's companion made a show of stretching.

"How about a little game of chess?" he asked with an indifferent air.

"I suppose," the grandmaster muttered.

The man leaned out of the compartment and hailed the conductor. A chess set appeared; he grabbed it with a haste that belied his feigned indifference, spilled out the pieces, chose two pawns and clutched them in his fists, then held out his fists to the grandmaster. On the bulge between the thumb and index finger of his left fist were the tattooed initials "G.B."

"Left," said the grandmaster, flinching slightly as he imagined blows from those fists, left and right.

He got White.

"We have some time to kill, right? Chess is just the thing on train rides," G.B. said genially as he set up the pieces.

They played quickly through a Danish Gambit, then things became complicated. The grandmaster looked at the board thoughtfully, making small, insignificant moves. A few times, possible mating patterns with his queen flashed before his eyes like lightning bolts, but he stifled them and just lowered his eyes, submitting to a faint nagging inner tune that buzzed like a mosquito.

G.B. droned tonelessly, " 'Brave Khas-Bulyat, poor is your hut . . .' "

The grandmaster was the personification of fastidiousness, of an austerity in dress and manners that is so characteristic of people who are vulnerable and unsure of themselves. He was young, and wore a gray suit, a light shirt, and a simple tie—a tie that, he alone knew, bore the Dior label. Somehow this little secret always gave the young, taciturn grandmaster a comforting feeling of warmth. His glasses, too, very often came to his rescue by keeping his shy, uncertain glance hidden from strangers. He despaired of his lips, which would typically quiver or distend into a pathetic little smile. He would gladly cover those lips as well, but that, unfortunately, was not yet acceptable in society.

G.B.'s play affected and distressed the grandmaster. The pieces on the left side were tangled up in a way that reminded him of the cabalistic images of charlatans. The whole left flank stank of toilets and disinfectant, of the sour smell of a barracks, of laundry hanging in the kitchen, even a whiff of castor oil and diarrhea from early childhood.

"Aren't you Grandmaster So-and-so?" asked G.B.

"Yes," confirmed the grandmaster.

"Ha ha ha, what a coincidence," G.B. exclaimed.

Coincidence? What coincidence is he talking about? This is incredible! How could this happen? I surrender, let me surrender, raced the grandmaster's thoughts in a panic. Then, seeing the point, he smiled.

"Of course, of course."

"Here you are, a grandmaster, and yet I'm forking your queen and rook," said G.B. He lifted his hand. The knight-provocateur was poised over the board.

A fork in the ass, thought the grandmaster. *Some fork! Grandpa had a fork that he never let anybody use. Property. Personal fork, spoon, and knife, personal plate and cuspidor. And remember that fur coat with the "lyre" pattern, that heavy overcoat that hung in the entryway though Grandfather almost never went out into the street. Grandpa's and Grandma's forks. Pity to lose the old ones.*

While the knight hovered over the board, possible precheckmating forays and sacrifices along luminescent lines and points again passed before the grandmaster's eyes. The knight, with the dirty-lilac flannel coming off its rump, was unfortunately too convincing, and the grandmaster shrugged his shoulders.

"You're giving up the rook?" asked G.B.

"What can I do?"

"You're sacrificing the rook for attack, aren't you?" asked G.B., still hesitating to put the knight on the desired square.

"Just saving my queen," muttered the grandmaster.

"You're not trying to trip me up?" asked G.B.

"No, you're a strong player."

G.B. gave his cherished fork. The grandmaster hid his queen in a sheltered alcove, a crumbling terrace with decaying carved stone columns and the rank autumn stink of rotting maple leaves. Here one could squat comfortably and wait it out. It was good here; anyway, it didn't hurt your pride. The moment he stood up and peeked out of the alcove, he noticed that G.B. had grabbed the rook.

The black knight's intrusion into the congested left flank was not particularly meaningful, but its occupation of the b4-square required some attention.

The grandmaster realized that in this variation, on this green spring evening, the myths of his youth would not suffice. True enough that glorious fools roamed the earth—sailor Billy, cowboy Harry, the beautiful Mary and Nellie, the pirate ships with their sails hoist to the wind—but the dangerous and real proximity of the knight to the b4-square was making itself felt. A struggle was in store, complex, subtle, fascinating, calculative. Ahead lay life.

The grandmaster won a pawn and took out his handkerchief to blow his nose. Those few moments of total privacy, when his lips and nose were hidden by the handkerchief, put him in the mood for banal philosophizing. *You strive for something*, he thought, *and then what? All your life you strive for something, and when victory finally approaches, it brings no joy. Take, for example, the city of Hong Kong, distant and so mysterious, yet I've already been there. I've already been everywhere.*

The loss of a pawn didn't much bother G.B., since he had just won a rook. His response was a queen move that gave the grandmaster heartburn and a momentary headache.

The grandmaster considered that there were still a few pleasures left for him. For instance, the pleasure of that whole long diagonal for his bishop. Pushing the bishop across the board would be a little like sliding headlong in a skiff as it splashed through the sunlit water of a suburban Moscow pond, from light to shade, shade to light. The grandmaster felt an irresistible passionate urge to seize h8: it was a square of love, a mound of love with transparent dragonflies hanging above it.

"Clever how you won back the rook. I screwed up," said G.B. in a low voice, only his last words betraying his irritation.

"Sorry," said the grandmaster softly. "Maybe we should replay the last few moves?"

"No no," said G.B., "no favors, absolutely not."

Sinking into strategic meditation, he began to hum, " 'Here is my dagger, here is my horse, here is my rifle . . .' "

Confronting the Enemy
◆

The turbulent summer love feast on h8 pleased but at the same time worried the grandmaster. He sensed that the center would soon be filled by an outwardly logical but intrinsically absurd accumulation of forces. Once again he would hear the cacophony and smell the chlorine of the left-flank corridors of that cursed distant memory.

"I wonder," said G.B. "Why are all chessplayers Jews?"

"Why all?" said the grandmaster. "I for one am not a Jew."

"Really?" said G.B. with surprise, then added, "I didn't mean anything by that. I myself am not prejudiced on that score. Just curious."

"And you?" said the grandmaster. "You're not a Jew, are you?"

"You must be kidding," G.B. muttered as he again became absorbed in his secret plans.

If I do this, he'll do that, thought G.B. *I take here, he takes there, then I go here, he replies like that . . . I'll finish him off in any case. Whatever he does, I'll break him. How about that, grandmaster-payoffmaster, you haven't got the guts to go up against me. I know your championships—all fixed. I'll crush you whatever you do, whatever it costs!*

"Well, I've lost the exchange," he said to the grandmaster. "But it doesn't matter, there's still a long way to go."

He started an attack in the center, and of course, as predicted, the center immediately became the scene of mindless, terrible activity. Here was non-love, non-welcome, non-hope, non-friendship, non-life. Chills of the flu, yellow snow again, postwar bleakness, itching body. The black queen in the center cawed like a lovesick crow, while next to it a kitchen knife scraped a tin bowl. Nothing so clearly demonstrated the senselessness and illusoriness of life as this position in the center. It was time to end the game.

No, thought the grandmaster, *there must be something more.* He put on a big tape of Bach piano music, and to calm himself with the pure monotonous sound of lapping waves, he left the dacha and went toward the sea. Above him the pine trees stirred, and beneath his bare feet was a slippery and springy covering of pine needles.

Recalling the sea, he began to study the position and, as with the sea, brought himself into harmony with it. Suddenly his soul was clear and light. Logically, like a Bach coda, he saw an approaching mate to the black king. The mating position, dimly lit but beautiful, was complete, like an egg. The grandmaster looked at G.B. Stolidly, like a bull, he was staring deeply into the rear of the grandmaster's position. He did not see the mate to his own king. The grandmaster kept silent so as not to break the spell.

"Check," said G.B softly, gingerly moving his knight. He could hardly contain the roaring within his body.

The grandmaster cried out and rushed to escape. Running after him, stamping and whistling, were the landlord of the dacha, Euripides the driver, and Nina Kuzminichna. Ahead of them and gaining on the grandmaster was Nochka the dog, who had been let off its chain.

"Check," G.B. said again, shifting his knight with a sigh of agonized longing.

The grandmaster was being led through a subdued crowd. Behind him, somebody was pressing a hard object into his back. A man in a black greatcoat with the G.B. insignia on its lapels was waiting in front of him. Step—half a second, another step—one second, another step—one and a half seconds, another step—two . . . Step up. Why up? Shouldn't these things be done in a pit? One must be a man. Is this necessary? How long does it take to put that stinking burlap bag over my head? It has become dark and difficult to breathe, and somewhere very far away an orchestra is playing, with bravado, "Khas-Bulyat the Brave."

"Mate!" cried G.B. like a brass trumpet.

"So I see," mumbled the grandmaster. "Congratulations!"

"Oof," said G.B. "Phew, I'm really sweating, it's really incredible, how the hell do you like that! Incredible: to slap a grandmaster with a mate! Absolutely incredible!" he guffawed. "Good for me!" He playfully patted himself on the head. "Oh grandmaster, dear grandmaster," he buzzed, putting his hands on the grandmaster's shoulders and giving them a friendly squeeze, "my dear young man, your little nerves just couldn't take it, right? Admit it!"

"Yes, yes, I broke down," the grandmaster hastily confirmed.

With a grand gesture, G.B. boldly swept the pieces off the board. It was old and cracked, and in places there were fragments of round stains that had been left by tea glasses of the railroads of long ago.

The grandmaster looked at the deserted board, at those sixty-four absolutely impassive squares with the capacity of accommodating not only his own life but an infinite number of lives, and that infinite alternation of light and dark squares filled him with reverence and a quiet joy. *I don't believe,* he thought, *that I've ever done a really mean thing in my life.*

"You know," complained G.B. with a sigh, "if I told this to people, nobody would believe me."

"Why wouldn't they believe you? What's unbelievable about it? You're a strong, tough player," said the grandmaster.

"No one will believe me," G.B. repeated. "They'll say I'm pulling their leg. How could I prove it?"

The grandmaster, slightly offended, looked at G.B.'s steep ruddy forehead. "Allow me to give you convincing proof. I knew I would meet you."

He opened his briefcase and took from it a large golden medallion the size of his palm. On it was finely engraved: THE BEARER HAS WON A GAME OF CHESS FROM ME. GRANDMASTER SO-AND-SO.

"All that remains is to fill in the date," he said, extracting engraving equipment from his briefcase and nicely inscribing the date on the medallion's edge. "This is pure gold," he said, handing it over.

"No fooling?" asked G.B.

"Absolutely pure gold," said the grandmaster. "I order quite a few of these medallions and always keep a supply in reserve."